HOW BEHAVIOR SPREADS

PRINCETON ANALYTICAL SOCIOLOGY SERIES

Damon Centola, Karen S. Cook, and
Peter Hedström, Series Editors

Feliz Garip, *On the Move: Changing Mechanisms of Mexico-U.S. Migration*

Emily Erikson, *Between Monopoly and Free Trade:*
The English East India Company, 1600–1757

HOW BEHAVIOR SPREADS

The Science of Complex Contagions

Damon Centola

PRINCETON UNIVERSITY PRESS
PRINCETON AND OXFORD

Published by Princeton University Press,
41 William Street, Princeton, New Jersey 08540

In the United Kingdom: Princeton University Press,
6 Oxford Street, Woodstock, Oxfordshire OX20 1TR

press.princeton.edu

ISBN 978-0-691-17531-7

Library of Congress Control Number: 2017956006

British Library Cataloging-in-Publication Data is available

Editorial: Meagan Levinson and Samantha Nader

Production Editorial: Deborah Tegarden

Text Design: Carmina Alvarez

Jacket art provided by the author; design by Meghan Kanabay

Production: Erin Suydam

Publicity: Julie Haav

Copyeditor: Gail Schmitt

This book has been composed in Palatino LT Std

Printed on acid-free paper. ∞

Printed in the United States of America

1 3 5 7 9 10 8 6 4 2

To my parents

Contents

Preface

This project began with a simple question: why do some social contagions seem to spread easily while others struggle to get going? For instance, why has HIV spread so rapidly through the world's population, but behaviors that can prevent HIV have not? The challenge with solving this kind of problem is that the spread of disease has become the default way of thinking about most kinds of social diffusion: one infected person can transmit the influenza virus to many others, who can in turn spread it to many more. Information is typically thought to spread in a similar fashion: one person can costlessly repeat a news story to many others, who can each in turn propagate it through a population. But if this is how diffusion works, why then do so many social movements take months or years to spread? Why do so many new technologies struggle to take off? And, why do disease-prevention strategies often fail to take hold? Can the lessons learned from viral diffusion be used to improve the spread of behavior, helping us to diffuse everything from social movements to innovative technologies?

To answer these questions, I spent the years during my PhD exploring the theoretical dynamics of how behaviors spread through social networks. These explorations led to some startling findings. There are many situations in which the most obvious ways to improve diffusion—for instance by increasing the network connectivity in a population—may actually wind up slowing it down. Indeed, for a large number of situations, the conditions that accelerate the viral spread of an epidemic can unexpectedly inhibit the spread of behaviors. These results turned the traditional wisdom about diffusion on its head, suggesting a new way of thinking about spreading in social networks. Increasing the channels for viral diffusion may in fact limit the extent of behavior change.

These theoretical results were published in collaboration with my PhD advisor, Michael Macy, in the *American Journal of Sociology*.[1] These findings, which provide the basis for chapter 3 of this book, led me to ask the more thoroughgoing question of whether this new theory of diffusion would hold up to empirical scrutiny.

Around the same time that I was thinking about how to apply this network theory of diffusion to a real-world process of behavior change, I had the good fortune to join the Robert Wood Johnson Scholars in Health Policy Program at Harvard University. There, my mentor Nicholas Christakis helped me to think up ways that I might test the theory of complex contagions. The challenge was that there were no methods available for testing network models of diffusion.

At that time, the idea of using the Internet to study social behaviors was just in its infancy, but after several months of sketching my ideas (and crossing most of them out), it finally became clear that it would be possible to conduct a causal test of this theory of diffusion using an Internet-based experiment. The study I conducted resulted in a paper published in *Science*, which provides the foundation for chapter 4 of this book.[2] This study also forms the basis of the discussion in the epilogue, in which I show how to apply these methods to a broader range of research topics.

The gratifying recognition that each of these papers received from the American Sociological Association, as well as from researchers in disciplines outside of sociology, encouraged me to present these ideas in a form that would make them accessible not only to mathematical sociologists and network scientists but also to a broader audience interested in understanding the conditions that can foster the diffusion of behavior through social networks. In turn, this led me to see how these ideas may be applied to a large variety of concrete situations and to appreciate how readily the results could be used to solve practical problems of diffusion. The second half of this book is dedicated entirely to these applications, which range in topic from selecting effective recruitment networks for collective action to identifying useful seeding strategies for public health interventions. I also address the implications for information brokers who span "structural holes" and what can be done to improve knowledge transfer across organizations. These applications in turn led me to see the more general implications of these ideas for public policy. I have since conducted several studies to test these policy ideas, and they form the basis for the discussion of social design in part 3.

HOW BEHAVIOR SPREADS

CHAPTER 1

Introduction

The promise of viral diffusion is all around us. We all know that new ideas can spread with the remarkable ease of a virus. Yet we also know that social innovations that can benefit society often fail to diffuse. The topic of this book is a new approach to using the pathways of network diffusion to accelerate social change.

A good example of a situation where this approach was successful was in Korea at the start of the 1960s. At the time, population growth rates were skyrocketing. Korea was facing an imminent population explosion. To intervene, the Korean government instituted a nationwide contraceptive initiative. Similar policy initiatives were attempted during the 1960s and early 1970s by the governments of several developing nations. They faced a similar problem. Living conditions were improving, but childbearing norms in rural households, in which families typically had five or more children, were still guided by traditional concerns of early life mortality.[1]

Most interventions were based on psychological models of behavior change. In some countries, mass-media campaigns shamed families for having too many children and attempted to induce contraceptive use by emphasizing individual accountability. The modest success of many of these programs stood in stark contrast to the Korean initiative, which surpassed all of its stated policy goals in less than twenty years. The success of this program signaled that a new way of thinking about public health interventions was on the horizon—a sociological way of thinking about how peer networks could be used to change social norms.[2]

The Korean intervention presented villages throughout the country with a menu of contraceptive options. Although Korea's program was nationally focused, its effectiveness hinged on villagers getting local exposure to contraceptive choices through social contact with their neighbors. Peer-to-peer networks of social diffusion successfully reached large numbers of adopters in many of the villages. When diffusion succeeded, women tended to adopt the same contraceptive methods as their contacts. This produced uniformity on contraceptive methods used within villages; however, there was a surprising amount of variation in the methods adopted across villages. Some were "IUD" villages, whereas others were "pill" villages, and still others were "vasectomy" villages. Interestingly, the particular method of contraception was not the determining factor for successful diffusion; rather, it was the network of social influence.[3] In the most successful villages, closely knit groups were linked together by overlapping social ties, which fostered the spread of contraceptive use throughout the community. The more studies that followed, the more findings supported the same basic conclusion— that social networks are the primary pathways for the spread of new social norms.[4]

An unexpected puzzle arose, however, from the fact the network pathways that were most successful for spreading behavior change were not the same networks that would be predicted by the theory of viral diffusion. While the viral model suggests that radiating networks of weak ties would lead to successful dissemination, it was instead overlapping patterns of spatial interaction that were the key to wide-spread adoption. In the decades since, scores of similar findings have surfaced in every field of diffusion research, from the spread of digital technologies to the mobilization of social movements. A growing catalog of studies has found that closely knit, densely overlapping networks are associated with the successful spread of innovative behaviors.

Today, the notion of virality animates the research agendas of hundreds of thousands of scientists worldwide, ranging from computer scientists and physicists, to sociologists and marketing scholars. Across many of these areas, lessons from the field of infectious-disease epidemiology provide a general orientation for studying behavioral contagions. The guiding assumption is that behaviors spread like viruses. The author of *The Tipping Point*, Malcolm Gladwell crystallized this idea: "I'm convinced that ideas and behaviors and new products move through a population very much like a disease does. This isn't just a metaphor, in other words. I'm talking about a very literal analogy. . . . Ideas can be contagious in exactly the same way that a virus is."[5]

This book offers a different perspective on diffusion. I show why the disease theory of diffusion does not work for understanding the spread of most behaviors and what this tells us about the kinds of social networks that are best suited for spreading innovations. This journey to discover how behaviors spread reveals the specific features of network structure that control the diffusion of behavior and, ultimately, shows how these features can be used to influence the process of social change. While research on diffusion often focuses on how to improve the qualities of a product or idea to make it more contagious, I consider situations in which the innovation itself cannot easily be changed. Instead, I focus on how changes to the social network of a population can transform a failed technology into a successful innovation. To demonstrate the impact of these ideas, this book is dedicated to providing practical solutions to problems of diffusion. The results offer a way of thinking about the network dynamics of social change that gives new life to the promise of using online technologies to promote sustainable changes in population behavior.

The examples used in this book vary widely, ranging from the diffusion of social media technologies to the spread of prophylactic measures for HIV to the growth of rebellion in post-Revolutionary France. The majority of examples are drawn from the diffusion literatures that I have been immersed in the longest—namely, the spread of health technologies and the mobilization of social movements. While on the surface these two topics seem to have nothing in common with one another, beneath the surface they have a shared logic of social influence. From a networks perspective, the common structures that underpin diffusion in both of these settings reveal the basic network characteristics that may be useful for improving the spread of behavior in a variety of contexts.

The findings here help to identify the kinds of networks that may be effective for spreading smoking cessation, as well as the network structures that can accelerate organizational change. These results show how to create online networks that can improve the adoption of new exercise behaviors. And they also reveal the differences between using social media to diffuse contagious memes versus to mobilize political activism. Here the dynamics of both informational and behavioral diffusion are explained within a framework that allows each to be understood on its own terms. The findings suggest a way for theorists and practitioners who are interested in diffusion to gain insight into when social networks will be helpful for spreading changes in behavior and how to make practical use of them.

One point worth stressing at the outset is that the approach here differs from approaches to social change that are based on the assumption that people's choices can be altered by exposure to the right kinds of messages. This is true in many circumstances. But the present approach is *collective* rather than *individual*. One surprisingly helpful way of thinking about this is by analogy with schooling among fish. Studying fish individually, it would be impossible to anticipate the complex schooling behaviors that they produce when they interact as a group. Similarly, studying people one at a time provides little insight into the collective dynamics by which new behaviors spread through a population. Diffusion, like schooling, is a collective social process that unfolds through the complex interactions of many interdependent actors. The approach adopted here is to study behavior change as we would study schooling—not as an individual phenomenon, but as a collective one. This perspective assumes that people are often in situations where the decisions they make are influenced less by the information they have access to, and more by the social norms that are common in their networks. The goal here is to show how these social networks may themselves be used to control the schooling process, and spread lasting changes in behavior.

ISN'T IT OBVIOUS?

Science has often been described as the development of new intuitions about how the world works. Commentary on the science of sociology has noted that while much of contemporary sociology can seem obvious today, it was not always so. Ideas that may seem bromidic now were once revolutionary approaches to thinking about social problems. The seemingly inevitable fate of successful ideas is to be absorbed into the body of scientific knowledge, eventually entering the popular lexicon, where they are reduced from novel intuitions to tacit features of everyday life. However, there are also scientific ideas that are so counterintuitive that they defy integration into the body of popular knowledge. These intuitions present such a challenging contrast with the expectations forged by a long evolutionary, cultural, and personal history that they are hard to hold on to even once they have been learned.

A quick example here will illustrate what is meant by a counterintuitive idea and how it can happen that a scientific discovery can remain counterintuitive even once it has been explained. Figure 1.1 shows a picture of two coffee tables. The intuition that I want to elicit concerns which of the two tables is longer. Look at each table and consider the ratio of its length to its width. What would you say it is? When

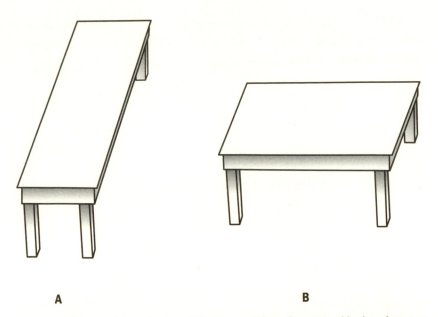

A   B

Figure 1.1 Adapted from Richard Thaler and Cass Sunstein, *Nudge: Improving Decisions About Health, Wealth, and Happiness* (New Haven, CT: Yale University Press, 2008).

I first saw this figure in the 2008 book by Richard Thaler and Cass Sunstein,[6] I guessed that the one on the left is perhaps 3:1 or 3.5:1, while the one on the right is closer to 1.5:1 or 1.25:1. Make your guess.

Now, take out your pen and lay it against the page. They are, in fact, the same table. Cognitive psychologists explain this illusion in terms of the way that the eye corrects (or fails to correct, depending on how you see it) for the orientation of the figures and the visual contrast created by the legs. Once you have measured the figures to your satisfaction and have internalized this new piece of knowledge, look away and then look back. Which table is longer?

The point is that despite having the right answer in mind, the objects nevertheless look the same as they did before. The bias in the perceptual system cannot be overcome by the knowledge that it is there. The value of scientific education is that once the bias is explained, a person can anticipate this kind of error and take precautions to avoid making mistakes in situations where it might matter. Whenever vigilance is surrendered, however, even if for a moment, a particularly persistent illusion can lead the mind to make unavoidable, and quite consequential errors in judgment.

This book is about just such an illusion, but not one in the perceptual science of psychology. Rather, it is about a similar kind of bias in our understanding of social networks. In particular, it is about a compellingly intuitive theory of diffusion that, like the apparent differences between the two tables in figure 1.1, is likely to be persistent. Nevertheless, the intuitive appeal of this idea notwithstanding, this book shows how this popular and intuitive theory of diffusion can go seriously wrong, leading to costly errors in our understanding of how behaviors spread through social networks. The intuitive theory I am talking about is called the *strength of weak ties*.

OUTLINE OF THE CHAPTERS

The basic idea of the strength of weak ties is that while our *strong ties*— that is, our friends and close family—all tend to know each other, our *weak ties*—that is, our casual acquaintances –connect us to remote parts of the social network. As the sociologist Mark Granovetter famously put it, "Whatever is to be diffused can reach a larger number of people, and traverse a greater social distance, when passed through weak ties rather than strong."[7] Our journey here starts in chapter 2 with the initial finding that launched my work into this topic—namely, that there is an unexpected problem with this remarkably influential theory of network diffusion.

The broad influence of this theory is due in part to the recent explosion of network science across disciplines such as physics, biology, and computer science, which ushered in a period of rapid discovery for understanding how the structure of social networks affects the dynamics of diffusion. What all of these fields have in common is a belief in the idea that a contagion, such as a virus, an idea, a meme, a method of contraception, a diet, a fashion, an emotion, an ideology, or a technology, can spread from one person to another. The guiding principle of all of this work is that the structure of social contacts can foretell how a contagion will diffuse through a population. The full impact of Granovetter's original insight was not realized until the physicists Duncan Watts and Steven Strogatz developed the *small-world* model, which demonstrated that bridge ties—that is, social links connecting otherwise distant people—can dramatically increase the rate of diffusion across social networks.[8] The strength of weak ties hypothesis and the small-world principle resonate with one another to present a unified and powerful view of how network structure controls the dynamics of social diffusion. The problem is that when we compare this view to a large body of empirical research on diffusion, a puzzle arises from the fact that while weak ties seem to improve diffusion in some cases, there are many other cases in which they do not.

The solution to this puzzle comes in chapter 3, with the finding that there is an important difference between "complex" behavioral contagions, for which transmission requires contact with multiple adopters, and "simple" informational and viral contagions, for which transmission only requires contact with a single source. Computational explorations show that when contagions are complex, because they are costly, risky, or involve some degree of complementarity, weak ties can slow down diffusion. This finding has implications for most of the contagions that social scientists care about, such as cooperation, social norms, marriage practices, health behaviors, voting behavior, technology adoption, and investment decisions, to name just a few.[9] It also means that social networks that accelerate the spread of an infectious disease can slow down the diffusion of its cure. This occurs because diseases, like information, are typically simple contagions that pass quickly along weak ties. Behavior change, however, typically is not.

With this finding, chapter 4 turns our attention from the mathematical world of computational experiments to the empirical world of behaviors spreading through human social networks. This is where we face a crucial challenge—devising a way to test this theory of diffusion empirically. For the vast majority of research on networks and diffusion, even the rudimentary task of identifying the existence of a diffusion process has been fraught with difficulties, to say nothing of being able to identify exactly how the structure of a social network may have altered it. Here the Internet is an invaluable ally for social research. Over the course of two years, an independent online community was constructed and populated with thousands of volunteers recruited at large from the World Wide Web. Techniques from small-group laboratory experiments were combined with tools from large-scale data science analytics to conduct an Internet-based social network experiment of how behaviors spread through online communities. The illuminating results from this study show that while weak ties were highly effective for spreading information, they slowed down the spread of behavior.

These results suggest that the rapid diffusion of information through weak ties may not tell much about the dynamics of behavior change. In fact, the more quickly that information goes viral, the less promising the outlook may be for spreading behavior. Thus, the finding that emerges from the intuitive distinction between simple viral contagions and complex behavioral contagions is the counterintuitive insight that the more weak ties there are in a network, the slower that innovations may spread.

In part 2 of this book, I use this theory of social contagions to address practical problems of diffusion. Chapter 5 shows the range of empirical settings to which the theory of complex contagions has been applied—from the spread of political hashtags on Twitter to the diffusion of smoking among teens.

Chapter 6 shows how these findings can be used to address the specific challenges that arise when innovators face social opposition. One application shows how public health interventions may be designed in order to trigger network cascades of behavior change in at-risk populations. Another application considers how social networks can be used to incubate the spread of an innovative technology in a population where an alternative product is already entrenched. In each case, the lesson is the same: clustering the early adopters together can increase the spread of innovation.

Chapter 7 turns to the topic of organizational performance and shows how the findings in this book challenge conventional wisdom about the value of information brokers for diffusing innovations. This chapter identifies the importance of *wide bridges* for spreading new behaviors and ideas across organizational boundaries. The discussion here also explores the origins of network structure. This chapter shows how the identities that people have within an organization can influence the structure of the networks that emerge, and demonstrates how organizational identities can be used to design networks that are effective for diffusion.

Building on these practical applications, part 3 takes a hands-on approach to constructing new forms of social capital online. Chapter 8 offers experimental findings on how to design social networks among strangers to increase the flow of new behaviors. The results highlight the importance of both social relevance and empathy in network ties and show how these factors can be strengthened within existing online settings by incorporating *homophily*—that is, similarity between social contacts—into the architecture of a social network.

Chapter 9 then turns to the difficult problem of how to control the kinds of behaviors that spread online. Social influence comes in all shapes and sizes, and there are some circumstances in which constructing influential networks may backfire by spreading undesirable behaviors. The relational context of social networks comes to the foreground here. The results show that sometimes the most intuitive network strategies for inducing behavior change can have the least desirable outcomes. To offer some guidance on how to avoid this, chapter 9 identifies how features of social comparison and social support in online network settings can determine the kinds of influences that people will have on each other's behavior. A policy experiment illustrates these ideas by showing how the design of relationships within an online community can catalyze, or inhibit, changes in physical activity.

By the end of this book, the discussion has developed from studying the effects of strong and weak ties on diffusion to demonstrating how the principle of social reinforcement gives new insight into the network dynamics of behavior change. The basic approach throughout is always the same: seeing how imperceptible changes in the structure of social relationships produce significant differences in collective outcomes. This method allows more than the understanding of individual behavior: it provides an appreciation of the unseen forces that guide the movements of collective behavior. The most promising finding is that the reasonable expectation that people will resist behavior change does not mean that people are incorrigible. Nor does it mean that diffusion will fail. Instead, this expectation reveals the pathways that behavioral contagions will need to follow if they are to flow through a population—and the strategies that can be used to make this process most effective.

PART I

Theory

Ideas and products and messages and
behaviors spread like viruses do.
—Malcolm Gladwell, *The Tipping Point*

CHAPTER 2

Understanding Diffusion

This book addresses a simple yet persistent problem. The things that we would like to spread often fail to diffuse. At the same time, the things that we want to prevent from spreading often succeed despite our best attempts to stop them.[1]

A good example of this problem, which has had catastrophic consequences worldwide, is the HIV/AIDS epidemic. The spread of HIV is unprecedented. Over the last thirty-five years, the disease has spread from the first diagnosed patient in 1980, to reach more than 37 million people worldwide. The unthinkable scale of this disease comes in part from its ability to diffuse through sexual-contact networks. If HIV were less effective at exploiting these network ties, it would be easier to stop; however, the challenges of preventing unprotected sex have contributed to making HIV/AIDS one of the most destructive pandemics in history.[2]

Surprisingly, one of the most effective prevention strategies for the sexual transmission of HIV is male circumcision. The procedure significantly lowers transmission rates from women to men, which can prevent infected individuals from unknowingly carrying the disease to multiple partners. For public health workers trying to prevent the further spread of HIV in sub-Saharan Africa, one primary tactic has been to encourage adolescents and sexually active adults to undergo the procedure.[3] But efforts to increase male circumcision rates have lagged in many countries due to religious practices and social norms that actively oppose it. This conflict is so acute that early efforts to promote circumcision in Kenya, where one in four adults was infected with HIV, resulted in NGO workers being violently removed from some of the most affected areas because of local backlash against the interventions.[4]

An intuitive way to address this problem is to devise an alternative prevention method that is less personally invasive and less culturally charged but nevertheless just as effective. The most exciting innovation in the last five years for HIV prevention has been the introduction of pre-exposure prophylaxis (PrEP) medications. A single daily pill of antiretroviral medication can be up to 90% effective in preventing infection. This highly potent medication can essentially eliminate HIV transmission without confronting any of the obstacles that challenge the spread of circumcision.[5]

Yet, in two recent PrEP trials with women in sub-Saharan Africa, the medication was found to be ineffective in preventing HIV. The problem was simply that very few participants actually took it. In one trial, only 30% of the women who were putatively taking the daily medication had any traces of the drug detected in their blood. This discovery rattled the HIV research community, which had not anticipated that there would be such serious problems with adherence. In subsequent interviews with trial participants, some women reported that they had feared that the PrEP medications—which are the same drugs used to treat HIV—might actually give them HIV, while others said they were concerned that if they took the medication, people in their community would think they had HIV and discriminate against them.[6] These views were common in the study population despite participants receiving informational counseling about the medication's safety and the importance of HIV prevention in their community. Thus, as with circumcision, diffusion efforts were frustrated by surprisingly high levels of resistance to the behavior.[7]

This basic problem of diffusion—that is, the failure to spread behavior—occurs whenever behavior change encounters resistance. Attempts to spread everything from vaccinations to innovative technologies to environmentally friendly business practices have faced similar difficulties. The less familiar an innovation is, and the more inconvenient, uncomfortable, or expensive it is, the greater the resistance will typically be, and the less likely it will be to diffuse.[8]

The typical solution to this problem has been to focus on the innovation itself by making the innovation easier to use, more familiar, and less costly. In many situations, these strategies can be effective. But, what happens when the innovation cannot be "simplified" into something more contagious? Sometimes cultural beliefs and normative entrenchment can create enduring opposition to change, particularly when that change challenges basic ideas about gender, status, or power.[9]

The University of Chicago anthropologist Michael Dietler, for instance, presents an interesting example of mud-brick houses failing to diffuse in Kenyan villages where poorly insulated thatched-roof housing was a constant source of hardship for families. Mud-brick houses were cheaper, required about the same construction time, and were much less difficult to maintain. However, the strength of the marriage bond in these villages was tied to a gendered division of labor in which women were dependent upon men to continually repair their dwelling. Mud-brick houses would eliminate this dependency and threaten to destabilize the marriage bonds in the village. It was not until village members saw the innovation successfully adopted by several households in a nearby community–where families found a way to maintain their system of marital dependence while assimilating the innovative housing technology–that the innovation finally spread to their village.[10]

Individuals who face the loss of privilege or power are expected to resist change, but even people who may benefit from change may not want to see a familiar system of relations that they understand be disrupted. As a result, technological and medical innovations—such as contraception, inoculation, irrigation, and even education—can face resistance if they threaten to disturb entrenched patterns of social relations.[11] This book offers a new approach to this problem. Instead of attempting to change the innovation, I focus on how changes to the social network of a population can improve the spread of innovative behaviors.

What was the difference between San Francisco, CA and Denver, CO that allowed gay bars to spread in one city during the 1970s and not the other? Why did private enterprise spread in the Wenzhou province of China and not in Shanghai? How was it possible for an anti-vaccination campaign in Marin County, CA to prevent families from immunizing their children, and what can be done about it?[12] The answers to these questions illustrate how the structure of social networks can be used to impede, or accelerate, the spread of behaviors. While it may not always be possible to alter behaviors to make them more attractive, it is often possible to identify and target social pathways that can increase the legitimacy and adoption of social change.

To make progress in understanding the vast number of situations in which this approach may be applicable, it is necessary to find a way of representing what is common in these situations without becoming mired in the specific details of each setting. Fortunately, there is such a general representation available: the network model of social diffusion.

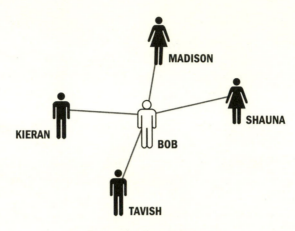

Figure 2.1 Ego Network

SOCIAL NETWORKS

Social networks have become a lingua franca for every ilk of social scientist—from archaeologists studying the spread of kiln and firing techniques in ancient India, to social psychologists studying the spread of reconciliation in the current Israeli/Palestinian conflict.[13]

One consequence of the use of network terminology across so many fields is that the term "social networks" has rapidly evolved over the last few decades. Confusion often results from the fact that it is now used in several different ways. A brief stage setting will be useful to explain how the term is being used here.[14]

Originally, social networks were ego networks, which consisted of a person, or ego (for instance, "Bob"), and his direct social contacts.[15]

In figure 2.1, the focal node of the ego network, Bob, has four contacts: Madison, Kieran, Shauna, and Tavish. Examining the traits of Bob's contacts provides some insight into Bob's patterns of association. Are most of Bob's friends male, female, or gender dysphoric? Are his friends the same race as he is, are they the same race as each other, or are they of mixed-race heritage? Do Bob and his friends have similar economic backgrounds and political beliefs?

While this is a rudimentary notion of a social network, it has been a useful way of detecting patterns of segregation and integration along a variety of characteristics, ranging from social and political beliefs to race, health, and religious values. There have been several important innovations in the last several decades that have pushed past the idea

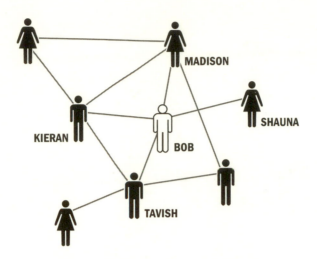

Figure 2.2 Friends of Friends Network

of ego networks; however, this basic approach to networks research is still used quite productively in several important areas of sociology. For instance, the ego network strategy has been used to study general trends of cultural and social change in the United States, and to discover patterns of peer influence in social support networks. Yet, despite its usefulness for many problems, this strategy confronts some notable limitations when it comes to identifying any process of diffusion that extends beyond the ego network.[16]

A major leap forward in thinking about social networks and diffusion came from Granovetter's work on weak ties. Building on ideas from Georg Simmel and others, Granovetter's thesis of the strength of weak ties emphasized that to understand the role of networks in social diffusion it was necessary to look beyond the ego network.[17] To understand Bob's beliefs and behaviors, there is more to the story than just who Bob is connected to. It also matters who Bob's friends are connected to.

As shown in figure 2.2, Bob's friends Madison and Kieran are connected to one another, while Shauna does not have any connections to the rest of Bob's neighborhood. The consequence of this structural pattern is that Madison and Kieran are able to pressure Bob to conform to behaviors that they agree with. And in turn, Kieran and Bob can then coordinate to pressure Tavish.

By contrast, Shauna is not subject to the same social pressures as the rest of Bob's friends and can thus be considered a weak tie in Bob's

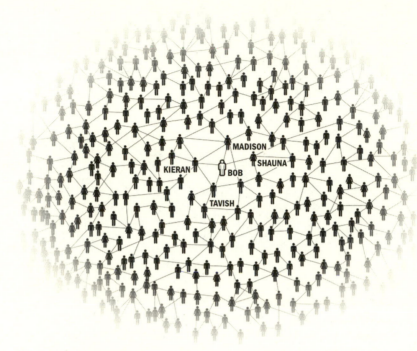

Figure 2.3 Bird's-Eye View of the Social Network

social network. As a result, the tie between Bob and Shauna can act as a valuable conduit for new ideas, information, and behaviors into Bob's neighborhood. The vast literature that has followed from this idea explores the implications of strong and weak ties for everything from strategic advantage in corporate exchange networks, to racial segregation in schools, to the spread of HIV.[18]

As influential as this step was, one more major leap forward in networks thinking was needed to reach the contemporary view of networks that is used here. This step was to look beyond the ego network, not just to Bob's friends and their friends but also to their friends' friends, and their friends' friends' friends, and so forth, all the way out to the rest of the population. This "bird's eye" view of social life—looking at the entire pattern of social connections across millions of people—provides a way of characterizing the large-scale structure of social relations within a society, as illustrated in figure 2.3.

To explore these massive social webs, new methods of computational analysis (such as network science and data science) have been imported from the natural and mathematical sciences into sociology. These tools provide new ways of characterizing the large-scale statistical properties of highly connected social networks. As a result, new concepts such as *small-world topologies* (networks with weak ties that shrink the degrees of separation between strangers) and *scale-free networks* (networks with highly connected "hubs" who link a population together) have become useful ways of thinking about how network structure can affect a population's collective behavior.[19]

Nevertheless, while the influx of new methods from the "hard" sciences has offered powerful new ways of studying social networks, it is important to keep in mind that these approaches are only useful here because their application bears a sociological origin. The intuition that the large-scale patterns of association in society can tell us something important about the behaviors that will emerge is an idea that dates back at least to Simmel's work on the interconnected web of group affiliations.[20] For more than a century, the idea has been firmly rooted in sociology that the underlying structure of social interactions in society can influence how social life will evolve. This is the idea that frames my approach, and motivates the belief that by understanding the network structure of a population, we can discover new ways to control the flow of behaviors across it.

THE NETWORK MODEL OF DIFFUSION

To represent the features of network diffusion that are found in most situations, a common approach is to study social contagions as we would study the spread of a pathogen. The simplest version of the network model of diffusion is to represent each person in the population as having two possible states. Either a person is *unactivated*, in which case they are "susceptible" to a contagion, or they become *activated* through social contact, in which case they are "infected" and can transmit the contagion to others.

Figure 2.4 illustrates a diffusion process that begins from a single person, Bob, who is the first person to become activated. This individual can be thought of as the "seed" person. He is patient zero. The seed is exogenously activated; however, all subsequent activation flows endogenously from Bob through his social contacts. Once Bob transmits the contagion to his neighbors, they become activated and can then activate their contacts, and so on, spreading the contagion through the network.

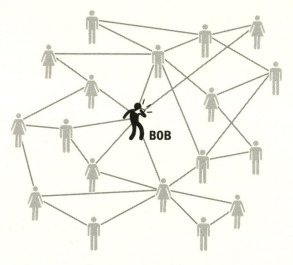

Figure 2.4 Patient Zero

There are many different kinds of transmission rules that can be used to determine how a contagion spreads from one person to another. The simplest transmission rule is that Bob will spread the contagion to all of his contacts. In turn, Bob's contacts will activate all of their contacts, and so on. Figure 2.5 shows how, following this simple transmission rule, a single activated seed in a connected network can result in a contagion spreading from person to person to reach the rest of the population.

For an infectious disease, knowledge of each person's network of contacts provides a map that can be used to trace the diffusion of a pathogen and to anticipate how many people are likely to become infected. One of the things that the network diffusion model is useful for is showing when and how this spreading process will unfold. Whether or not there will be an epidemic outbreak of an infectious disease often depends upon the pattern of connections through which the disease can be transmitted.

When this model is applied to the spread of behavior, it is common to assume that once an individual is activated, she stays activated. In public health settings, this is referred to as a *one-and-done* intervention. Circumcision works this way, as does the polio vaccination. An individual only needs to become activated once to remain "treated" for life.

Condom use, however, is different. Condom use is effective only if people maintain the behavior.[21] Similarly, preventative screenings, PrEP

Figure 2.5 Diffusion of a Social Contagion

medications, diabetes treatments, and malaria medication all require regular maintenance in order for individuals to be considered activated.

The differences between these alternative modes of activation–that is, one-and-done versus long-term maintenance–and what they imply for effective strategies for promoting network diffusion, are important for almost every kind of spreading process and will therefore be explored in detail in the following chapters. Fortunately, the network model of diffusion can be used to study all of these various forms of activation, making it a useful way to explore everything from measles-mumps-rubella (MMR) inoculations, to emotional contagions, to brand loyalty.

Given the complexity of diffusion processes in the real world, the simplicity of the network model is what makes it so appealing. It represents any situation in which social contacts are channels of transmission for the spread of behavior. Looking carefully at a network, it is possible to identify how the structure of connections can alter the process of diffusion, giving us new insight into the question, how do social networks influence the spread of behavior?

FROM WEAK TIES TO SMALL WORLDS

The most famous answer to this question comes from Mark Granovetter's strength of weak ties theory. "Strong" and "weak" have a double meaning in Granovetter's usage. One meaning is relational (at the dyadic level), the other is structural (at the population level). The relational meaning refers to the interpersonal strength of the tie as a conduit for influence. Weak ties connect acquaintances who interact less frequently, are less invested in the relationship, and are less readily influenced by one another. Strong ties connect close friends or kin whose interactions are frequent, affectively charged, and highly salient to each other. Strong ties increase the trust we place in close informants, the exposure we incur from contagious intimates, and the influence of close friends. As Everett Rogers noted, "Certainly, the influence potential of network ties with an individual's intimate friends is stronger than the opportunity for influence with an individual's 'weak ties.' "[22]

Granovetter also introduced a second, *structural* meaning. The structural strength of a tie refers to the ability of a tie to facilitate diffusion, cohesion, and integration of a social network by linking otherwise distant nodes. Granovetter's insight is that ties that are weak in the relational sense—such that the relations are less-salient or frequent—are often strong in the structural sense—such that they provide shortcuts across the social network. Although casual friendships are relationally weak, they are more likely to be formed between socially distant actors with few network neighbors in common. These "long-range ties" between otherwise distant nodes provide access to new information and greatly increase the rate at which information propagates, despite the relational weakness of the tie as a conduit.

Granovetter observed that when two people have a strong connection to a third person, they are also likely to have a connection with one another. There are several reasons for this structural regularity. One reason is that we tend to be similar to the people we know well, so these people also tend to be similar to each other, making it likely that they will form a tie. We also tend to share social contexts with our strong ties (for example, we belong to the same churches, neighborhoods, schools, and so on), which means that they also tend to share these contexts with each other and are likely to meet. Moreover, since we interact frequently with the people we know well, it is likely that they will be part of the same interactions together. As illustrated in figure 2.6, the closer that Bob is with Tavish and Keiran, the more likely it is that a tie will form to close the triad.[23]

This means that a person's strong ties tend to be located within "closed triads"—that is, social triangles in the network. A common way for network scholars to study this is to ask, "what fraction of each person's friends are connected to each other?" The answer tells the level of local "clustering" in a person's neighborhood, which also tells the average strength of the ties there. Thus, relational affect translates into network structure, and vice versa. Strong ties tend to be clustered, and

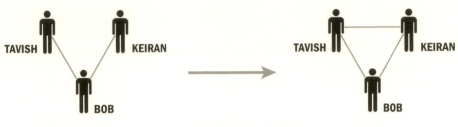

Figure 2.6 Triadic Closure

clustered ties tend to be strong. Correspondingly, network ties that span long social distances tend to be weak ties, and weak ties tend to be long.

Viewed from the *relational* perspective of each individual, strong ties are the most important links in the social network. They are proximate, trusted, and familiar, and therefore the most influential for diffusion. However, from the *bird's eye* perspective of the entire network, strong ties also tend to be bunched together in redundant clusters of interlocking triangles. Consequently, for a contagion to spread from one part of a network to another across strong ties, it has to travel through lots of clustered neighborhoods to get there.

Figure 2.7 shows an example. Let's say that Maya, shown in black in the far left panel, needs to hire a new programmer and wants to use her "word of mouth" network to spread the news of her job opening. Figure 2.7 illustrates how information about Maya's job will spread through a clustered social network. Everyone in this network has four

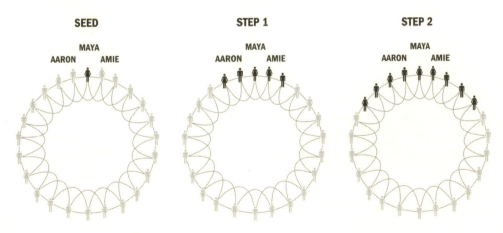

Figure 2.7 Diffusion in a Clustered Network

neighbors, two ties on the left and two ties on right. In the far left panel in figure 2.7, Maya acts as the "seed" for initiating the diffusion process. She tells all of her close friends about the job then asks them to tell all of their close friends about it, and so on. In the first "step" of this diffusion process, shown in the middle panel, Maya activates her four immediate contacts, shown in black. Then, in the second step, shown in the panel on the far right, each of Maya's contacts tells each of their contacts about the job. Ideally, Maya would like to see this word of mouth process go viral, so she can quickly find the right person.

However, there is a problem. The problem is that many of the ties among Maya's friends wind up reaching back to people who have already heard about the job from Maya. In Step 1, Maya told both Aaron and Amie about the job opening; then, in Step 2, they both spread the information to their neighbors. But since Aaron and Amie are connected to each other, they both wind up sending redundant messages to each other in Step 2. Signals that should go to new people are wasted going to people who already know about the job. It would have been much more efficient if Maya's friends had network ties to other people instead of to each other.

These wasted signals are an inevitable consequence of diffusion in a clustered social network. In networks with lots of triangles, two steps outward often equals one step back. If we play this out repeatedly, step after step, it becomes clear that while strong ties have high levels of subjective relevance for each person, they also have a high level of objective redundancy for the network as a whole. This makes them highly inefficient for diffusion.

Weak ties, by contrast, are relationally the least important contacts in each person's ego network. People connected by weak ties are often not very similar to each other, nor do they typically interact frequently or substantively. Subjectively, they are often the least noticeable features of a person's social landscape.

However, Granovetter observed that this is also what makes them so important for diffusion. The fact that weak ties are not embedded in the network of strong relations gives them a tremendous structural power. While strong ties tend to be clustered into triangles of shared friends, weak ties branch randomly throughout a population.[24] A key feature of Granovetter's insight is that structure, not affect, plays the major role in diffusion. Once affect is removed, the purely structural effect of adding weak ties to a network is to create shortcuts that link distant regions together.

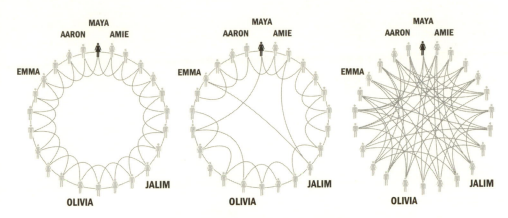

Figure 2.8 The Small World Model

This idea is illustrated in figure 2.8 using the small-world network model. From left to right, the three panels in figure 2.8 show how introducing weak ties into a clustered population changes the network's capacity for diffusion. The clustered network on the far left-hand side in figure 2.8 is the same network that we saw in figure 2.7. Maya and her friends are connected in overlapping neighborhoods, and everyone has four contacts, two on the left and two on the right. From left to right, the panels in figure 2.8 explore what happens to the network when clustered ties are "rewired" to create weak ties.

Moving from the far-left panel to the middle panel, we can see that a few of the local neighborhood ties are broken and then randomly reconnected to other people in the population.[25] While Emma and Jalim used to be many steps away from each other, they are now connected directly. These random connections create "shortcuts" that reach farther across the network than the ties they are replacing. The importance of these long ties for diffusion is that now instead of information about a new job having to travel many steps to get from Maya to Olivia, it can now travel between them in only two steps. Less clustering in people's ties translates into faster access to the population.

A common way of talking about this is in terms of the "degrees of separation" between people, a notion that was made popular by the Pulitzer Prize–nominated play, *Six Degrees of Separation*.[26] The play highlights the power of a random tie to bind together the diverse members of a society who might otherwise never have any contact with one another. It is the same idea here.

In the small-world model, each connection can be thought of in terms of a handshake. The degrees of separation is the number of handshakes that it takes, going from contact to contact, to travel from one randomly chosen person, through all of the intervening friends of friends, to reach another randomly chosen person.

If we measure the average degrees of separation in a network, it tells how "small" the world is. The term "small world" refers to a network where it is possible to get between any two people in just a few handshakes. Highly clustered networks are usually "large worlds"—it typically takes hundreds or thousands of handshakes to get across a large network.

Consider, for example, the networks shown in figure 2.8, but much bigger—say, with 80,000 people in them. In a clustered network like the one shown on the far left of figure 2.8, the degrees of separation will be on the same scale as the size of the population. So, if there are 80,000 people in the network, the average degrees of separation will be several thousand steps. It will take thousands (and possibly tens of thousands) of handshakes to get between any two people.

But when clustered networks are rewired to create long ties, it reduces the number of redundant ties in each person's neighborhood and transforms the global topology from a clustered, large-world network into a randomized small world.[27] In figure 2.8, the far-right panel shows that when this rewiring process is complete, there is no longer any clustering in people's neighborhoods—every tie is a weak tie.

For Maya's word-of-mouth campaign, this means that each step out from Maya—to her friends, and her friends' friends, and so on—reaches exponentially more people than it did before. This model provides an elegant mathematical explanation for the "six degrees of separation" principle.[28] In a small world network, the distance between any two people is on the same scale as the *logarithm* of the size of the network. Thus, the degrees of separation between people stays incredibly small even as the population size becomes vast. As a result, even in a population of 80,000 people, the typical degrees of separation between any two people is reduced from several thousand steps to around four steps. Even if there are one billion people in a population, on average everyone is still only less than ten handshakes away from each other!

This idea–and the observation that it is big news for diffusion–underpins Granovetter's theory of the strength of weak ties. Decades before the small-world model, when Granovetter first proposed the strength of weak ties, none of these ideas had been articulated so

Figure 2.9 Diffusion in a Large World

clearly.[29] However, Granovetter's insight rests upon the notion, held in common with the small-world model, that increasing weak links across a network can accelerate diffusion by dramatically increasing each individual's exposure to the population. The stunning result from the small-world model is to show just how dramatic this increase can be. For a diffusion process that starts from a single seed, a smaller world with a greater fraction of weak ties markedly increases the number of people that a contagion will reach on every step into the network. Thus, weak ties can transform a spreading process from a slow spatial wave that cascades gradually across a population into a global virus that explodes suddenly throughout a social network.

To see what this means for Maya's word of mouth campaign, figures 2.9, 2.10, and 2.11 show these dynamics in action. These "computational experiments" use the same three networks shown in figure 2.8—a clustered spatial network (shown in fig. 2.9), a partially rewired network with a few weak ties (shown in fig. 2.10), and a random network composed entirely of weak ties (shown in fig. 2.11). In each figure, the time series for the diffusion process is shown progressing from left to right. The elapsed time for each diffusion process is indicated by the calendar above each of the panels.

At the beginning of each of the three experiments, all of the nodes (except the two initial seeds) are unactivated, as shown in gray. They have not yet adopted the behavior. The two seed nodes are shown in black. They are the social innovators—namely, Maya and Aaron—who initiate the diffusion process. Diffusion follows a basic social

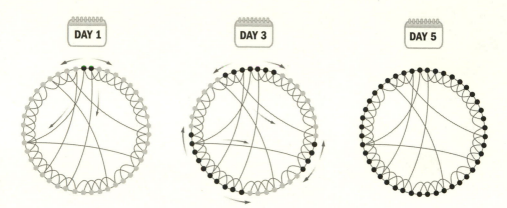

Figure 2.10 Diffusion with Weak Ties

transmission rule. As with any word-of-mouth process, the only way that persons can become activated is by coming into contact with an activated neighbor. When activated, nodes turn black and pass the word along to their neighbors. Diffusion continues until the social contagion has spread through the entire network.

Just as in figures 2.7 and 2.8, in these simulations everyone has four neighbors, that is, two neighbors on the left and two on the right. Figure 2.9 shows that when the diffusion process is initiated, information spreads from the seed nodes to the neighbors on both sides. From there, it spreads to the neighbors' neighbors, and so on around the network. By the end of the diffusion process in figure 2.9, it takes fourteen days for word of mouth to spill over from one neighborhood to the next, until it ultimately reaches the entire population.

Things get more interesting when we add some weak ties. Figure 2.10 repeats the diffusion experiment, except this time a few of the connections have been randomly rewired to create long-distance ties in the network. It is important to remember that the overall number of ties remains the same—everyone still has four neighbors. The only difference is that there is slightly less redundancy because a few of those neighbors are no longer connected to each other.

At the start, the diffusion process initially unfolds as before. Word of mouth spreads out spatially until it hits one of the long-distance links. It then jumps across the network and begins to fan out across the new area until it hits another long-distance link and jumps again. Each long tie allows information about the job to spread to an untouched

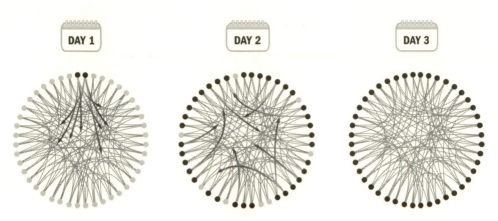

Figure 2.11 Diffusion in a Small World

region of the network. The result is that word of the job spreads much faster than it did before. Instead of taking fourteen days to reach everyone in the network, now it only takes five days.

What happens if we add more weak ties? Figure 2.11 repeats the same experiment in a completely random network, in which all of the ties have been rewired. In this network, redundancy is minimized, giving each person maximum exposure to the network. As in all the previous experiments, every individual has four contacts, but now there is no clustering in the neighborhoods. Consequently, as the diffusion process gets going, each new person that is reached creates exponentially more new exposures than before.

The results show the stunning effects of weak ties on diffusion. On the first step, word of the new job jumps from the seed nodes to activate eight new individuals, who in turn spread the information to thirty-two other individuals. The social contagion spreads simultaneously to all parts of the social network. From there, it only takes one more step before everyone in the population is activated. Only two days after Maya tells people about the job, she is able find her ideal candidate, Olivia, who learns about it from a friend of a friend.[30]

These stunning dynamics tell an unambiguous story about the powerful effects of long distance ties for diffusion. Although long ties are affectively weak, they are structurally strong. They perform the impressive social function of binding a large and diverse network together, replacing inefficient, neighborhood-based pathways with efficient cross-cutting ties that accelerate the spread of social contagions.[31]

As Granovetter put it, "Whatever is to be diffused can reach a larger number of people, and traverse a greater social distance, when passed through weak ties rather than strong."[32] It is difficult to overstate the impact of this idea. For every field of diffusion research, from the transmission of pathogens to the growth of social movements,[33] the lesson is the same: weak ties accelerate the spread of social contagions, and small worlds are far better for diffusion than large worlds. This intuitive theory of network diffusion stands behind tens of thousands of contemporary studies of social spreading. With this intuition firmly in hand, the topic we turn to next is what this theory reveals when we compare it to empirical studies of how behaviors spread.

AN EMPIRICAL PUZZLE FOR THE STRENGTH OF WEAK TIES

Social movements are perhaps the most studied examples of network diffusion in sociology. As Robert Putnam wrote, "Social networks are the quintessential resource of movement organizers. Reading groups became sinews of the suffrage movement. Friendship networks, not environmental sympathies, accounted for which Pennsylvanians became involved in grassroots protests after the Three Mile Island nuclear accident. [And, s]ocial ties more than ideals or self-interest explain who was recruited to Freedom Summer, a climactic moment in the civil rights movement."[34]

When a social movement expands from the initial activists to the new recruits, each wave of participants becomes the front line of new recruiters. As Granovetter noted, weak ties intuitively accelerate this process by allowing a recruitment drive to reach outside close friendship networks to attract attention from broader segments of the population. Particularly when a social movement is risky or dangerous, and most people are initially unlikely to join, large-scale mobilization depends upon recruitment networks that can activate weak ties that will increase the movement's exposure to the population.[35]

It is puzzling, then, that social movements often do not follow the path predicted by the theory of weak ties. Contrary to the intuitive expectation from the above simulations, studies of collective action consistently report that mobilization spreads spatially, like a wave front, propagating through clustered networks, rather than exploding globally, like a virus, jumping across long-distance ties.[36]

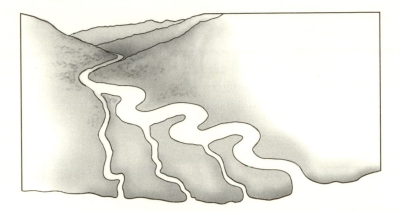

Figure 2.12 River with Branching Distributaries

A particularly striking example of this pattern of spreading comes from Roger Gould's study of the Paris Commune revolts.[37] The revolution began in the small, tightly knit urban communities of post-Revolutionary Paris. As the movement grew, instead of exploiting long ties to excite revolutionary action in new areas of the city, the movement travelled spatially, cascading across the densely populated urban neighborhoods.

For the theory of weak ties, this is a very strange pattern of growth to understand. Consider, by analogy, how a river flows from its source in the highlands down to its mouth by the ocean. As shown in figure 2.12, as the main branch of the river flows toward the mouth, smaller rivers, called distributaries, often exploit opportunities to branch off and flow more quickly down to the sea. These branches are analogous to weak ties—they are shortcuts that the river can take to jump from the main branch, which is wide and winding and relatively slow, to quickly reach the ocean.

What Gould observed is tantamount to watching a flood of new water flow down the main branch while completely bypassing all of the distributaries. It is baffling. Indeed, it is a law of mechanics that in any physical system material flows always exploit all of the open pathways, particularly the most efficient routes.[38] Gould's results indicate that the human dynamics of diffusion do not seem to obey this law.

Rather, Gould's description of the spread of mobilization through Paris suggests that the revolution passed through each of the local neighborhoods before reaching distant parts of the urban population.

Gould's account seems unnaturally slow. Long ties, like the distributaries of a river, create opportunities for a social movement to leap outside of geographical constraints to excite activism in new parts of the population. This ability of long-distance ties to escape the limitations of geographic space is what underlies fears about the epidemic spread of infectious diseases and animates the promise of viral marketing strategies. In stark contrast to this way of thinking about diffusion, Gould's description is remarkably two-dimensional. Yet, despite the fact that the diffusion process was limited to slower, geographic pathways, it nevertheless grew into a tidal wave of revolutionary action.

From a networks perspective, it is hard to make sense of this story. A diffusion process that restricts its own access to the broader population should not grow so effectively. In general, the rule is: greater exposure equals greater diffusion. As Granovetter put it, "We may surmise that since the resistance to a risky or deviant activity is greater than to a safe or normal one, a larger number of people will have to be exposed to it and adopt it, in the early stages, before it will spread in a chain reaction. Individuals with many weak ties are, by my arguments, best placed to diffuse such a difficult innovation."[39] Thus, a diffusion process that fails to exploit weak ties, and therefore limits its own exposure to the population, is likely to eliminate its own best chances of success.

Decades later, however, a similar spreading dynamic was observed in the growth of trade unionization in Northern Europe. Census measures from 1890 to 1940 show the near-universal expansion of trade unions across Sweden's political districts. Similar to the Paris Commune, the rapid spread of the movement was not accelerated by long-distance jumps across the social network. Instead, mobilization traveled largely through spatial ties. Contrary to the intuitive picture of rapid diffusion offered by the strength of weak ties, Peter Hedström found that overlapping residential networks and clustered neighborhoods were responsible for the large-scale success of the movement. He concluded, "Spatial properties and network densities are likely to influence considerably both the speed of a mobilization process and the success of a movement in organizing the relevant population."[40]

A more recent example of this same anomalous pattern of diffusion is found in Doug McAdam and Ronnelle Paulsen's study of Freedom Summer, in which they document the work of civil rights activists who fought to protect minority voting opportunities in the 1964 national elections. Participation in the collective action involved traveling to Mississippi during a time of violence and oppression. It was incredibly

dangerous. Participants faced confrontations with lethal force. Nevertheless, these activists managed to mobilize a recruitment drive that drew
people from across the country. This is a particularly striking case of mobilization because participants were recruited primarily through word
of mouth. For this kind of campaign, weak ties are naturally expected
to be highly effective for getting the word out and for activating interest among large numbers of people who otherwise would not have had
direct social contact with the movement. Yet, despite the fact that weak
ties offered an obvious advantage for rapidly increasing the movement's
exposure, McAdam and Paulsen concluded that membership grew primarily through recruitment networks composed of strong ties.[41]

For the theory of weak ties, each of these examples is anomalous.
Why would a diffusion process spread through strong ties and clustered
neighborhoods rather than exploiting farther-reaching weak ties? While
these examples are anomalous, they are not uncommon. Similar observations have been made in studies of everything from innovation diffusion to social epidemiology. This pattern of "low-dimensional" spreading has been found in the diffusion of social cooperation, protest
events, the spread of consumer goods, the diffusion of birth-control
methods, the growth of violent-crime epidemics, the spread of institutional norms, the adoption of cultural practices, and the propagation of
industrial technologies. In fact, this inefficient pattern of spreading is
so prevalent that Lisa Berkman and Ichiro Kawachi finish their introduction to the field of social epidemiology by concluding that dense
neighborhood networks and cohesive social settings are the most likely
places for the rapid spread of innovative health behaviors.[42]

Considered altogether, these anomalies confront us with an empirical
puzzle. Long-distance ties are the social pathways along which contagions spread most effectively. Yet, the empirical literature on diffusion
consistently finds that social contagions skip over weak ties, spreading
instead through less efficient networks. Like a river that leaves its distributaries dry, these diffusion processes oddly use the longest, slowest
channels to run their course. What does this mean for the strength of
weak ties? And, ultimately, what does it tell us about the networks that
are best for diffusion?

CHAPTER 3

The Theory of Complex Contagions

There is an elegant solution to the empirical puzzle that confronts the strength of weak ties. It suggests that this puzzle is merely a problem of counterfactuals; that is, although we may observe in a given empirical setting that a behavior spreads quickly through a spatially clustered population, that does not necessarily mean that spatial networks are the most effective pathways for diffusion. Isn't it possible that the same contagion would spread even more effectively in another network structure? For instance, while Gould's study of the Paris Commune reports that mobilization diffused spatially, perhaps this pattern of spreading was due to the fact that there were simply no weak ties in those social networks. It would be like a river with no distributaries. The reason the contagion did not flow outside the main branch is the simple historical fact that there were no other branches for it to follow.

Thus, the reason that empirical studies have found that spatial networks and strong ties are effective for diffusion may simply be that there were no other pathways for these diffusion processes to exploit. The counterfactual hypothesis is that *had there been* more weak ties in those empirical networks, those diffusion processes would have followed more efficient pathways. In which case, weak ties would have allowed each of those diffusion processes to spread even faster and farther than they did. So, goes the argument, the networks that happen to be observed in a particular empirical example of diffusion may not actually tell us much about the networks that are best for diffusion.

The computational experiments in chapter 2 support this counterfactual hypothesis. Maya's word-of-mouth campaign diffused effectively in a spatial network, but it was able to spread exponentially faster in a network that was rewired to increase the number of weak ties. To see whether this counterfactual hypothesis can in fact explain the empirical anomalies that confront Granovetter's theory of diffusion, this chapter uses computational experiments to test the counterfactual hypothesis. Against this hypothesis, this chapter also tests a competing view that argues that these empirical anomalies are due to heterogeneity in the kinds of contagions that propagate across social networks. According to this view, long-distance ties will improve the spread of *simple* contagions, which can be transmitted from a single contact, but they will not help to spread *complex* contagions, which require contact with multiple sources of activation. The differences between simple and complex contagions are explained below in terms of the social mechanisms that create resistance to adoption. In other words, the reason behaviors may not spread like diseases is that they require legitimacy, credibility, or complementarity in order to be adopted.

In what follows, the strength of weak ties theory is tested against this alternative view. The results show that as networks are rewired to become ideal conduits for the spread of simple contagions, they become less suitable for spreading complex contagions. To explore the scope of these findings, this chapter concludes by testing the robustness of these results under conditions that increase the realism of the computational experiments. These robustness tests show that there is a broad class of situations in which the disease model of diffusion does not explain the spread of behavior.

SIMPLE AND COMPLEX CONTAGIONS

In their study of Freedom Summer, McAdam and Paulsen observed that "the fact that we are embedded in many relationships means that any major decision we are contemplating will likely be mediated by a significant subset of those relationships."[1] This passage offers useful insight into the important distinction between being exposed to a behavior—and knowing it is an option for you—and actually deciding to adopt that behavior for yourself.[2] There are many situations in which contact with a single activated individual is sufficient for exposure but not for transmission.

Thus, it is useful to make a distinction here between the kinds of contagions for which a single exposure is sufficient for transmission, and the kinds of contagions for which transmission requires several sources of reinforcement. For infectious diseases, such as the influenza virus, a single exposure is often sufficient. Even though there may only be one person in my network who has the flu, if that person sneezes on me, I may catch it. If I in turn sneeze on others, they can also become infected, and so on. At no point did anyone need to be convinced to get sick. Measles is an even more telling example. Nearly every contact

Figure 3.1 Simple Contagion

between a sick person and a susceptible one will lead to transmission of the virus.

This is also the way that most information travels. Valuable information, for instance about changing weather conditions or new media events, spreads easily from person to person, as does more banal information about the score of a sporting event. If I learn the score of today's playoff game, I can easily repeat it at a party. Anyone who hears me also learns the score and can just as easily spread this information to others. No one needs to be coerced or pressured to adopt the informational contagion or to spread it. News propagates effortlessly through a network. For this reason, diseases and information are typically simple contagions, which only require a single activated contact for transmission.

Figure 3.1 illustrates this simple spreading dynamic. When a new contagion reaches a focal individual's neighborhood, she becomes activated and then spreads the contagion to the rest of her neighbors. While not every interaction between an infected person and a susceptible one will necessarily lead to a new activation, each exposure constitutes a positive probability of transmission, and extended contact increases the likelihood that a single activated individual will spread a simple contagion to each of her contacts.

By contrast, social movements, complex information (such as urban legends, or rumors that require confirmation), social norms, medical and health-related behaviors, innovation adoption, and large capital investments are different. They typically involve some kind of cost (financial, psychological, or reputational), risk, or complementarity, which increases an adopter's dependence on other people's decisions. The costlier, higher risk, or less familiar a behavior is, the more that the decision to adopt depends upon social confirmation.

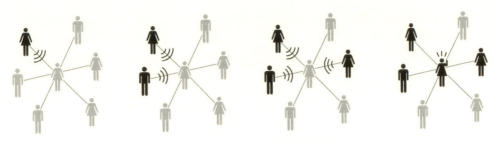

Figure 3.2 Complex Contagion

For this reason, any meaningful behavior change is likely to be a complex contagion—that is, one requiring contact with multiple sources of reinforcement in order to be transmitted. For a complex contagion, a person's "threshold" for adoption is defined as the number of activated contacts required to trigger her activation. Figure 3.2 illustrates these threshold dynamics. Because the focal individual initially resists adopting a costly new behavior, she requires several of her contacts to adopt it before she will. Her threshold for activation can only be overcome if she receives sufficient social reinforcement from her network to encourage her to adopt.[3]

Thus, while multiple *exposures* to the same infected individual may be sufficient for simple contagions to spread, multiple *sources* of exposure are needed to diffuse complex contagions. As McAdam and Paulsen put it, "Any major decision . . . will likely be mediated by a significant subset of [our] relationships."[4]

THE MECHANISMS OF COMPLEXITY

The more one reflects on this idea, the more apparent it becomes that most of the behaviors that we are interested in—such as investing in a market, choosing a career, selecting a neighborhood, adopting a high cost technology, choosing a method of contraception, joining a social movement, joining a church, and voting—are complex contagions. This is because the more that is at stake with a decision, the more dependent people are on receiving social confirmation. The less certainty there is, the more valuable social proof becomes. And the greater the reputational or financial cost of a decision, the more social reinforcement is needed to encourage adoption.

There are abundant examples of behaviors whose transmission requires exposure to more than one source. The willingness to repeat a bizarre urban legend, the adoption of unproven new technologies, the lure of educational attainment, the attractiveness of participating in risky migrations or social movements, the decision to exit formal gatherings, or the appeal of avant-garde fashion all may depend upon having contact with multiple prior adopters.[5]

There are at least four "social mechanisms" that explain why a complex contagion might require exposure to multiple sources of activation: strategic complementary, credibility, legitimacy, and emotional contagion.

Strategic complementarity: The value of a behavior increases with the number of others who adopt it.

Simply knowing about an innovation is rarely sufficient for adoption.[6] In situations where there are "network effects," the economic value of a choice can depend upon how many other people have made the same choice. The classic example of this is communication technologies. A single fax machine is not very useful. There is no reason to get a fax machine unless you know people who already have one. One person alone is not likely to convince you that it is worth the large capital expenditure; however, as more contacts have fax machines, the relative value of a fax machine increases. As more people adopt, the complementary value of the technology can turn it from a luxury item into a necessity.

The same is true of telephones, hand radios, email accounts, and social media accounts. The more people who adopt a social technology, the greater its inherent value is for everyone. The same dynamics also hold for participation in collective action. Studies of strikes, revolutions, and protests emphasize the positive externalities of each participant's contribution.[7] The costs and benefits for investing in public goods often depend on the number of prior contributors—the "critical mass" that makes additional efforts worthwhile. Complexity is an essential feature of any diffusion process that relies on complementarity to create value for future adopters.

Credibility: The more people who adopt a behavior the more believable it is that the behavior is beneficial or that it is worth the cost of adoption.

Innovations often lack credibility until adopted by people we know. For example, James Coleman found that doctors were reluctant to adopt medical innovations until they saw their colleagues using it. M. Lynne

Markus found the same pattern for the adoption of media technology, and Viswanath Venkatesh found that the decision to adopt new supply-chain technologies and management strategies relied on confirmatory evidence from peer institutions. The need for credibility can also increase the complexity of people's willingness to adopt new beliefs and attitudes. People's willingness to spread new urban legends and transfer folk knowledge generally depends upon multiple confirmations of the story before there is sufficient credibility to repeat it to others. The need for social confirmation may be greater when a story is learned from a socially distant contact—in order to allay concerns that surprising information is nothing more than fanciful invention of the informant. This is often the case with reputation effects. A single individual may be the source of misinformation about a colleague, but confirmation from multiple sources can reinforce a new reputational belief.[8]

Legitimacy: The more people who adopt a behavior, the greater the expectation is that other people will approve of the decision to adopt and the lower the risk of embarrassment or sanction.

Having several close friends participate in a collective action often increases a bystander's acceptance of the legitimacy of the movement. Similarly, people's decisions about what clothing to wear, what hairstyle to adopt, or what body parts to pierce are also highly dependent on legitimation from others who are doing the same. People are equally attentive to social expectations when adopting standards for their health and exercise routines. The same logic also applies to the importance of peer reinforcement in the growth of new markets. In part, this is because social proof reduces an individual's exposure to risk. In general, the uncertainty that attends large capital investments, forecasting decisions, and support of controversial social views can be allayed by seeing others adopt the behavior. The need for social reinforcement may thus be greater when there are reputational consequences of a behavior. There is safety in numbers. The reputational consequence of a wrong decision can be reduced if others also make the same decision.[9]

Emotional contagion: The excitement associated with adopting a behavior increases with the number of others who adopt it.

Most theoretical models of collective behavior—from action theory to threshold models to cybernetics—share the basic assumption that there are also expressive and symbolic impulses in human behavior that can translate into emotional, rather than deliberative, forms of social contagion. The communication and amplification of emotional energy in these settings typically emerges in socially concentrated gatherings where multiple people reinforce each other's excitation and expression of shared emotive states. The dynamics of emotional contagion have been observed in settings ranging from sporting events, to acts of cruelty, to the formation of philosophical circles.[10]

In light of the variety of social mechanisms that can give rise to complexity in behavioral transmission, the question I turn to now is what implications complexity may have for how behavior spreads through social networks.

COUNTERFACTUAL EXPERIMENTS WITH COMPLEXITY

To see what effect, if any, the complexity of a contagion has on the process of network diffusion, the small-world model from chapter 2 can be used to test the counterfactual hypothesis from the strength of weak ties. Like the computational experiments in the previous chapter, diffusion can be studied first on a clustered network and then observed as long ties are introduced and the degrees of separation in the network are reduced. At the end of this chapter, I will also explore what happens when we relax the simplifying assumptions of the small-world model to include more realistic features of empirical social networks.

To start with, a proper test of the strength of weak ties is to keep everything the same as it was before, with one exception. This time, we will assume that the contagion is complex.

To continue with the example from chapter 2, let's suppose that Maya's word-of-mouth campaign worked and that she has hired a new programmer and finished her software development project. Now she wants to use the same word-of-mouth strategy to diffuse her product. Instead of spreading information about a new job, this time Maya and her business partner, Aaron, are attempting to diffuse a new desktop application for people to install on their computers. So, this time, instead of one social contact being sufficient to transmit the contagion, each person requires confirmation from a second source of activation before being willing to adopt. In every other way, the computational experiments are the same as before.

The first experiment is shown in figure 3.3. It uses the same clustered network that we began with last time, in which every person has four

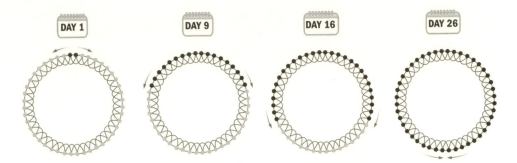

Figure 3.3 Diffusion in a Large World

neighbors, two on the right and two on the left. The nodes shown in gray indicate the actors who have not yet adopted the behavior. The two individuals shown in black—namely, Maya and Aaron—are the seeds who introduce the contagion into the population.

In the clustered network, the complex contagion spreads much like it did before. It cascades from neighborhood to neighborhood across the population. But notice that even though the behavior spreads to the entire population, it spreads more slowly than the simple contagion did. This time, it takes twenty-six days to spread because each person must wait for confirmation from a second source before they are willing to adopt the behavior themselves.

This slow-but-successful pattern of diffusion seems to lend credence to the counterfactual hypothesis. Because the complex contagion spreads so slowly through the spatial network, a few changes to the network topology will probably help to speed things up. For Maya and Aaron, who may face competition once their product is released, faster is better—getting the word out more quickly will hopefully translate into faster adoption. And based on the slow rate of diffusion in figure 3.3, there's a lot of room for improvement. Reducing the size of the world by adding a few long ties should be able to help out quite a bit—perhaps even more than it did for the simple contagion.

Figure 3.4 shows what happens when the network is rewired with a few weak ties. Instead of spreading faster, the contagion slows down! How can reducing the redundancy of network ties slow down a diffusion process? This seems like a paradoxical result—reducing the degrees of separation in a network should increase the rate of diffusion.

Before worrying too much about this, we can here take advantage of the fact that we have a counterfactual model. We can explore the

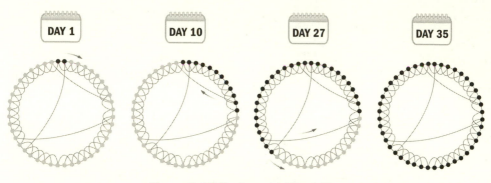

Figure 3.4 Diffusion with Weak Ties

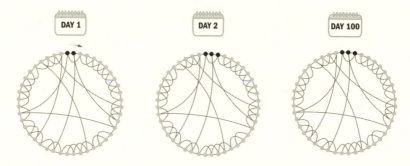

Figure 3.5 Diffusion with More Weak Ties

dynamics of diffusion a bit more and see what happens when some additional weak ties are added. If we're lucky, we can use the model to push past this bump in the road and see if a little more rewiring solves the problem.

But when more long ties are added, things get worse. Instead of helping to get diffusion going, diffusion stops entirely (figure 3.5). Moreover, adding even more long-distance ties does not help—diffusion has stopped and nothing seems to change that. For Maya and Aaron, the lesson is perplexing. All the strategies that worked so effectively for recruiting their job candidate completely failed when it came to diffusing their product.

In fact, the only way to make the product spread effectively is to go all the way back to the spatial network that we started with originally. Making the world smaller seems to cause irreparable problems for the spread of a complex contagion. To explain this puzzling result, we need to understand why long-distance ties would not help diffusion. For

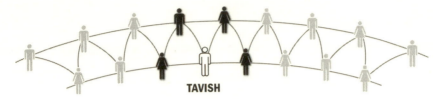

Figure 3.6 Tavish's Neighborhood

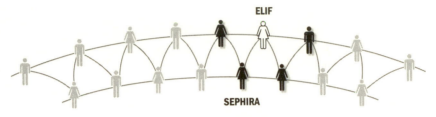

Figure 3.7 Elif's Neighborhood

simple contagions, each long-distance link presents an opportunity for the contagion to jump across the network and discover new targets of activation. However, for a complex contagion, a signal that travels across a long tie arrives alone, without any social reinforcement. Consequently, the first problem with adding long ties to the network is that they do not create useful pathways for complex contagions to diffuse. But there is also a second problem, which is worse; in addition to not helping, they also hurt diffusion.

To see why, figure 3.6 zooms in to show a segment of the clustered network from figure 3.3. The focal individual, Tavish, is shown in white, and his four neighbors are shown as black nodes. Correspondingly, figure 3.7 shows the focal individual, Elif, in white, and her four friends are highlighted as black nodes. In figure 3.8, the two white nodes, Ashley and Sephira, are the shared friends, or common neighbors, between Tavish and Elif. They form a *wide bridge* between the neighborhoods, which is highlighted in the figure. This wide bridge consists of multiple ties from Ashley and Sephira that connect Tavish's neighborhood to Elif's neighborhood. This bridge is the pathway for social reinforcement and behavioral diffusion between the two neighborhoods.

For most theories of simple diffusion, a bridge between two neighborhoods is generally assumed to consist of a single tie. However, if transmission requires multiple contacts, then an effective bridge must consist of multiple ties. Hence, we can measure a bridge not only by its

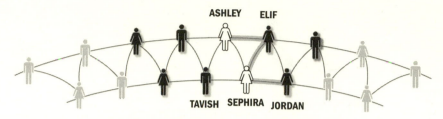

ASHLEY ELIF

TAVISH SEPHIRA JORDAN

Figure 3.8 A Wide Bridge Between Neighborhoods

length (that is, the distance that is spanned by the bridge) but also by its width (that is, the number of ties it contains).

While simple contagions spread most effectively when bridges are long, complex contagions depend on bridges that are wide. The width of a bridge between two neighborhoods is defined as the number of overlapping ties between them.[11] In figure 3.8, the bridge between Tavish's neighborhood and Elif's neighborhood consists of three ties: Ashley to Elif, Sephira to Elif, and Sephira to Jordan.

This bridge is wide enough to allow a minimally complex contagion—one requiring two sources of activation—to travel from Tavish's neighborhood to Elif's neighborhood. To continue the example of Maya's software initiative, if Tavish and all of his friends start using Maya's new technology, reinforcing signals from Tavish's friends Ashley and Sephira can convince Elif that she should adopt the technology too. But this is not sufficient for the contagion to spread farther. If the technology is costly or unfamiliar, Elif's other friends may also require social proof in order to adopt. The additional connection between Sephira and Jordan widens the bridge between the neighborhoods. Together, Sephira and Elif can convince Jordan that she should try Maya's new software. Once Jordan and Elif both adopt, they can spread the innovation to Elif's other friends. As the technology spreads from Elif's friends to her friends' friends, and so on, wide bridges act as the invisible channels of social influence that transmit behavior change across the social network.[12] These are the pathways through which complex contagions propagate.

Figure 3.9 shows what happens when a few of these bridge ties are rewired. As the number of long-distance ties increases, the average bridge width narrows. While Tavish and Elif now both have new connections to other parts of the population, they also have fewer ties to each other's friends. They still have one friend, Sephira, in common, so

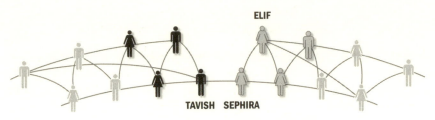

Figure 3.9 Rewiring Reduces Bridge Width

there is still a tie between their neighborhoods. Information can still spread between them. However, Tavish and his friends no longer have the same amount of influence in Elif's neighborhood. While Elif and her friends can learn about an innovation from Sephira, this information does not come with the necessary social reinforcement to convince Elif and her friends to adopt. Thus, while word of Maya's product may spread, the product itself may not.

Ever since Granovetter's pioneering work on diffusion, bridges have been thought of as long, narrow ties that connect distant parts of a population.[13] The reason that the width of these bridges has been less appreciated is that wide bridges impede the spread of simple contagions. Wide bridges create redundancies that slow simple diffusion. Thus, for simple contagions, too much clustering means that there are too few long ties, which slows down the diffusion process; while for complex contagions, too little clustering means that there are too few wide bridges, which not only slows down diffusion but can prevent it entirely.

This means that there are many situations in which efforts to create more efficient pathways for information diffusion may inadvertently erode the networks of social reinforcement that are necessary to maintain behavioral influence. This has implications for any setting in which accelerating the flow of information may unintentionally undercut the goal of information diffusion, such as to grow group solidarity, spread complex technical knowledge, diffuse new social norms, or achieve widespread mobilization for a social movement.[14] While Granovetter argued that "whatever is to be diffused" will spread most effectively through weak ties, the main finding here is that we cannot generalize from the spread of simple contagions to the diffusion of complex contagions.[15]

A NEW TAKE ON SPATIAL DIFFUSION

These lessons offer new insight into the widely observed tendency for social movements to spread spatially. Beginning with McAdam's seminal study of Freedom Summer, spatial patterns of mobilization have been a consistent finding in social movement research. Hedström's study of the early labor movement in Sweden shows that participation spread locally, from one residential neighborhood to another. In China, dormitory housing arrangements structured social ties in a way that allowed for easy diffusion of student dissent. Similarly, the close quarters of inner-city settlements in the Paris Commune promoted the emergence of violent revolts.[16]

Spatial dynamics are also found in studies of innovation diffusion, as in William Whyte's study showing that consumer adoption of air conditioning units spread spatially through the residential neighborhoods of Philadelphia. Similar patterns of spreading are also found in the diffusion of new organizational forms, as described in a recent study of the growth of private manufacturing in China.[17]

These empirical studies point to the relational property of spatial networks that makes them conducive to social, political, and cultural diffusion—namely, *physical proximity*. This is needed for the spread of communicable diseases that require physical or respiratory contact, fashions and technological innovations that require visual contact, and sensitive information that requires face-to-face communication. As Hedström suggested, "The closer that two actors are to one another, the more likely they are to be aware of and to influence each other's behavior."[18]

This analysis shows something different. It reveals a structural property of spatial networks—wide bridges—that has received far less attention. The results here suggest that complex contagions may favor spatial networks not only because the ties between nodes are physically short but also because the bridges between neighborhoods are structurally wide. While physical proximity can make the connection *relationally* strong, it is the width of the bridge that makes the connection *structurally* strong for the propagation of complex contagions.

Spatial networks have historically been seen as facing a trade-off between having strong relational value but poor structural reach. Conversely, weak ties have poor relational value but excellent structural reach. By Granovetter's lights, structural reach, not relational value, is the key to successful diffusion. The findings here, by contrast, suggest that spatial networks may offer both a relational strength and a structural advantage for improving diffusion. For complex contagions, clustered networks of strong ties may be highly efficient pathways for diffusion across a large and diverse population.

THE ROBUSTNESS OF DIFFUSION

The implications here are exciting. We can already begin to see what these results might mean for the best strategies for designing public health interventions, for mobilizing collective action, or for structuring relationships between organizations to increase scientific collaboration and cultural exchange. Part 2 of this book pursues these implications in depth. The rest of this chapter is dedicated to answering the questions that many readers may be wondering about at this point.

To start with, it is reasonable to wonder how to translate the lessons from the small-world model into implications for the real world. The small-world model is a highly stylized, highly abstract representation of social networks. There are no families, no best friends, and no enemies. Furthermore, real spatial networks are not typically laid out as circular lattices, nor do network ties typically form through random rewiring. Thus, while this model is well known and widely used, it is also artificial. There is a noticeable lacuna between the implications that may be drawn from the model of small worlds and the implications that will be useful for understanding, and perhaps influencing, real-world diffusion processes. To close this gap, we would like to know more about how the results on complex contagions hold up once we start making things more realistic.

Real-world social networks, for instance, are not uniform lattices in which everyone has the same number of ties. What happens to the results if more variation is introduced into the distribution of network "degree" (that is, the number ties each person has)? Also, in real-world networks, the degree distribution is often skewed. Some people (called "hubs") have disproportionately more ties than other people. What happens if we test the diffusion dynamics of complex contagions on networks with hubs? Additionally, the model also assumes that all ties are equal. There is no "strength" or "weakness" in the network ties. But, of course, the strength and weakness of ties are basic features of Granovetter's original conception of networks. So, what happens to the results if tie strength is put into the model?

Another thought is that the results on complex contagions seem to hinge on the fact that when a shortcut is added, a local bridge is reduced. In the small-world model, ties are rewired to create shortcuts. But, there must be other ways of increasing the number of weak ties. What if, instead of rewiring the ties in the network, shortcuts are instead introduced by adding more ties to the network? In that case, local bridges would still be wide, and there would be long-distance ties as well. What happens to diffusion then?

Another consideration is that in all of the simulations so far, the thresholds have been uniform throughout the population. In the simple-contagion model, everyone had a threshold of one. Then, in the complex-contagion model, everyone's threshold was increased to two. What happens if you introduce more variance into the threshold distribution, so that some people have lower thresholds and some people have higher ones? How does this affect diffusion?

Moreover, instead of people's thresholds being drawn from a random distribution and then fixed, people themselves might also be a little bit random. What if thresholds are probabilistic instead of deterministic? That is, what if a person's threshold for adoption can vary over time? What happens then? Finally, what about status? If some people have higher status than others, how does that affect the diffusion of complex contagions?

The more we think about it, the more questions we can come up with. I spent a lot of time on this project thinking through these questions and others, trying to figure out whether the dynamics of complex contagions are an artifact of the small-world model, or whether they are a bona fide property of diffusion in the real world.

To address each of these questions in detail, the following pages show how the model was changed to incorporate realistic dimensions of networks and persons into the study of complex contagions, and what they mean for the process of social diffusion. (To foreshadow a bit, the results turn out to be highly robust.) Most of the time, these changes do little to alter the dynamics of diffusion reported above. This consistency is due to the clarity and power of the small-world model and the incisiveness with which it captures the essential features of network topology that control diffusion.[19] Still, there are several exceptions where introducing greater realism into the model unexpectedly strengthens the results on complex contagions. The more realistic the model becomes, the more useful wide bridges typically are for diffusion.

The following pages explore the dynamics of diffusion as the model is elaborated to include the following: skewed degree distributions (or hubs), increased tie density, status differences, variations in thresholds, and variations in tie strength. Once we are satisfied with the robustness of the results, chapter 4 then turns to the question of how to test these findings experimentally.

HUBS, HEALTH, AND INDUSTRY INERTIA

One of the most common features of empirical social networks is that some people are better connected than others. In a series of computational explorations of network connectivity by Lázló Barabási and his colleagues in 1999 and 2000, they identified an interesting class of networks, called scale-free networks, which have extreme distributions of connectivity.[20] These are social topologies in which the best-connected individual may have a hundred times, or even a thousand times, more connections than most other people in the population. Barabási's basic idea was that while most people have only a few ties, highly connected ("high-degree") hubs play the essential role of binding a population together.

Even though empirical social networks are unlikely to be as dramatically skewed as Barabási suggested, his model nevertheless offers useful insight into the role that highly connected individuals can play in the diffusion of social contagions. For instance, consider a piece of new health information about cholesterol or diabetes. A single hub can inform hundreds of contacts, who can in turn spread the word to others. The downside of this remarkable accelerant for diffusion is that hubs have also been argued to be a primary pathway for the rapid spread of HIV and other sexually transmitted infections. As Gladwell and others have observed, hubs are a perfect vehicle for spreading simple contagions.[21]

To mitigate the downsides that can arise from this, it would be useful to know if hubs could be equally effective for spreading desirable changes in health behaviors, such as condom use or other prophylactic behaviors. To see whether skewed social topologies might affect the spread of complex contagions, I tested the spread of a minimally complex contagion (that is, with a threshold of two) on a scale-free network in a population with 40,000 actors. Because of the extreme skewness of the degree distribution, most actors had only five contacts, while a small number of individuals had several hundred connections. A network generation algorithm was used to create a highly clustered scale-free network. A rewiring algorithm was then used that preserved the degree distribution while the network was rewired. In other words, the degree distribution in network was kept constant as the level of clustering in the network was changed. This made it possible to test the independent effects of clustering on diffusion while maintaining a scale-free network.[22]

These explorations of degree heterogeneity present a special opportunity to think about thresholds for adoption. When degree is uniform (for instance, everyone has 6 neighbors), then a threshold of two is equivalent to requiring that 33% of a person's contacts adopt before they will. Correspondingly, if everyone has eight neighbors, then a threshold of two means that everyone requires 25% of their neighbors to adopt before they will. But if everyone has a different number of neighbors, it becomes a little more complicated to think about the meaning of complexity. For a person with 3 neighbors, a threshold of two means that more than half of their neighbors need to adopt before they will. But for a person with 200 contacts, two neighbors constitute a mere 1% of their neighborhood.

To make sure that we understand how these features of thresholds interact with degree heterogeneity, I ran two sets of tests to evaluate the effects of hubs on diffusion. The first set studied absolute thresholds, which rely only on the number of activated neighbors, regardless of the size of the neighborhood. I studied the spread of a minimally complex contagion across scale-free networks as they were rewired. The second set used a fractional representation of thresholds.[23] This means, for instance, that everyone has a threshold of 30%. Thus a contagion that is complex for some people (that is, requiring two or more activated contacts to trigger adoption) will not be complex for others. For a person with 3 ties, a threshold of 30% translates into a simple contagion—that is, only one contact is needed to trigger adoption. However, for a person with 100 ties, much more reinforcement is required—30 activated contacts are needed to trigger activation. Thus, when thresholds are fractional, hubs are harder to activate.

Both ways of representing thresholds—absolute thresholds and fractional thresholds—are useful for understanding diffusion processes. For instance, in a health context, the decision to use condoms may be based on a belief about what is normatively required. This is a situation in which the fraction of contacts who adopt a behavior may be more important than the absolute number. This fractional representation of thresholds is also found in McAdam and Paulsen's idea that people rely on a "significant subset" of their relationships when making important decisions.[24] Nevertheless, there can also be situations in which thresholds for adoption rely primarily on the number of adopters, regardless of a person's neighborhood size. For instance, repeating an urban legend may require confirmation from only two or three people. Regardless of how many people you know, hearing the story two or three times may be sufficient to believe it.

In the first set of computational experiments, I studied the diffusion of a contagion with an absolute threshold of two. This minimally complex contagion spread effectively across the clustered scale-free network. However, as the scale-free network was rewired, diffusion was less successful. The drop-off in success was not as severe as it had been before. In the experiments discussed above, which used a spatial network, randomization caused success rates to drop off precipitously. The addition of just a few long ties transformed the entire network from one that was capable of spreading complex contagions to one in which they could not spread at all. However, in the scale-free network, increasing the fraction of long ties reduced the reach of the diffusion process but did not stop it entirely. This happened because the contagion would occasionally activate a hub. With low levels of rewiring, residual clustering in the hub neighborhood enabled the hub and a few of its neighbors to collectively spread the contagion to the rest of the hub's followers. This created a sizable number of adopters. However, even a modest level of additional rewiring prevented the contagion from spreading beyond the hub's immediate neighborhood. Figure 3.10 shows why.

Most people only had a few contacts. For the vast majority of the population, activation required having a large fraction of their neighborhood activated (that is, two out of an average of five contacts). Unlike hub neighborhoods, the outlying neighborhoods were connected by minimally overlapping connections—sometimes with only a single wide bridge between them. As shown in figure 3.10, in these low-degree neighborhoods, even a little bit of randomness could disrupt the long chains of reinforcement necessary to keep the contagion spreading. A few rewired ties could break the connection that linked hundreds of low-degree neighborhoods to one another. With additional rewiring, even the hubs could not help to spread the contagion, and diffusion stopped entirely.

The second set of experiments, which used fractional thresholds, showed more dramatic results. Even slightly rewiring the scale-free network destroyed any chance of the contagion spreading. Using a threshold of 25% made the contagion minimally complex for the majority of individuals, who had five neighbors. For anyone with fewer

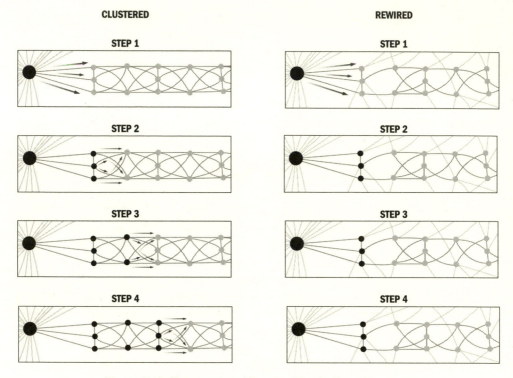

Figure 3.10 Clustered and Rewired Scale-Free Networks

neighbors (that is, four or less), the contagion was simple and could be adopted from a single contact. However, a hub with 200 contacts required coordinated adoption by fifty neighbors before the hub would adopt. Without clustered ties in a hub's neighborhood, it was impossible to get enough local coordination to trigger adoption by the hubs. Thus, once bridge width was eroded even a little bit, hubs became irrelevant for the diffusion process.

These results have important consequences for thinking about the role of hubs in diffusion more generally. When thresholds are absolute, adoption depends only on counting the number of activated neighbors; however, when thresholds are fractional, people are also influenced by the non-adopters. In other words, while hubs can act as *outgoing* sources of influence *to* a lot of people, they are also exposed to *incoming* influences *from* a lot of people. For a simple contagion, this only accelerates the rate of diffusion. The fact that hubs are exposed to lots of people means that they can be activated more quickly, dramatically increasing the reach of a diffusion process. For complex contagions, things often work differently.

Although hubs are exposed to nearly everything passing through a network, they are also aware of all the people who are not adopting a behavior. These non-adopters are countervailing influences that can offset the signals from any adopters. Network clustering can help a diffusion process by allowing peripheral nodes to coordinate with each other to convince a hub to adopt. Without clustering, however, it becomes challenging for a few peripheral adopters to influence a hub's behavior when the hub is also aware of all the other contacts exerting countervailing influences against the behavior.

To see how these advantages and disadvantages of hubs play out in the diffusion of new technologies, let's compare the adoption of an innovative technology by a Fortune 500 manager—who has hundreds of peer contacts—to the adoption of the innovation by a less connected manager at a small start-up company. Because the Fortune 500 manager is a hub in the network, she will be able to discover, very early on, any innovative technologies that are relevant to her business. By contrast, the start-up manager, with only a few dozen professional contacts, is far less likely to hear about the innovation early on.

At the same time, the well-connected manager will also be subject to strong pressures from her large number of contacts who have not yet adopted the innovation. Pressure from these non-adopters can create a form of social "inertia" that impedes action. Because the highly connected Fortune 500 manager can see that the innovation is not widely accepted, and because she knows that so many people are watching the choices she makes, her abundance of social ties can prevent her from acting quickly. Consequently, while the Fortune 500 manager may be first to discover an innovation, she may be among the last to adopt it.[25]

By contrast, the start-up manager may have the very same threshold for adopting the innovation, but because she has fewer contacts, she is far less likely to be pulled into the inertia of existing industry norms. The start-up manager has less pressure from countervailing forces and can therefore more easily be convinced to adopt the innovation.[26]

Thus, a useful observation for innovation diffusion is that well-connected hubs, who are best positioned to easily discover innovations, may also be the biggest roadblock to their rapid dissemination. The only way around this blockage is for reinforcing chains of wide bridges composed of less connected individuals to propagate innovations through peripheral network channels.[27] While these chains of low-degree individuals can be highly effective for diffusion, they are also highly sensitive to randomization. Weak ties can easily erode the wide channels of reinforcement necessary for the successful diffusion of a new technology. Thus, one implication of complexity for networks with hubs is that while increasing the skew of the degree distribution in a network can give individuals much faster access to information, it can also make the network much more sensitive to disruption from weak ties.

INCREASING DENSITY AND THE PROBLEM OF EXPOSURE

A recurring theme in the findings on complex contagions is that rewiring network ties reduces bridge width. Perhaps one way to solve this problem is to leave bridge width alone. Instead of rewiring existing bridges to create long ties, what if we simply add new ties to the existing social network? In that case, simple contagions can use the newly added long ties to jump across the network, while complex contagions can still spread through the unperturbed wide bridges in the underlying lattice. Doesn't this solve all of our problems?

It is a good idea, and there are a couple of situations in which this suggestion can work quite nicely; however, it also introduces a few new problems that land us back where we started. The key finding here is that it depends on how we think about thresholds. If thresholds are absolute, then adding long ties to the network can absolutely help. Indeed, the ideal solution is to add every possible tie to the network and simply connect everyone to everyone else. In a network where everyone knows everyone, diffusion becomes very easy. Even if everyone has a threshold of two, as long as there are two people anywhere in the network who have adopted, everyone will know about it at the same time, and everyone will adopt at once. The same conclusion holds if thresholds are increased to three or four. The problem of diffusion is solved. Unfortunately, the reason this seems too good to be true is that it is.

The first, most obvious problem with this solution is that people have a limited amount of time to give to their network ties. If there are increasing numbers of weak ties in people's contact networks, it is unlikely that people will spend as much time interacting with their strong ties. And, going to the extreme, in a population with hundreds of millions of people, if everyone is connected to everyone else, people are still likely to have only a small number of contacts with whom they interact directly and who are able to influence them.[28]

The second, more fundamental problem comes from seeing what happens when we move from absolute thresholds to fractional thresholds. For a contagion with an absolute threshold, like an urban legend, the more people someone is connected to, the more likely it is that reinforcing sources of activation can be found. But this assumes that people ignore the non-adopters. The problem is that most of the time people do in fact pay attention to countervailing influences. For instance, if there are normative or reputational factors at stake in an adoption decision, a couple of adopters in a sea of non-adopters do not provide much confidence that others should adopt too.

To test the effects of increasing network density on the spread of complex contagions with fractional thresholds, I conducted a new set of counterfactual experiments in which I began with a spatial lattice and allowed the network density to increase. Rather than rewiring existing ties in the network, the underlying lattice was left unchanged, and weak ties were instead added to the network. Each simulation started with a spatial network with 40,000 actors in which everyone had eight contacts. Diffusion was studied using a minimally complex contagion (that is, a threshold of 25%, requiring two out of eight neighbors to adopt).

The contagion spread easily in the spatial lattice. However, when long ties were added to the network, diffusion began to slow down. Similar to the findings for hubs, the more ties that people had, the more reinforcement they needed in order to be convinced to adopt. At the same time, the growing number of weak ties in people's neighborhoods increased the number of countervailing influences that they were exposed to. The consequence for diffusion was that the underlying wide bridges in the spatial network were no longer able to provide enough reinforcement to overcome the countervailing influences from increasing numbers of weak ties. Thus, as neighborhood sizes increased, diffusion stopped.

STATUS IN FASHION

Another important feature of social networks that has not been considered yet is that there are often status differences between people. With some notable exceptions, theoretical models of network diffusion do not typically take status into account.[29] One reason for this is that a casual way of thinking about status is as the inverse of susceptibility. A person with a low threshold could equally be described as someone who is connected to people with high status. However, this is not very satisfying, and in many ways, it misses the point of status, which is that a single individual can influence everyone he or she comes into contact with—even though those same people may not be easily influenced by anyone else.

To see what effect status differences might have on the dynamics of complex contagions, I wanted to incorporate status into the model a meaningful way. My approach was to select some people in the population to be more influential and others to be less so. The people who were selected to be high status "opinion leaders" could instantly influence anyone who was connected to them.[30] For instance, the fashion mogul Elle MacPherson can directly influence all of her contacts. Importantly, even though most of these contacts might not be as influential as Elle, they also may not be so easily influenced by someone other than Elle. So, to keep things balanced in the model, the influence of everyone else in the population (that is, the low-status individuals) was reduced to compensate for the increased influence of the high-status nodes. Thus, while Elle can directly influence her followers, it would take a lot of her followers to influence her.

My first idea was to randomly select a few individuals to be opinion leaders and then to introduce a few activated seeds into the network and see what happens. I tried using both opinion leaders and regular Joes as seeds to see whether it made any difference for diffusion. However, either way, status did not do much. The results were nearly identical to what was observed before.

So, to give the opinion leaders a serious chance to make a real impact, status differences were distributed throughout the population so that every neighborhood in the network had at least one opinion leader. Thus, in a population with 40,000 actors, in which everyone has eight neighbors, this means that there are 5,000 opinion leaders. What would this do to the dynamics of diffusion?

It turned out that diffusion was more dependent upon wide bridges than it had been before. Increasing the fraction of long ties in the population by even a moderate amount stopped diffusion entirely. To see why, suppose that an opinion leader influences of all her contacts by getting them to adopt a new fashion. The problem is what happens next. How likely is it that the neighbors of the opinion leader will be able to keep spreading the fashion to others? As shown in figure 3.11, in a random network, the low-status individuals have no friends in

Step 1

Step 2

Step 3

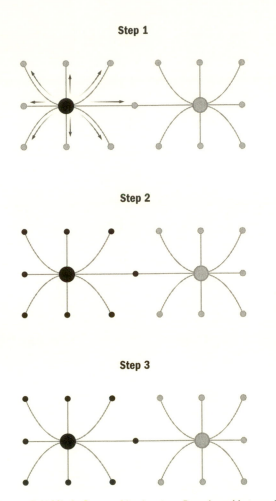

Figure 3.11 High-Status Nodes in a Random Network

common. Thus, they cannot coordinate their efforts to spread the new style to others, so diffusion stops with them.

Because the acolytes are relatively low status, it requires more of them to keep spreading the behavior to others. Even in a clustered network, this makes diffusion challenging. While any individual can be convinced to adopt a new fashion by a single opinion leader, it would take several low-status contacts to convince them to try it.

As shown in figure 3.12, diffusion beyond the opinion leader's immediate neighborhood depends heavily on the existence of wide bridges, which allow lower-status individuals to reinforce each other's

Step 1

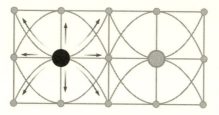

Step 2

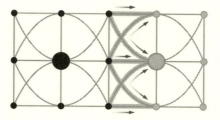

Step 3

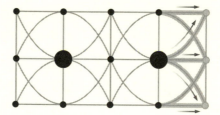

Figure 3.12 High-Status Nodes in a Clustered Network

efforts to spread innovative behaviors farther into the network. The greater the status inequality in a network is, the more important wide bridges are for enabling the regular nodes to work together to spread the influence of opinion leaders to other parts of the social network.

THRESHOLDS IN TECHNOLOGY ADOPTION

A different kind of assumption that also seems particularly important is not the influence that people have, but rather their susceptibility to influence. Thus far we typically have assumed that everyone in the population has exactly the same threshold for adoption. Empirically, thresholds typically vary from person to person and can be expected to follow some kind of normal distribution, in which there are a few individuals who are highly susceptible, a few who are incredibly obstinate, and most who have a moderate level of resistance to a new behavior.[31]

To see how this distribution of thresholds might affect the dynamics of complex contagions I conducted a large number of computational experiments that explored the space of potential variation. The main finding is easy to understand. Using a Gaussian distribution with a moderate standard deviation, the mean of the threshold distribution governs the basic dynamics of diffusion.[32]

This means that if the mean of the distribution is low (that is, on average, people have a threshold of one) it is probable that a moderate amount of randomization can improve the dynamics of diffusion. An example of this kind of situation is the diffusion of a new app that is free and fun to use. Most people just need to find out about it in order to download it. Although there may be some late adopters who require social reinforcement, these individuals do not affect the overall dynamics of diffusion. This kind of contagion will usually spread very effectively from person to person through long ties. This logic holds for moderate levels of randomization, such that occasional sticking points in the diffusion process (due to highly resistant individuals) can still be overcome by social reinforcement from several contacts. However, these improvements in diffusion from long ties can break down in a completely random topology, where obstinate individuals may be able to block a diffusion process from spreading. When these simulations were extended to include threshold distributions where individuals have more resistance to adoption, the results show that as soon as the mean of the threshold distribution increases to two, long ties become less useful. In general, if the mean of the threshold distribution is high enough that on average people require two or more sources of activation for adoption, then increasing levels of randomization are likely to lead to failed diffusion. As the mean of the threshold distribution increases, the dynamics of diffusion become increasingly dependent upon wide bridges throughout the network.

These observations raise a related question: what happens to diffusion if individuals' thresholds can change over time? There may be times when a person who would otherwise resist a behavior might have a moment of weakness, or a change of heart, and be triggered to adopt based on a single exposure. Conversely, early enthusiasm for a technology may fade, and a person might subsequently abandon a behavior that they had previously adopted.[33] These considerations are important not only for thinking about the maintenance of a behavior but also for thinking about how far a diffusion process will spread throughout a population.

Unlike the computational experiments discussed above, in which individuals' thresholds were fixed, I also conducted a large number of computational experiments in which the temporal dynamics of individual susceptibility were studied with a probabilistic threshold model. In this model, individuals' decisions to adopt were randomly drawn every time they considered the behavior. I was surprised to find that the results were essentially the same as what was found for fixed thresholds, above. The mean of the probability distribution governed the overall dynamics of diffusion.

If the average expectation of the probability distribution was that actors could typically become activated by a single contact, then randomization could improve diffusion. On the other hand, if the average expectation was that people would normally require reinforcement from two or more contacts, then the behavior would typically spread as a complex contagion and randomization could impede diffusion. Actors who became momentarily susceptible to activation from a weak tie (that is, "turned on" from a single contact) would also subsequently "turn off" when their thresholds reverted back to the expected value. Unless people were embedded within clustered networks that provided them with social reinforcement from fellow adopters, any momentary diffusion across a long tie could quickly disappear when thresholds returned to normal. As above, the higher the mean of the probability distribution, the easier it is for long ties to disrupt diffusion.[34]

STRENGTH AND WEAKNESS OF TIES
IN COLLECTIVE ACTION

Finally, perhaps the most obvious feature of the real world that has been omitted so far is the strength and weakness of ties. Up to this point we have assumed that all ties have the same strength, regardless of length. This is a reasonable assumption for disease diffusion. In a sexual contact network, an infected individual can transmit a pathogen just as easily through weak ties as through strong.[35] Similarly, for most information diffusion, weak ties are effective conduits for spreading everything from news of a job opening to information about a natural disaster.

It is often different for complex contagions. The weaker the tie, the less influence a contact is expected to have. This is why Granovetter distinguishes between relationally weak ties connecting distant acquaintances, and relationally strong ties that connect close friends who all know one another.[36] To see how the strength and weakness of ties affects the dynamics of diffusion, I followed Granovetter's original formulation, in which all ties in the network are labeled as either strong or weak. Clustered neighborhoods were made into strong ties, and long distance links into weak ties.

To formalize this in the model, strong and weak ties were assigned relative weights, which determined how much influence they had for triggering an individual's threshold. To be conservative, clustered (strong) ties were assigned a weight of 1, and random (weak) ties were given a weight of 0.5. Thus, for a *simple contagion*, for which an individual had a threshold of one, a single strong tie would be sufficient to trigger adoption, but two weak ties would be required.

Bringing the small-world model into line with Granovetter's original notion of strong and weak ties significantly increased the importance of wide bridges for diffusion. Consider the example of recruitment to a collective action. Someone who may require reinforcement from only one close friend to be convinced to join the collective action would require contact with two casual acquaintances. This means that weak ties are effective for recruitment only when they come with social reinforcement—and that's assuming that joining the collective action is a simple contagion. Reinforcement becomes more important when thresholds are increased. If the contagion is minimally complex (that is, a threshold of two), a potential recruit would require reinforcement from two close friends to be convinced to join the collective action; yet, it would take four acquaintances to have the same effect.

Wide bridges have the relational benefit of also being strong ties. For complex contagions, this makes wide bridges not only structurally necessary but also relationally efficient. They transmit complex contagions using only the minimal amount of social reinforcement. Rewiring a social network to increase the fraction of weak ties not only reduces the overlapping ties in each neighborhood but, because each tie is weaker, also increases the number of ties required to achieve the necessary level of social reinforcement. For both reasons, introducing weak ties into the network prevents the diffusion of complex contagions.

In sum, regardless of whether long ties are added to a network or rewired, whether decisions are probabilistic or deterministic, or whether ties have relational strength, increasing the fraction of long ties in a network can prevent complex contagions from spreading. The structural advantage of clustered networks for diffusion is that they not only create more reinforcing support for a new behavior, they also protect a new behavior from premature exposure to countervailing influences that are likely to slow down its adoption.

To see what these results mean in practice, chapter 4 takes up the task of studying how real behaviors spread through human populations. To do this, I develop an experimental method for testing how behavioral contagions diffuse through online social networks.

CHAPTER 4

A Social Experiment on the Internet

Decades ago, Granovetter offered remarks on the importance of empirically testing threshold models of collective behavior. Although Granovetter candidly confronted the realities of just how challenging it would be to collect the necessary data, he nevertheless suggested some ways it might be done.[1] It was not until recently, however, that a series of methodological studies revealed that network diffusion itself may be a mirage. The causal identification of how behaviors spread in social networks—that is, who influences whom, in what order, and why—is nearly impossible to deduce from traditional observational approaches. Even the simple task of identifying the existence of a diffusion process has been shown to be out of reach in many situations.[2] If it is this hard to show that diffusion exists, then determining how the structure of a social network may have altered a diffusion process seems entirely unapproachable.

Nevertheless, this is what we are setting out to do. Here I have adopted an experimental approach to studying diffusion using social communities on the Internet. Online it is possible not only to observe the causal process of diffusion, but also to identify how changes in network structure may directly impact the rate at which new behaviors are adopted.

THE CHALLENGES OF DIFFUSION

Why is it so hard to study diffusion empirically? One reason is that a satisfactory test of the theory of complex contagions must meet all four of the following requirements: large populations, complete adoption data, complete network data, and replication.

Large populations

For many kinds of social systems, size matters. It is not that more is better, it is that more is different. The dynamics of collective behavior in a small group is often qualitatively different—in some cases the opposite—from that of a large group.[3] However, the good news is that if a population is large enough that it is above an identifiable critical point, the results generalize to larger population sizes all the way up to the theoretical limit of infinity. Perhaps the simplest way of saying it for our purposes is that small populations cannot be small worlds. It is a scope condition of the small-world model that networks must be sparse—that is, the population size must be significantly larger than the average neighborhood size.[4] Consequently, in order to study the dynamics of network diffusion in small worlds, populations need to be large.

Complete adoption data

Once we have a large population, the first thing we need to know about it in order to study diffusion is the actual sequence of adoption decisions that takes place as a behavior spreads through the network—that is, we need to know who adopted from whom, and in what order. Moreover, it is also necessary to ensure that each adoption decision is due to social influence and not to other factors that may be unobserved, such as economic changes, informational exposures, or exogenous influences. For instance, if an economic windfall hits a segment of the population (for example, because new manufacturing jobs are created in a region), several connected people may all independently adopt an innovation within a few days of each other without there being any network diffusion between them.

Complete network data

Just as important as tracking the chain of adoptions through the network is also being able to observe all of the people who were exposed to a contagion but failed to adopt it. In other words, we also need to be able to track all of the pathways along which a contagion did not spread. Thus, we need to know the entire social network for a population. Otherwise, it may appear that most people are adopting, while in fact the vast majority of people who are exposed to a contagion do not adopt.[5]

In addition, we need to make sure that the network structure can be identified independently from any of the confounding relational variables that could also affect diffusion, such as interpersonal affect (tie strength), social similarity (homophily), frequency of interactions, shared informational exposures, or other factors that can provide alternative explanations for why there is transmission across network ties. For instance, if people in clustered networks have stronger emotional bonds than people in random networks, then any differences in diffusion may be due to the strength of ties and not to the width of bridges.

Replication

Finally, let's say that all three of the above requirements are satisfied. Take, for example, a population in which 100,000 people are connected in a social network and a contagion is observed spreading from person to person through the network. How many observations of diffusion are there? The answer is, one. The unit of observation for diffusion is not a person but, rather, a population. One observation cannot tell us whether a population's network structure had any effect at all on the collective outcome. Additional observations of successful diffusion need to be repeated in several independent populations that all have the same network structure. And, of equal importance, the same diffusion process must also be observed spreading less successfully in several other independent populations whose network structure is different. In other words, both the successes and the failures need to be replicated. Only when we have all of these observations of diffusion replicated across multiple independent populations can we conclude that network structure has a causal effect on social diffusion.

What is clear at the outset is that there is no obvious way to proceed. Each of these requirements is difficult, and meeting all four of these at the same time seems impossible. Fortunately, over the last several decades a great deal of progress has been made developing new methods for studying social behavior. Small group experiments have shown that it is possible to study how social interactions can lead to reproducible patterns of social influence and behavior change.[6] At the other extreme, new methods from data science have made it possible to study how large-scale changes in population behavior may arise. If we can extract the best features from each of these approaches, it may be possible to identify a way of combining them that will allow us to move the study of diffusion forward.

The ideal approach would be to take the control and theoretical precision offered by small group experiments and combine it with the scale, observational precision, and natural setting that comes from data science. If we can do this successfully, it would provide a way to satisfy all of the requirements for an experimental test of social diffusion. Wanting to find out if this was possible, I set out to build a social experiment on the Internet.

A SOCIAL EXPERIMENT ON THE INTERNET

For an experimental design to work, it has to be experienced as natural by the participants. If they think the setting is artificial, then their behavior there is likely to be shaped by that perception. A related challenge is to figure out how to control the structure of people's social networks without them knowing it. As in everyday life, the pattern of our social networks is invisible, and yet it is nonetheless able to influence our choices and behaviors.

My approach to building an Internet experiment was to find a setting in which people were already actively communicating with strangers. This would make it possible to create communication networks for people without the ties seeming artificial. Additionally, I was looking for a setting in which people's online interactions could result in a meaningful behavioral choice. This choice needed to be one that could be measured directly, and, ideally, it would also be a behavior for which it would be possible to eliminate exogenous influences so that each instance of adoption could be traced back to the signals from previous adopters.

Under those conditions, it would be possible to observe the spread of a real behavior through a social network while also having complete control over the network structure. Of course, even if it is possible to build such a study, that does not mean that it will confirm the theoretical idea that motivated it. But disconfirmation of an idea is as scientifically important as confirmation, so even having the possibility of testing this theory of diffusion—whatever the result—was a big step forward.

There were a few ideas for where to start. One idea was that investment websites might provide a setting in which it would be possible to study how people influence each other's behavior when choosing stocks. Alternatively, commercial media sites might offer a setting in which it might be possible to observe how people influence each other's movie downloads or product ratings. Other options included using a shopping site to study social influences on the products people buy, or using a job-posting site to study how people's social networks influence the resumes that are used or the jobs that are applied for. However, after exploring a large variety of options, health and lifestyle websites stood out as the most attractive setting for an experiment, for several reasons.

First, I was struck by the sincerity and commitment that participants on health sites exhibited in their interactions with strangers. A staggering wealth of sensitive medical data, protected by the Health Insurance Portability and Accountability Act, is exchanged in these settings—including medication details, health diaries, MRI and CAT scans, medical reports, and physician referrals. Most of this information is uploaded, shared, followed, and commented on by people who have never met face-to-face. Yet, these interactions can influence patients' decisions to take medications, join medical trials, and change physicians.[7] On even the most rudimentary health sites, where members simply give advice about exercises, diets, and resources for getting screenings, participants were inexplicably eager to share and to learn from each other. If this eagerness to engage with strangers could be reproduced in an experimental setting, it could be used to study how social networks influence behavior change.

The second reason for choosing a health setting is that health behaviors are important. Investment behaviors, job search, and product adoption are also important; however, the decision to get a cancer screening can be life altering. Not to mention the life-saving decision to get vaccinated or the life-threatening decision to try a new medication.

Third, health behaviors and health outcomes are widespread and often social. Only a select group of people actively invest in the stock market, and the people who do invest can make their decisions without social input. By contrast, in every walk of life people make health decisions that affect them and those around them. From the spread of infectious diseases to the treatment of chronic illnesses, health decisions and health outcomes affect us all, and most often cannot be divorced from the social influences that we are exposed to.[8]

Finally, the distinction between simple and complex contagions is particularly poignant in a health setting. The deadly HIV infection can diffuse quickly across long ties in sexual contact networks. So can information about lifesaving PrEP medications. However, there is an important difference between the diffusion of health information and the diffusion of health behavior. Long-tie networks, which can quickly spread both new infections and new information, may not spread new behavioral norms. Entirely different kinds of networks (networks of wide bridges) may be needed to make unknown prophylactic treatments into accepted behaviors.

For all of these reasons, a health setting seemed like an opportune place to conduct an experimental study of behavioral diffusion. My strategy was to look for behaviors that people were already engaging in online and to select one that could be the focal behavior for this study.

Looking around at various popular commercial sites to get ideas, a common theme that kept emerging was that websites would offer their members the ability to participate in health communities where they could share recommendations with each other. Despite the fact that these communities were artificially created, and often anonymous, the social interactions on these websites were surprisingly natural. This "artificial but natural" principle became the model for this experimental design.

The next question was how to build an online community that people would actually want to join. The answer came in the form of a partnership with Graham Colditz at the Harvard Medical School, who had been running a very successful cancer-screening website through the Harvard Center for Cancer Prevention. Tens of thousands of unique visitors a month would voluntarily come to the website Your Disease Risk to complete online health surveys that provide risk assessments for various forms of cancer.

The idea was to build on the principle of health screening to study the behaviors that people would naturally be expected to do afterward. For instance, after receiving a risk assessment, most patients receive recommendations for activities to try, topics to learn about, and lifestyle options to explore. The problem is that they rarely follow up on them. This study was designed to see whether providing people with the right kinds of social networks would promote the spread of a particular kind of follow-up behavior.

The online health community that I constructed was called the Healthy Lifestyle Network. Participants were recruited from a link that was placed on the final assessment page of the Your Disease Risk site. Additional subjects were also recruited from health assessments on commercial websites, such as Prevention.com, Men's Health, and Women's Health, and from advertisements that were used to attract participants from these commercial websites. Subjects were not paid to participate but were offered the opportunity to join a health community in which they could learn about new health resources from other participants.

The advertisements highlighted that the community would be a social experience for participants and that it would provide them with opportunities to follow up on their health interests and concerns. This recruitment strategy was an important feature of the experimental design since it created the expectation for participants that they would meet and interact with strangers on the site. Further, it set up the expectation that these interactions would lead to opportunities to adopt new behaviors. Thus, although the social environment was artificial, it was designed to be a natural setting for participants to have interactions with strangers who might influence their behavior.

It is useful to think about what this means from a sampling perspective. Participation was limited to people who speak English, who are computer literate, and who care about their health. There are many, many people who could not participate in this study but who are very important to reach. This study was designed to see whether even the easy-to-reach people, who have interests in health, might nevertheless have their behaviors determined by the structure of their social networks. Given the recruitment strategy that was used, the "null hypothesis" is that just about anyone who would take the time to sign up for the Healthy Lifestyle Network would also be interested in using the health resources that were sent to them. The experiment was designed to show that even among this interested and easy-to-reach population, the structure of the social networks through which helpful resources flowed would significantly affect whether those resources were actually used.

To make this test as real as possible, it was essential that the network itself remain invisible to the participants. This is because in the real world, people have no information about what the large-scale topological structure of their social networks looks like. People typically know with whom they interact directly—although even ego-network reporting is often surprisingly unreliable—and they often have some sense of who their contacts interact with. Yet, beyond that, people know very little about what the large-scale structure of the social network is. Nor do they care. What matters to all of us is our immediate social world. The design of the experiment was set up to preserve this "local" view of the social network. The strategy was to bring people into the study in a way that would get them excited about their immediate social contacts but not give them any information about the scale or structure of the larger social network. Of course, the theory of complex contagions hypothesizes that despite the fact that the large-scale structure of the social network is not directly observed, it can nevertheless be a direct cause of whether or not people change their behaviors.

What had to be figured out next was a natural way of bringing participants into the experiment that would allow them to (1) create an identity in the online community, (2) be randomly assigned to a social network of peers, and (3) take part in the diffusion process.

Creating an identity

Participants arrived to the study through a web page that gave them a fun, easy-to-understand overview of the Healthy Lifestyle Network. The three IKEA-style graphical panels told participants what would happen: they would choose a username and avatar, they would be matched with peers in the social network, and then they would have opportunities to share and receive recommendations for new health resources.

When participants clicked on the Get Started link, they were asked to provide their email address and to agree to the informed consent. The informed consent assured the participants that no personal or identifying information would be revealed and explained that all interactions would be anonymous. Once participants completed this page, they were then officially enrolled in the study and were able to create a username and select an avatar to represent themselves in the community. Finally, to complete their profiles, participants were asked to select a set of health goals and interests that would be used to identify other members of the community who would be most useful for them. Once participants completed all of these steps, they were then placed into an experimental trial, where they were randomized to one of two social networks, as shown in figure 4.1.

Assigning participants to social networks

Each experimental trial consisted of two populations—one clustered network, and one randomized network—both of which were the same size and in which everyone had the same number of neighbors. The clustered-network condition was designed to be similar to a spatial network. It had neighborhoods composed of clustered ties with wide bridges between them, which linked the population together. The random-network condition was created by rewiring the clustered network to maximize each participant's exposure to the population. As discussed in chapters 2 and 3, the rewiring procedure ensured that each node in the random network maintained the exact same number of neighbors as in the clustered network (that is, a uniform degree distribution), while simultaneously reducing clustering in the network and eliminating redundant ties within and between neighborhoods.[9]

The networks themselves were created before the study began. Then, when subjects arrived at the study, they were randomly assigned to one of the network topologies, as shown in figure 4.1. Subjects were first

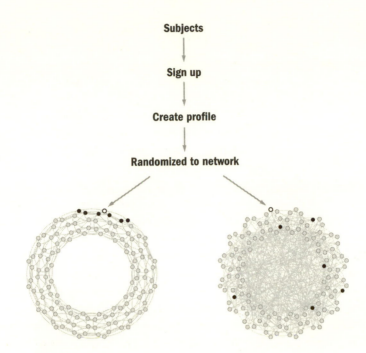

Figure 4.1 Participant Registration and Randomization

randomized to one of the two networks, and then they were randomized to occupy one of the empty nodes in that network. A participant's immediate neighbors in the network constituted their "health buddies" in the Healthy Lifestyle Network. From the ego-network perspective of participants in the study, all they knew was that they had a set of health buddies to interact with. From this perspective, the two experimental conditions were indistinguishable from each other. However, from a bird's-eye perspective, it was possible to see how the large-scale topological structure differed across each of the populations. Importantly, participants could not alter the social topology in which they were embedded (for example, by making new ties or dropping existing ones). The networks that participants had when the study began were the same networks they had when it finished.

The illustration in figure 4.1 shows focal individuals (unfilled circles) being randomized to each experimental condition. The black nodes in each network correspond to each focal individual's neighbors (or health buddies). In the clustered network, these neighbors share overlapping contacts with each other, creating wide bridges to the nearby neighborhoods. By contrast, in the random network, there is no redundancy in the neighbors' contacts, creating maximal exposure to the network and increasing the number of people whom the focal actor can reach in two steps. Gray nodes indicate individuals who are not connected to the focal node.

In each trial, newly arriving subjects were randomized to experimental conditions until both networks were completely populated. Once both networks were full, the experimental trial was nearly ready to run. There was one more step, and then the diffusion process would be initiated.

The final step was to show all of the newly registered participants their "buddy pages." The buddy page displayed each participant's username, avatar, and health interests, as well as the usernames, avatars, and health interests of their health buddies. In both conditions, health buddies were matched to have similar interests. Because both networks in each trial had neighborhoods of the same size, subjects' buddy pages in both conditions were structurally identical, showing the same number of neighbors in each case.

In total, 1,528 subjects participated in the Healthy Lifestyle Network study (fig. 4.2). There were six experimental trials overall, each one consisting of a clustered spatial network and a corresponding randomized network. In each trial, both networks had the same size, degree distribution, and density. In Trial A, both networks contained 98 people, and each person had six neighbors. In Trials B, C, and D, both networks contained 128 people, and each person had six neighbors. Finally, in Trials E and F, both networks contained 144 people, and each person had eight neighbors. This assignment of subjects to conditions yielded a total of twelve experimental populations–six embedded in clustered spatial networks, and six embedded in random networks.

Initiating a diffusion process

Diffusion was initiated by selecting a random "seed node" in each network to send a message to its network neighbors encouraging them to adopt a health-related behavior—namely, joining a health forum website. Each message took the form of an email that indicated the adopter's user information and provided a web link to the health forum's registration page. Each new person who adopted the behavior (that is, each new member who registered for the health forum) automatically sent invitation messages to their health buddies inviting them to adopt. From there, if any of those people also adopted, messages were then sent to their health buddies, and so on, generating a diffusion process across the network.

The messaging system was designed to supply a precise record of the adoption sequence, providing a time series of the spread of the behavior through each population. Messages were sent to a participant only if one of their neighbors joined the forum. The more neighbors who adopted, the more reinforcing signals a participant received. At most, subjects could receive up to one message from each of their health buddies.

When subjects clicked on the link in the invitation email, it took them to the registration page for the health forum website. In order to get access (that is, to officially adopt the behavior), participants were required to complete a registration form. This was an important part of the experimental design.

The registration form was fairly simple—participants were asked to enter information about their health interests, fitness background, and lifestyle. However, the length and difficulty of this form offered a useful control parameter for determining the complexity of the diffusion process. For instance, if the registration form was removed, then clicking the email link would be sufficient to join the health forum. This would make adoption essentially an effortless behavior, which would likely be a simple contagion.[10] Conversely, if the registration form was several pages long, or if the information that was requested was highly confidential (such as requesting participants' social security numbers), this would increase the level of social reinforcement that would be needed to convince participants to adopt the health forum—making the diffusion process more complex.

For this study, it was important for participants to encounter enough resistance so that adoption of the behavior was not trivial (such as just clicking on a link), but it was also important that registration was easy enough that it would be possible to observe a real diffusion process without having to spend many months fine-tuning the registration page. An easy solution was to use a registration form with enough questions so that people had to scroll down (that is, below the fold of the screen) to complete the form. This is a fairly low bar for adoption and thus makes for a conservative test of the theory of complex contagions. Still, I was surprised to find that even the small "cost" of registering for the health forum created a sufficiently large barrier to adoption that many subjects who clicked on the email link when they first received a health-buddy invitation subsequently left the registration page without

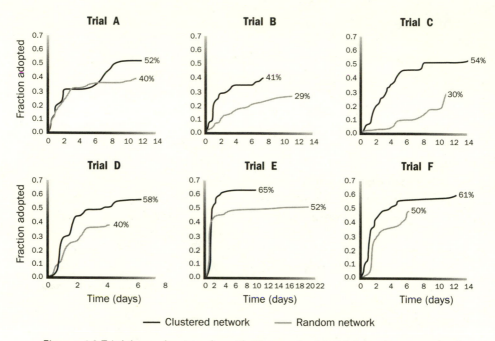

Figure 4.2 Trial A used networks with 98 people, in which each person had six neighbors; Trials B, C, and D used networks with 128 people, in which each person had six neighbors; Trials E and F used networks with 144 people, in which each person had eight neighbors.

joining. Only after they received additional invitations from other health buddies did those participants come back and register.

Once subjects adopted, what was their experience like in the health forum? Inside the forum, adopters could visit and review hundreds of health resources related to lifestyle, fitness, nutrition, smoking cession, and weight loss. Participants could evaluate and share these resources, as well as see the resources commented on by their health buddies who had adopted. This content was available to all adopters of the health forum.

All of this activity inside the forum could not actually affect the diffusion experiment. Once subjects registered for the forum, their actions could not result in any additional emails being sent, nor could they receive additional emails from their health buddies. Another way of saying this is that joining the health forum was a binary and irreversible adoption decision (that is, one-and-done). As described above, this design resulted in a single message being sent to each of the adopter's unactivated health buddies and then ended their interactions with them.

The health forum itself operated as a stand-alone website. To make the forum as useful as possible, adopters could continue using it as long as they wanted to, and they were able to return to the site and log back in as many times as they liked. For several months after the experiment was completed, the forum continued operating as a freely available web resource for the adopters. Each time they returned, the forum would display current information about their health buddies' activities, along with updated ratings and information about the health resources that were available.

Yet, perhaps the most important thing about the health forum is that it was constructed exclusively for this experiment. It was impossible for people outside of the Health Lifestyle Network study to find out about it or to join it. The only way to adopt was to receive an invitation from a health buddy. Thus, each time a subject adopted, it was possible to trace the sequence of prior adoptions that led to their decision.[11]

In each trial, the starting time (time = 0) for each diffusion process corresponds to the instant when the seed node was activated in each network and the initial signals were sent. In all trials, the diffusion process was allowed to run for three weeks.

WATCHING BEHAVIOR SPREAD

The results were illuminating. In every trial, the behavior spread with remarkable ease through the clustered social networks—starting out locally, then spilling over to nearby neighborhoods, and ultimately percolating through the population. Figure 4.2 shows the complete time series of diffusion for all twelve networks in the study. Each panel corresponds to a unique experimental trial, in which the dark line shows the clustered network, and the light line shows the random network.

Because each network is an independent observation, the statistics here are very easy to do. Each network provides a single data point corresponding to the final number of adopters. To see if network structure significantly affected the success of diffusion, we can collect all six data points for final adoption in the clustered networks and compare them to the corresponding six data points from the random networks. The simplest and cleanest test to run is a nonparametric evaluation of whether the data points from the clustered networks are consistently greater than the data points from the random networks. Even without a statistical test, the conclusion is obvious.

Every trial showed the same thing—clustered networks significantly improved the reach of the diffusion process. To get a sense of how big this improvement was, we can look at the average performance of all the networks across each of the trials. The results show that on average the behavior was adopted by 53.77% of the population in clustered networks, whereas it was adopted by only 38.26% of the population in the random networks—clustered networks produced an average increase of 40% in overall adoption ($p < 0.01$).

Going a step further, we can extend this analysis to consider not only the final reach of these diffusion processes but also their speed. To do this, we can repeat the same nonparametric statistical procedure as above, but this time we can compare the total rate of spreading in each network by measuring the average number of nodes activated per second from the start of each diffusion process until its conclusion.

Even without a formal analysis, the slopes of the curves in figure 4.2 tell a clear story. Clustered networks significantly accelerated the spread of adoption in every case. In fact, across all six trials, the average rate of diffusion in the clustered networks was more than four times faster than it was in the random networks ($p < 0.01$).

We can conclude that adoption of the health forum spread both farther and faster in the clustered social networks than in the random ones. Moreover, because each network in the study provides an independent, controlled observation, these results offer a causal conclusion: clustered networks significantly improved the spread of behavior.[12] To understand how this is possible, it is useful to take a closer look at exactly how diffusion unfolded in each of the networks.

Figure 4.3 shows the actual spreading process for both networks, side by side. The sequence of panels (from left to right) shows an elapsed time series of the health forum spreading through a clustered network and a corresponding random network. For both sequences, the left panel shows the start of the diffusion process with a single seed node, shown in black. The rest of the population is shown in white. The temporal progress of diffusion in each network is shown in a series of five panels. When a person adopts, the node turns black, and their links are darkened to highlight the activated pathways of exposure that lead from the adopters to the rest of the population.

In the random network, the most immediate thing to notice about diffusion is how quickly the signals (shown by activated links) reach the rest of the population. In just a few steps, nearly everyone has been exposed to the health forum. The dark lines in figure 4.3 show the

CLUSTERED

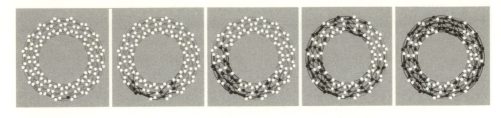

RANDOM

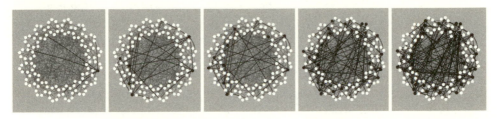

Figure 4.3 The Spread of Behavior in Online Social Networks

impressive speed of information diffusion, which is the hallmark of weak ties and small worlds. Less redundancy creates more exposure. However, while word of the health forum spread quickly in the random network, adoption did not.

By contrast, in the clustered network, messages spread locally. Instead of signals fanning out simultaneously to different parts of the population, they circled back into the same clustered neighborhoods where they originated. This redundancy created a spatial concentration of messages in the network, which generated far fewer initial exposures but nevertheless translated into greater numbers of adopters.

Once each neighborhood became saturated, the behavior then flowed to nearby neighborhoods, cascading across the population. Over the next couple of weeks, each of the diffusion processes followed a pattern of spatial diffusion that was remarkably similar to those documented by Torsten Hagerstrand, Peter Hedström, and David Strang and Sarah Soule.[13] As Roger Gould observed in his study of the Paris Commune:

> The process by which neighborhoods influenced each other through overlapping enlistments can only be analyzed by considering the entire network of overlaps. Each neighborhood simultaneously affected and was affected by the levels of resistance in

other neighborhoods, both directly (to the extent that it was directly linked to each of these neighborhoods) and indirectly (to the extent that each of these other neighborhoods was itself influenced by still other neighborhoods, and so on). In other words, the influence process occurred not just between isolated pairs of neighborhoods, but through chains of neighborhoods linked directly and at various removes. The interdependence of resistance levels across residential areas was thus intimately tied not only to the quantity, but also to the structure of overlapping enlistments.[14]

The similarities between the growth of a social movement in nineteenth-century Paris and the diffusion of a behavior through an online health community suggests an important generality underlying the dynamics of spatial diffusion. As suggested in chapter 3, the effectiveness of spatial networks for diffusion may be due in no small part to how they structure social interactions. Relational factors aside, the results from these experiments show that placing people into clustered patterns of association—whether in an urban neighborhood or in an online community—can significantly improve the spread of behavior.

THE HUMAN SIDE OF DIFFUSION

To understand the human side of these network dynamics, it is useful to start from the fact that the theory of complex contagions is based on an individual-level model of behavior change. We can therefore turn to an individual-level analysis of subjects' behaviors to see whether the explanation offered by the theory of complex contagions—that is, that people require social reinforcement—can provide some insight into why diffusion unfolded as it did in the online networks.

There are at least two social mechanisms that might explain why adoption of the health forum would be a complex contagion. The first is credibility. Even a behavior as simple as joining an online health forum requires a commitment of time and effort. The user has to register for the website, search around the various pages, and see what is useful. While the first message that a participant receives creates awareness of the health forum, the decision to adopt may require some degree of social proof to convince a potential adopter that the site is not a waste of time. The more contacts who adopt, the more credible the health forum is, and the more likely it is that the website will be a useful tool for finding new health resources. The second mechanism is complementarity. The more people who join the health forum, the greater the number of user-contributed ratings and recommendations the site is expected to have, and the more benefits a user can expect to receive from health buddies participating in the forum. For both of these reasons—that is, credibility and complementarity—receiving invitations from multiple contacts is expected to increase the likelihood that participants would pay the "costs" of adopting.

To see whether joining the health forum was indeed a complex contagion, I tested participants' likelihoods of activation after receiving different numbers of health-buddy invitations. This was done by comparing the likelihood that people would adopt after one signal to the likelihood that they would adopt after receiving a second, third, and fourth reinforcing signal.

The effects of social reinforcement on adoption behavior were clear. Participants were 67% more likely ($p < 0.001$) to join the forum after receiving a second signal than after receiving only one signal. Additionally, when this same comparison was made between the likelihood of adopting after two signals versus after three signals, the results showed that receiving a third signal increased the likelihood of adoption by 32% compared to receiving only two signals ($p < 0.05$).[15] Joining the health forum was indeed a complex contagion.

There was also a positive effect of receiving four invitations instead of three on the likelihood of adoption, but the significance of this effect was limited due to smaller sample sizes. What I found most insightful from these analyses was that more signals did not create a saturation effect, nor did they reduce the likelihood of adoption. Receiving additional signals had a consistently positive effect on individual adoption rates.

These findings offer some insight into why diffusion was more successful in clustered social networks.[16] Clustered networks concentrated the signals from adopters into a localized sequence of reinforcing messages, which offered evidence for both the credibility of the health forum and its increasing complementary value. This process transformed ostensibly redundant social ties into effective pathways for the spread of behavior.

ADOPTION VERSUS MAINTENANCE

To take this analysis one step further, we can think about what these dynamics of diffusion might mean for the level of commitment that individuals had to the behavior once they adopted it.[17] In chapter 2, I discussed some of the differences between a one-and-done adoption process versus behaviors that require continued maintenance. Male circumcision and measles-mumps-rubella vaccinations are one-and-done, while condom use and diabetes treatments require maintenance. Similarly, buying a Mac Airbook is a one-and-done behavior, but staying committed to the OS X operating system requires maintenance.

In the context of health behavior, it would be very useful to know whether these experimental results on adoption provide any insight into the effects of network structure on the maintenance of behavior. Fortunately, one of the benefits of the health-forum website was that I was able to keep it available for use by participants even after the diffusion study had been completed. Adopters could keep returning to the health forum for months after they had initially joined. The website maintained an automatic record of every adopter's return visits, providing an excellent way to see whether the dynamics of social reinforcement had any long-term implications for maintenance.

To measure the effects of social reinforcement on participants' engagement with the health forum, I grouped adopters by the number of invitations they received from their health buddies, and then I compared how many times the members of each group returned to the health forum. Recall that participants could not receive messages from their health buddies once they had adopted. So this test was really looking to see whether the reinforcing signals that triggered adoption may have also had an effect on long-term engagement.

Each grouping contained all and only the adopters who had received exactly that number of signals: group 1 contained adopters who received exactly one signal; group 2 contained adopters who received exactly two signals, group 3 contained adopters who received exactly three signals, and so forth. The primary comparison was between the "early adopters," who adopted after one signal (group 1) and the adopters who required multiple signals (groups 2–5).

For the members of group 1, a single activated contact was sufficient to trigger them to join. In this group, only 12% of adopters ever returned to the health forum: 10% came back once, and the remaining 2% returned a second time. None of the early adopters came back more than twice. The early adopters provide a baseline expectation for the likelihood that participants would return to the health forum. This baseline could then be compared to the other groups to see if social reinforcement had any effects on participants' likelihood of making return visits.

Compared to the 12% of early adopters who returned to the forum, 34% of subjects who adopted after two signals returned at least once; 9% came back twice, 1% came back three times, and 1% came back four times ($p < 0.001$). These effects were not only significant but also became stronger with greater levels of social reinforcement. Adopters who received three signals had a 40% return rate; 9% of them came back twice, 10% came back three times, and 1% came back four times ($p < 0.001$). Engagement with the forum continued to increase with the amount of reinforcement that participants received. Subjects who adopted after receiving four signals came back 41% of the time ($p < 0.001$), and subjects came back 45% of the time when they adopted after five signals ($p < 0.01$).[18]

In light of these findings on commitment, it is useful to emphasize the difference between correlation and causation. Unlike the experimental results on diffusion, which provide causal evidence for the effects of network structure on the spread of behavior, the results on commitment show a correlation between receiving reinforcing signals for adoption and the likelihood of being more engaged with the adopted behavior. There are many possible explanations for this correlation—perhaps people who are laggards in the adoption process also tend to be more committed to the behaviors that they adopt. Or, perhaps the opposite is true. Perhaps early adopters are more likely to stick with a behavior, but reinforcing signals from multiple neighbors provide people with added incentives to get the most out of the behaviors they adopt. A different explanation for these correlations is that participants' greater commitment to the health forum was a result of the complementary value that came from having more contacts who were adopters. In other words, the more reinforcing signals that a person received, the more reason there was to keep using the forum to see what other people contributed.

While none of these explanations is definitive, strong correlations between social reinforcement and engagement with the forum suggest a connection between network structure and behavioral commitment.[19] In offline settings, clustered social networks may help to promote behavioral maintenance because of the *relational* strength of strong ties—close friends and long-term interactions help to enforce behavioral commitments. However, the findings here show a *structural* reason why clustered networks may increase long-term engagement. Clustered networks provide reinforcing signals that strengthen both the credibility and complementarity of a behavior. For adopters, there may be added value for sticking with a behavior that others are participating in as well.

Supporting this conclusion, the overall analyses of return visits for each group show that participants who were the hardest to convince to join were also the ones who were the most committed after they joined. Participants who adopted after two invitations were 135% more likely to return to the health forum than participants who adopted after only one invitation. Further, subjects who adopted after three signals were 185% more likely to return, and those who adopted after four signals were 190% more likely to return to the forum ($p < 0.001$). The suggestive implication is that the factors that make a behavior complex—such as the need for credibility or the added value from complementarity—may also make behaviors "sticky" once they are adopted.

This implication may also suggest that actors who have the most resistance to adopting a behavior may be the most committed to it once their thresholds are finally triggered. In other words, if, for instance, adoption depends on being convinced about the complementary value of a technology, then once there is sufficient reinforcement to trigger adoption, there may also be sufficient complementary value to make the technology difficult to abandon. The factors that create resistance to a behavior before adoption may also become the reasons for sticking with it after adoption. For this reason, there may be many cases in which complexity is not necessarily a limitation on a diffusion process but rather a necessary hurdle to overcome in order to generate lasting behavior change.

This experimental study of diffusion reveals a new way of using online settings to study how population structure can shape people's behavior. The potential this offers for studying a variety of new and previously untested questions is exciting, and is explored in greater depth in parts 3 and 4 of this book. While these methodological advances are promising, this is not to say that this approach is without limitations. For instance, there were several shortcomings of this experimental study that need to be addressed when considering its broader implications. A key limitation in the design of this experiment is that in the real world, unlike in this study, adopting a new health behavior is often extremely difficult. To adopt behaviors such as getting a vaccination, going on a diet, starting an exercise routine, or getting a screening, people may be required to pay the costs of time, deprivation, or physical pain. By contrast, the effort it took to sign up for the health forum was relatively minimal. So, how do the results from this online setting translate into implications for offline health behaviors? Because of the greater costs and challenges that are faced when making decisions about vaccinations or lifestyle changes, the need for social reinforcement is expected to be greater in those situations. This suggests that the results from this study are likely to be conservative. The greater need for social reinforcement in those cases indicates that the diffusion of real-world health behaviors is likely to depend even more on networks that provide social reinforcement than did the diffusion dynamics observed in these experiments.

An additional constraint of this experiment was that participants did not have any direct communication with their health buddies or information about their identities. This made it possible to isolate the effects of network topology on the dynamics of diffusion without the presence of confounding variables, such as tie strength. However, it also raises the question of what the strength of the effects of network topology would be when allowed to interact with other factors that affect interpersonal relationships. For instance, previous studies of diffusion have suggested that factors such as homophily and strong interpersonal affect may help to improve the spread of behaviors. As discussed in chapters 2 and 3, these features of social networks tend to be highly correlated with the formation of clustered social ties.[20] Thus, if there is an interaction effect of tie strength or homophily, it is likely to reinforce the value of clustered networks for diffusion. Consequently, my expectation is that these reinforcing factors would serve to amplify the observed effects of clustered social networks in promoting the diffusion of complex contagions.

These findings offer a new way of thinking about spreading in social networks: redundancy, more than reach, may be a key factor for diffusing innovations. Starting from the observation that behavior change is more likely when people receive social reinforcement from multiple sources, these results show that this individual-level observation translates into a network-level phenomenon whereby large-scale diffusion can reach more people and spread more quickly through wide bridges rather than long ties. Perhaps the most unexpected finding from this experiment is that clustered social networks may be a valuable structural ally not only for promoting the diffusion of challenging new behaviors, but also for increasing their maintenance.[21] To see how widely these results may apply, part 2 of this book explores the practical uses of these findings in applied settings where there is an interest in promoting the spread of behavior.

PART II

Applications

All politics is local.

—Tip O'Neill, former Speaker of the US House of Representatives

INTRODUCTION TO PART II

The ideas developed in this book draw upon a trade-off between the efficiency of long ties for spreading information and disease versus the effectiveness of wide bridges for spreading behaviors. There are nuances to this trade-off, as in situations where networks that are effective for spreading norms also become, as a result, more effective for spreading diseases. Nevertheless, throughout these chapters I have emphasized a line of demarcation that places information and disease into one category and behavior into the other.

The fundamental distinction to be made here, however, is not between viral contagions versus behavioral ones, but rather between the vast number of pathogenic, informational, and even behavioral contagions that propagate easily across long ties versus the universe of social contagions that require multiple sources of reinforcement in order to spread. This distinction challenges the familiar idea that the disease model of diffusion can be generically applied to the spread of behaviors. Here, too, there are nuances. It is clear that there may be times when behaviors do indeed spread as simple contagions, and there may even be times when diseases spread as complex contagions.[1]

It is not hard to come up with examples of simple behaviors for which a single contact is sufficient for transmission. For instance, while driving on a single-lane road, every driver's speed may be determined by the one car at the front of the group. Another familiar example is the decision to watch a viral video. Without any need for social reinforcement, a video from an acquaintance may be watched and forwarded to others. It is easy to come up with dozens of other examples of trivial behaviors that are simple contagions. However, in each example, it is also easy to see that as soon as a behavior becomes less trivial—for instance, because it involves a greater level of risk—it quickly becomes a complex contagion.

If, for example, the lead driver on a single-lane road is going very fast, the drivers behind are not likely to be convinced that they should drive fast, too. Similarly, if a link to a viral video opens a connection to a website with odd security protocols, the recipient will likely hesitate before following the link or before agreeing to install new viewing software into her browser. The decision to proceed requires being convinced that it is safe. In other words, while there are limitless examples of trivial behaviors that are simple, behaviors that are even moderately consequential are typically complex.

The implications of complexity extend to an enormous range of human and nonhuman activity in which the spread of collective behavior depends on stable channels of social reinforcement. The dynamics of complexity have been found in the behavior of bacteria colonies, ant armies, and honey bee swarms, and in the case of the latter, they have even been shown to produce nearly optimal levels of collective intelligence in a swarm's behavior.[2] Across all of these settings, complexity in social diffusion is harnessed through network structures that provide stable channels of social redundancy.

To see how widely these results may apply, the following chapters show how to make use of these findings for promoting diffusion in practical contexts. Chapter 5 illustrates the broad range of empirical settings in which research on complex contagions has been usefully applied. Chapter 6 explores the implications of these findings for situations in which innovators face entrenched opposition, such as contested public-health interventions and industry competition. Chapter 7 then turns to the implications of these findings for institutional contexts in which managers must make the best use of their organizational networks to spread innovative behaviors.

CHAPTER 5

Complex Contagions in Other Contexts

In the last few years, studies of complex contagions have explored a wide range of empirical domains using a variety of research methods, from field experiments on the diffusion of agricultural technologies in Malawi to large-scale observational studies on the spread of political donations online.[1] A primary focus of recent work has been to uncover the specific factors in online networks that give rise to complexity in diffusion.

A recent study of diffusion on Twitter, for instance, found that whether hashtags spread as simple or complex contagions is determined by the subject matter of the tweets. Political hashtags, such as, #TCOT (which stands for "Top Conservatives on Twitter") and #HCR (which stands for "Health Care Reform") were "riskier to use than conversational idioms . . . since they involve publicly aligning yourself with a position that might alienate you from others in your social circle." These hashtags exhibited high levels of complexity, with most people requiring contact with up to five or six adopters before adopting a new political hashtag, "with repeated exposures continuing to have unusually large marginal effects on adoption."[2]

By contrast, less controversial hashtags, such as idioms, were found to be simple contagions. The idiom hashtags "#cantlivewithout," "#dontyouhate," and "#musicmonday" typically spread from person to person with only a single contact. Similar results have been found on other social media sites, such as Facebook and Skype, indicating that the determining factor for whether diffusion is simple or complex is not the particular domain in which diffusion takes place but, rather, the kind of social contagion that is spreading. Whenever adoption involves risk, complementarity, or normative acceptance, social reinforcement is typically needed for the spread of behavior.

Not surprisingly, the successful spread of politically contentious hashtags through Twitter is due in part to the structure of the Twitter communities in which they diffused. The regions of the Twitter network where these social contagions spread effectively were composed of clustered, overlapping ties. Related studies of political activism on Twitter—such as the diffusion of hashtags about social movements—have also found that densely connected Twitter networks, where messages are likely to be reinforced from several contacts, are the communities in which these hashtags have the greatest reach. A consistent finding throughout these studies is that highly central individuals, who are typically very effective for diffusing idiom hashtags, are less important than densely interconnected peripheral individuals for the spread of politically radicalized hashtags. Interestingly, these interlocking peripheral communities are associated both with greater propagation of activist messages and with greater turnout at protest events.[3]

MOBILIZATION OF SOCIAL MOVEMENTS

The implications of complexity for political diffusion and mobilization on social media offer useful connections to the more established tradition of research on social movements. In particular, the association between riskiness and complexity in political tweets is suggestive of Doug McAdam's important work on the differences between "high risk" and "low risk" forms of collective action.[4]

Many well-known forms of collective action are high risk, such as protest against an authoritarian regime, where participants face the threat of imprisonment, torture, and death. Yet, not all collective action is so dangerous. The field of social-movement research ranges from low-risk peaceful gatherings supporting environmental sustainability to violent conflicts with police and fellow citizens over civil rights. The role of social networks in mobilizing these different kinds of social-movement efforts is likely to be determined by the degree of risk (or cost) associated with a particular event.[5]

A clear implication of the results on simple and complex contagions is that low-risk/low-cost collective action will spread more effectively through networks of long, narrow ties than through wide bridges. The reason for this is that barriers to participation in low-risk/low-cost collective action are more associated with access than with resistance. Even minimal contact with an individual who has joined an action can provide social incentives for participation. While many people may support a cause, the challenge that activists often face is spreading the word about an event. The more weak ties that are activated, the more people who will have some social connection to the event and will therefore be likely to attend.

McAdam takes this idea one step further and suggests that weak ties may also help to mobilize low-risk/low-cost collective action by providing social incentives to people who are apathetic about the cause itself. Imagine, for instance, an antiwar concert at a local beach. The concert is easy to attend and entails no risk, but some people may simply have little or no interest in the cause. While these people may have a low threshold for attending the event, they are unlikely to participate. Recruitment by a friend can give them a social incentive to show up. As McAdam (1986) put it, "Given the relatively low cost and risk associated with the [event], [a] hypothetical recruit is likely to attend, even if he is fairly apathetic about the issues in question. And this, I suspect, is true in most instances of recruitment to low-risk activism. Some crude calculation of social [value] as against personal costs prompts people to participate in safe, relatively cost-free forms of activism."[6]

The more weak ties there are in each adopter's network, the easier it is to spread social incentives to new recruits. Consequently, the smaller the world is, the more effective a word-of-mouth campaign will be for recruiting lots of people who would otherwise have had no reason to participate. Thus, for low-risk/low-cost collective action, the classical wisdom about network diffusion holds true. Increased network exposure is the key to recruitment.

The opposite, however, is true for high-risk or high-cost collective action. For instance, as an *International Herald Tribune* article on radical activist groups in South Korea reports, "Radical thought is passed on in clandestine 'study circles,' groups of students who may come from the same high school or hometown or church. These study circles . . . serve as the basic organizational unit for demonstrations and other protests."[7] The more risk that is associated with a mobilization effort, the more that success depends upon close-knit networks to establish trusted relationships and provide social reinforcement for participation. Correspondingly, the more weak ties there are in a social network, the easier it is for information to be leaked, and the less effectively people can be organized.[8] In these situations, weak ties in the network can slow down the rate of recruitment to high-risk collective action by increasing the risks associated with discussing movement activities.

A different kind of insight into the role of social networks in organizing high-risk collective action comes from taking the (hostile) point of view of the organization or government that is being opposed. Hannah Arendt was one of the first scholars to make the connection between the logic of social control and a strategic view of social networks.

In *The Origins of Totalitarianism,* she observed that citizens under a totalitarian regime are allowed to live and interact in a web of casual, weak-tie associations. Strong-tie networks—in which people interact with one another in trusted, close-knit groups—are actively discouraged by the regime. A cultivated atmosphere of suspicion prevents cohesive networks from forming and inhibits the growth of a network infrastructure capable of supporting high-risk collective action.[9]

From an unflinchingly strategic point of view, this network-based approach to social control follows a clear and disturbing logic. Complex contagions pose a threat to the regime; however, simple contagions are useful. The diffusion of state propaganda and the solace of pluralistic ignorance can flow easily through the web of weak-tie contacts. A weak social infrastructure thus encourages compliance with the dominant regime while actively preventing the reinforcement necessary to mobilize dissent.

The main lesson of complexity for social-movement mobilization is that social networks that offer significant advantages for some kinds of collective action will create substantial obstacles for others. As McAdam wrote, "If the complexity of the recruitment process is to be recognized, it cannot be assumed that there is a single dynamic that determines entrance into all forms of activism. At the very least, the costs and risks attached to the form of activism being studied should be specified insofar as they are likely to affect the precise mix of factors that produces participation." The network implications that arise from high-risk and low-risk collective action apply broadly to mobilization strategies that target traditional friendship networks, as well as to mobilization efforts using online networks and social media channels.[10] Both online and off, the networks that are best for mobilizing a collective action will depend on its degree of complexity.

DIFFUSING DIGITAL INNOVATIONS

These network implications also apply to mobilization efforts aimed at spreading new media technologies. Many technologies are low cost and low risk in the sense that they are inexpensive (often free) and do not involve a great deal of complementarity or opportunity cost. These technologies can be expected to diffuse most effectively across long ties. However, when technologies involve either a greater financial cost, or, as in the case of most social media technologies, they are free but they have such high levels of complementarity that they are useless unless lots of one's friends and contacts are using them, unilateral action entails a greater risk of wasting one's time and effort or incurring the opportunity costs of social exclusion. The most well-known examples of complementary social media technologies, such as Facebook, Twitter, and Skype, have consistently been found to be complex contagions, diffusing most effectively through clustered peer-to-peer networks that provide social reinforcement.[11]

Within more elaborated forms of social media, such as the massively multiplayer game of Second Life, the process of social diffusion within the virtual world is mediated by complex relationships that often involve subtle features of social interactions, such as reputation effects, bargaining and exchange histories, and social exclusion. Nevertheless, diffusion within this virtual world tends to follow the same structural logic found in other online settings, such as Facebook and Twitter.

In Second Life, innovative assets shared among users, such as novel hand gestures (like the "Aerosmith gesture"), spread more effectively through clustered peripheral networks than through highly centralized hubs.[12] This finding is reminiscent of the results that were found for political hashtags on Twitter, which also spread more effectively through clustered peripheral ties than through hubs. The mechanisms underlying the complexity of diffusion in these two cases are similar, but not identical. In the Twitter networks, complexity was driven by the social risks of posting politically contentious messages. In Second Life, the complexity of asset diffusion was driven by the normativity of hand gestures. Hand gestures require coordination. They are only useful to have if lots of one's peers are using them, too. Consistent with the findings in chapter 3 on degree heterogeneity, hubs were harder to activate in Second Life because their thresholds for adopting hand gestures were fractional instead of absolute. Highly connected individuals required greater numbers of peers to adopt before they would.

In virtual social settings, the design of a social environment can delimit whether diffusion is likely to emerge at all. Some settings may, by design, eliminate the potential for complex contagions to propagate. For instance, the social-news aggregator Digg places a premium on users sharing novel content with one another. This makes it unlikely that users will share content posted by their peers and prevents users from sharing content posted by multiple peers.[13]

At the other end of the spectrum, the design of social media sites can also strengthen the dynamics of social diffusion. Sites like Facebook and Twitter provide ready-made communication tools—such as Share and Retweet buttons–that accelerate the spread of simple contagions through their networks. The dynamics of diffusion become more complex, however, when the spread of digital artifacts requires users to pay costs of time and effort in order to adopt them. For instance, a recent cultural innovation that diffused across three million Facebook users—namely, placing an "equality sign" within a user's profile photo—was found to be a complex contagion, requiring social reinforcement in order to be transmitted.[14]

There were two factors underlying the complexity of the contagion in this case—cost and legitimacy. First, adopting the innovation required users to manually change their profile photo. While this involved only a modicum of technical skill and personal effort, it was nevertheless more demanding than clicking a Share button. Second, the contagion itself was considered to be politically contentious since it signaled support for same-sex marriage. Like political hashtags on Twitter, adoption of the innovation involved "displaying an opinion that is unpopular . . . [, which] creates the risk for conflict and contention" within a person's Facebook community.[15] Thus, the legitimacy of the behavior was a factor in users' willingness to adopt it. In light of these findings, researchers characterized the diffusion of the equality sign as a form of online social movement since it involved the risks of social exclusion and peer sanction common to many forms of political activism.[16] An interesting implication of the need for legitimacy is that social reinforcement was most effective at triggering adoption of the equality sign when it came from diverse members of a user's network. Reinforcing signals from many different kinds of contacts indicated greater normative acceptance of the behavior, which lowered the social risks associated with its adoption.

COMPLEXITY IN HEALTH

Similar dynamics of social reinforcement have also been found to accelerate the spread of health behaviors. Among runners, for instance, new exercise habits spread most effectively when athletes come into contact with several fellow runners who have all adopted the same routine.[17] Complexity in the dynamics of health extends from the spread of the most desirable behaviors, like exercise, to the least desirable ones, such as smoking. An analysis of smoking behavior in the Framingham Heart Study shows that the likelihood that a smoker will quit smoking, versus continue smoking, depends on which behavior is reinforced by their social contacts—in part because smoking is often explicitly social and thus shaped by the dynamics of social norms.[18]

A more recent analysis of complexity in smoking behavior, using data from the National Longitudinal Study of Adolescent to Adult Health, examined the dynamics of abstention under conditions where smokers could revert back to smoking after quitting. The diffusion of smoking cessation was highly dependent upon reinforcing clusters of "quitters" in the social network. The presence of both pro- and anti-smoking norms in the population increased individuals' dependence on reinforcement from peers because of actors' susceptibility to counter-vailing social influences from smokers who exerted their own norma-tive pressure on group behavior. Similar dynamics of complexity were also found in online networks. An examination of peer interactions in QuitNet—a social media platform for smokers trying to quit—showed that smokers were more likely to abstain when they were given rein-forcing contact with several abstinent users.[19]

An interesting twist in the relationship between complexity and health comes from a recent series of studies that unexpectedly found that clustered social networks could increase a population's vulnerabil-ity to the spread of infectious diseases.[20] While clustered social networks are normally inefficient for spreading simple contagions, like the mea-sles, these studies found that anti-vaccination attitudes (or "anti-vaxxer" norms) were complex contagions, which spread very effectively through networks composed of wide bridges. Clustered networks pulled people into patterns of mutual reinforcement on the anti-vaxxer norm, which created stable pockets of susceptibility to viral infection. The high sus-ceptibility of these anti-vaxxer communities, in turn, made the entire population vulnerable to the epidemic outbreak of an infectious disease. Strangely, this means that clustered social networks can thereby be-come better conduits for disease diffusion than random networks. An interesting new direction for research on this topic examines how health behaviors, health attitudes and infectious diseases may interact in a broader, multilayered network of both simple and complex contagions.[21]

Taken together, these implications of complexity suggest several new directions for future research. Some of these implications are concern-ing, whereas others are optimistic. All of them identify important op-portunities for exploring how the complexity of contagions can impact the dynamics of social diffusion. Chapter 6 applies these ideas to situa-tions in which diffusion encounters opposition. The discussion there shows how the results from the preceding chapters can be used to de-velop network strategies for overcoming resistance to the spread of innovations.

CHAPTER 6

Diffusing Innovations That Face Opposition

Even beneficial behaviors can encounter strong opposition. We must admit that this is often reasonable. It is natural to expect that social confirmation from several people might be needed before someone makes the decision to try an experimental medical procedure or adopt an unusual diet. Indeed, it is not only reasonable, but in many cases desirable, that people are cautious when making these kinds of choices. Nevertheless, this reluctance creates enormous difficulties for scientific dissemination efforts, public health campaigns, and innovation diffusion efforts, in which innovative ideas challenge existing social norms. There are many times when it would be useful to have a strategy for circumventing these social barriers to diffusion. This is where the results on complex contagions may be helpful.

Consider, for instance, a public health intervention in which a small number of individuals in a population are given personal incentives to lose weight. How should these individuals be chosen? Can they be chosen so that their change in behavior will influence others to also lose weight? What if there are existing norms that create resistance to the new weight-loss behavior? This chapter shows how the insights from the previous chapters might be applied in these kinds of situations. Specific network strategies for selecting a small number of "seed" individuals may be able to greatly increase the number of people who are ultimately reached by an intervention.

Similarly, consider a setting in which an entrepreneur attempts to diffuse an innovation that challenges an incumbent technology. As with a public health intervention, even a beneficial innovation can face strong opposition from an entrenched competitor. This chapter shows how the structure of the social network can be used to initiate the successful spread of a "challenger" technology.

Practical suggestions for how to improve diffusion in these situations come in the form of two simple ideas:

1. Clustered seeding can speed up the spread of a contested public health intervention.
2. Clustered networks can create "incubator neighborhoods" that allow a challenger technology to outcompete an established competitor.

In both cases, the main lesson is the same: increasing early adopters' access to the network can backfire, leading to failed diffusion. Behaviors that face entrenched opposition can spread more effectively when early adopters have less exposure to the network.

STRATEGIES FOR SEEDING A CONTESTED PUBLIC-HEALTH INTERVENTION

Unlike the online experiments described in chapter 4, in many public health settings social networks are well established and therefore difficult to explicitly change. As a result, the pressing question to answer for many interventions is, what is the most effective way to "seed" a new behavior into an established population? Here, computational experiments (that is, simulations) can show how the choice of seeding strategy impacts the spread of an intervention through public-health networks.

The network data used in these simulations come from two well-known sources, the National Study of Adolescent to Adult Health (that is, Add Health), and the Framingham Heart Study.[1] The approach adopted here is of someone who is responsible for developing an intervention in which several people are "treated" in the hopes of spreading a sustainable change in behavior. From this interventionist point of view, the goal is to seed a small segment of a population in a way that stimulates change in the greatest number of people. The results presented below are from computational experiments that were conducted on the three empirical health networks shown in figure 6.1.

The first two networks are from the Add Health data set, which contain (A) 1,082 people and (B) 1,525 people, respectively, [2] and the final one, C, is from the Framingham Heart Study and contains 2,033 people.[3] In every case, intervention strategies were tested to see how introducing a challenging new health behavior into the social network—for instance, condom use or regular exercise—would translate into sustained changes in behavior. The selection of these particular public health networks is based on their availability and large size.

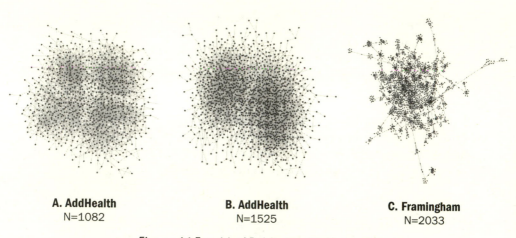

A. AddHealth
N=1082

B. AddHealth
N=1525

C. Framingham
N=2033

Figure 6.1 Empirical Public Health Networks

In each simulation, a small number of seeds were chosen for treatment. Similar to the computational experiments from chapters 2 and 3, the seeds were created by exogenously activating nodes in the network who could then transmit the behavior to their neighbors. Unlike the previous computational experiments, however, here the focus is not just on adoption but also on long-term engagement. Condom use and regular exercise are not one-and-done behaviors; they require maintenance. In these simulations, as in many public health interventions, individuals could abandon the behavior at any time if they did not receive sufficient social reinforcement to maintain it.

The experiments began with the activation of the seeds, who were the "treated" individuals. Other actors in the population decided whether or not to adopt the behavior based on whether their thresholds for activation were triggered by their activated neighbors. In the first two experiments, using the Add Health networks, actors required at least 40% of their neighbors to be activated in order to adopt. The last experiment, using the Framingham network, tested the effects of higher thresholds for adoption—actors required at least 60% of their neighborhood to be activated in order to adopt.[4]

In these simulations, actors resisted the intervention. Non-adopters put pressure on the adopters to abandon the intervention behavior. This pressure also affected the treated seed nodes. After the behavior was seeded and began to spread through the network (that is, after five rounds), if the countervailing pressures from the seeds' neighbors were too great, then the seeds themselves would abandon the behavior. Thus,

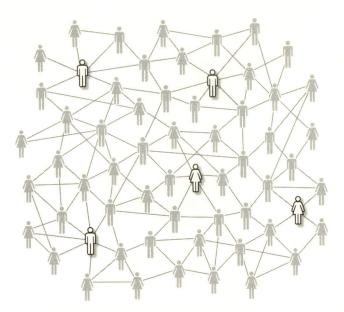

Figure 6.2 Random Seeding

starting on round six of each simulation, the seeds were just as susceptible to social influence as everyone else.[5]

The seeds' thresholds were the same as everyone else's—in the first two simulations, 40% of the seeds' neighbors needed to be activated in order for the seeds to maintain the behavior, and in the third simulation, 60% of the seeds' neighbors needed to be activated in order for them to maintain the behavior. For the duration of each simulation, every individual's decision—to maintain the behavior or to abandon it—depended on whether they had a sufficient fraction of activated neighbors.

Random seeding

The first seeding strategy that was attempted was to "go viral" by maximizing the seeds' exposure to the network. This strategy was implemented by randomly selecting a small fraction of nodes in each network to become treated seed nodes for the intervention. In each of the Add-Health networks (Networks A and B), the seed group comprised 10% of the population, which was selected at random to receive the intervention treatment; in the larger Framingham network (Network C), the seed group comprised 15% of the population. Figure 6.2 shows an illustration of the random seeding approach. In each network, the seeds (shown in

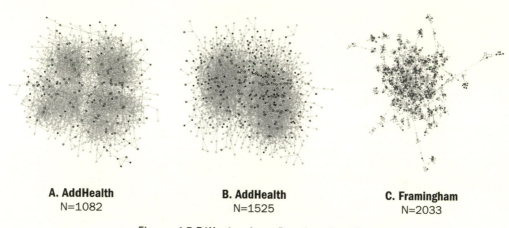

A. AddHealth
N=1082

B. AddHealth
N=1525

C. Framingham
N=2033

Figure 6.3 Diffusion from Random Seeding

white) were surrounded by untreated neighbors (shown in gray), giving the intervention maximum exposure to the network.

Figure 6.3 shows the resulting level of adoption after the first five rounds of the model. This figure shows how far the intervention behavior spread through each of the three networks while all the seeds were still activated. White nodes indicate activated seed nodes, and black nodes indicate newly activated adopters. Gray nodes are individuals who were not activated.

During the initial stages of diffusion, the intervention spread with modest success. At first, this spreading process appeared as if it might keep going; however, it was cut short once the treatment effects wore off for the seeds. At round six, the seeds began to require social support in order to maintain the new behavior. At this point, many of the seeds began to abandon the intervention. This initiated a downward spiral of participation. Once the seeds abandoned the behavior, so did their neighbors, and their neighbors' neighbors, and so on. A cascade of attrition flowed through each of the networks, as almost all of the adopters who were activated during the initial diffusion process subsequently reverted back to their old behavior.

Figure 6.4 shows the end result of this process. In the first AddHealth network, the final adoption rate dropped to 2.7%—far below the size of the initial 10% seed. In the second AddHealth network, final adoption also dropped below the initial seed, reaching 6.6%. And in the Framingham network, activation plummeted from the initial 15% seed, down to 2.3% of the population.

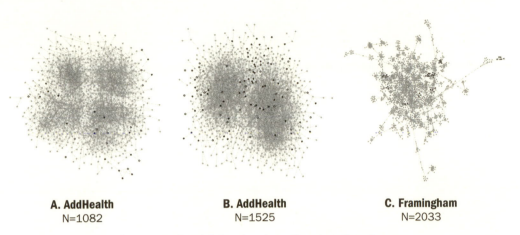

A. AddHealth	B. AddHealth	C. Framingham
N=1082	N=1525	N=2033

Figure 6.4 Final Adoption from Random Seeding

The random seeding approach suffered from a couple of weaknesses. The first was that because the treated individuals were initially the only adopters in their neighborhoods, it was up to them alone to convince their neighbors to change their behavior. Because the seeds were in the minority, they were fighting against the majority influence in each neighborhood. The "social inertia" in each case was pulling the seeds' neighbors toward not adopting.

The second weakness of this seeding strategy was more serious. Because the inertia in each neighborhood was pulling the population toward inaction, only a few of the seeds' neighbors ever adopted the behavior. Most of them did not. Thus, once the treatment effects wore off—and the seeds began to require social support to maintain the behavior—they were trapped by the same inertial forces that affected everyone else in their neighborhood, leading most of them to abandon the behavior.

While the random seeding strategy gave the intervention maximum exposure to the population, it also left the seeds without any support. The consequence was that seeds faced strong countervailing influences from their neighbors, making them highly prone to recidivism.

Clustered seeding

The appeal of the random seeding strategy is based on an intuitive idea that comes from the disease model of diffusion: namely, more exposure creates better diffusion. But the findings on complex contagions suggest that a neighborhood-based approach that limits the seeds' exposure

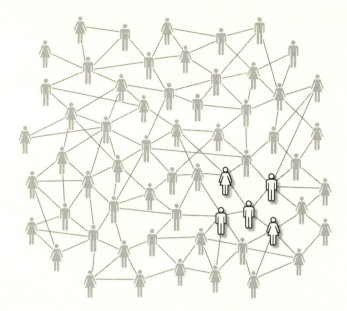

Figure 6.5 Clustered Seeding

may be more successful.[6] So, I ran another set of experiments to test this new strategy. This time, rather than selecting individuals at random from the entire population, I instead selected a few neighborhoods in the population and then "treated" all the members of these neighborhoods with the intervention.

Figure 6.5 shows an illustration of the clustered seeding approach. To make sure that the results from these experiments could be compared to the first set of experiments, the neighborhoods were chosen so that the total number of activated seeds was identical in both the clustered seeding experiments and the random seeding experiments. The only difference between the two experiments was that previously the seeds had been chosen at random, giving them access to the entire population, whereas this time they were clustered together in local neighborhoods. Figure 6.6 shows the resulting diffusion of the intervention behavior after the first five rounds of each simulation.

The clustered seeding approach produced a significant increase in the overall spread of the behavior. In each of the simulations, reinforcing pressure from the seeds created a cascade of adoption that poured out into each of the networks. While this is promising, prudence requires that we wait to see what happened once the effects of the

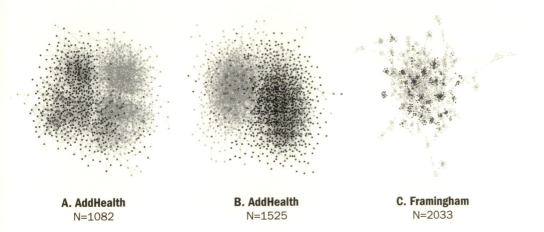

A. AddHealth
N=1082

B. AddHealth
N=1525

C. Framingham
N=2033

Figure 6.6 Diffusion from Clustered Seeding

intervention wore off, at round six. Did the behavior unravel as it had before? Figure 6.7 shows the results. When the treatment effects wore off, there was almost no change in the number of adopters. In every network, the intervention had become self-sustaining; the behavior "locked in" to become a stable social norm.

The success of the clustered seeding strategy is due to the fact that the seeds provided reinforcing support for one another to maintain the behavior. Within each seed neighborhood, the density of activated individuals put the balance of social inertia in favor of the new behavior instead of against it. Once the treatment effects wore off, lock-in on the treatment behavior prevented recidivism within the seed neighborhoods.

Outside the seed neighborhoods, reinforcement worked in a similar way.[7] Seeds were able to work together to recruit their shared neighbors. Once these neighbors adopted, they could, in turn, coordinate their efforts both with the seeds and with each other to recruit additional neighbors. This process created a reinforcing network of support that extended far beyond the seed neighborhoods.

Over several hundred trials of these experiments, clustered seeding produced a 180% average increase in final adoption in the first AddHealth experiment, a 90% average increase in final adoption in the second AddHealth experiment, and a 440% average increase in final adoption in the Framingham experiment.[8]

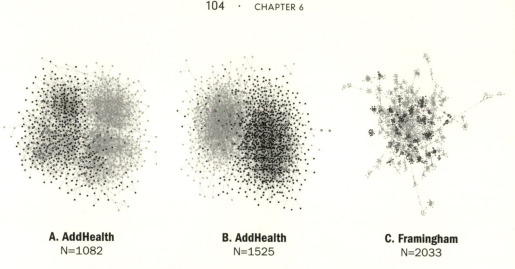

A. AddHealth
N=1082

B. AddHealth
N=1525

C. Framingham
N=2033

Figure 6.7 Final Adoption from Clustered Seeding

The main lesson from these computational experiments is that when a population is inclined to resist an innovation, clustering the seeds together can be a useful strategy for initiating diffusion. As the innovation spreads, reinforcement among the seeds and their shared neighbors creates local lock-in on the behavior in each new part of the network. The more locally entrenched an intervention becomes, the greater reach it can have throughout a population, and the more successful it is likely to be.[9]

It is particularly useful to see how well this strategy works for maintaining the behavior once it starts to spread. A clustered seeding approach turns the dynamics of social inertia from an obstacle to diffusion into a resource for creating stable lock-in on behavior change. This approach to spreading an innovation may appear slow when compared with the viral spread of a simple contagion; however, it can be surprisingly effective for initiating diffusion in situations where hard-to-maintain behaviors face entrenched opposition.

USING INCUBATOR NEIGHBORHOODS TO DIFFUSE TECHNOLOGICAL INNOVATIONS

In addition to the seeding strategy, the structure of the social network can also play a decisive role in determining whether an innovative behavior can successfully challenge an entrenched social practice. Even a superior innovation may be unable to gain a foothold in a population when everyone has already coordinated on a competing alternative. In this kind of situation, network clustering can be the difference between a successful innovation and a failed technology.

Consider, for instance, the spread of a new social media platform, for which the value of the technology is determined primarily by the number of other people who are using it. We can think of this in terms of a coordination problem in which actors are deciding between two platforms, A and B, where there is a high level of complementarity in their choices.

Let's assume that option A is the better platform. It offers a better interface and it is easier to use. However, we can also assume that everyone in the population is already using option B. Since B is the universally adopted incumbent, it is the desirable choice. Let's also suppose that individuals in the population are adventurous. They occasionally make brief "experiments" in which they try out new social media platforms. While it is easy to try out a new platform, it can also be costly because time spent learning how to use one platform is also time away from participating in the other one. So, while these experiments afford people the chance to discover a better option, they also create the unwelcome risk of social exclusion from falling behind in the rapid sequence of posts and responses among their peers. In a world where everyone is using platform B, a curious individual who briefly experiments with option A will soon find that she fails to coordinate with her friends who are all using B. Without any social encouragement to keep using the new alternative, this individual will quickly abandon her experiment and revert back to the norm of using option B.

It may also happen at some point that two contacts accidentally coordinate, and both experiment with the innovative option at the same time. These individuals can reinforce each other's choice of option A. From this accidental coordination, these friends may both find that they enjoy using option A, and agree to try to spread the innovation to others. As in the seeding study above, let's assume that we are faced with the problem of these innovators attempting to diffuse option A. The obvious challenge for their diffusion initiative is that the same social network where they want to spread option A is also the locus of entrenchment on option B.

While this problem of diffusion is similar to what we saw above in the seeding experiments, there is an important difference here. This time, everyone has unlimited access to both A and B and can try either option at any time. Both technologies are freely available and known to everyone from the start. Thus, while the seeding experiments showed how to use an exogenous seeding strategy to initiate diffusion, this example shows how the structure of the social network can be used to initiate diffusion endogenously.

Let's start by considering a random network. The first thing to notice is that in a random network, experimenters have the best opportunity to expose lots of people to the innovation. If two neighbors both attempt to spread option A to their other neighbors, a random network will maximize the number of new "targets" that they both reach. For a simple contagion, this would work beautifully to spread the innovation. When there is entrenched opposition, however, widespread resistance to the innovation creates complexity in the diffusion process that turns these exposures from assets into liabilities.

In a random network, the two experimenters are not likely to have any friends in common. Consequently, when they each interact with their other friends, they will not be able to coordinate with each other to reinforce the innovation. This creates two problems for their diffusion initiative. The first problem is that it is hard for them to spread the innovation. Since option B is the incumbent, the experimenters' neighbors receive reinforcement for option B from all of their contacts. Without coordinated effort from the experimenters, their neighbors are likely to ignore the experimenters' attempts to advance option A. The second problem is that the random network makes it less likely that the experimenters will both keep using option A. This is because the experimenters will receive countervailing influences from all of their other contacts, encouraging both of them to revert back to the established norm of using option B. The experimenters' momentary shared success with option A will quickly be overwhelmed by the social influences forcing them to return to the popular platform.[10]

The potential for social change is improved considerably by moving to a social network in which there is a high level of clustering in the neighborhood structure. In a clustered social network, two experimenters who coordinate on option A are likely to have friends in common. They can therefore reinforce option A among their mutual contacts. If any of these shared neighbors switch to the new platform, these new adopters can then help to reinforce the initial experimenters' continued use of option A.

Going one step further, the shared friends of the experimenters are also likely to share other contacts in common. Thus, these new adopters can coordinate both with each other and with the experimenters to convince other shared friends to switch to option A. The experimenters and their neighbors can thereby form a local pocket of social reinforcement on option A. This neighborhood can act as an incubator for the growth of the innovation.

The key advantage of a clustered network is that the process of "dyadic" coordination (between two people) is embedded within the more enduring structure of a "triad" (between three people). As a result, two experimenters who coordinate on a new option can quickly solidify neighborhood support for the innovation through interactions with their mutual contacts. A "challenger" technology can thereby gain an initial foothold into a population, despite widespread entrenchment on a competing alternative. From this initial pocket of innovation, wide bridges of social reinforcement can carry the innovation from neighborhood to neighborhood. Once this spreading process gets going, clustered networks buttress against the forces of recidivism that might threaten to bring people back to the established norm of using option B.

As Simmel stated, "A dyad depends on each of its two elements. For its life it needs both, but for its death, only one. The dyad therefore, does not attain the super-personal life which the individual feels to be independent of [one]self. As soon, however, as the there is a sociation of three, a group continues to exist even in case one of the members drops out."[11] In other words, clustered networks create stability in a diffusion process. If a group of neighbors converges on option A, even if one neighbor "defects" back to option B the others will continue to reinforce the group's use of A. The innovation will "stick" at the group level despite any individual lapses in behavior.

For diffusion, this means that clustered neighborhoods protect a complex coordination process from being derailed by accidents and deviations that would easily destroy an agreement that formed across long ties. Long ties are dyadic in nature and thus can be broken by a single individual. Wide bridges, however, are conduits of behavior change that are "super-personal" and are therefore stable structures for the spread and maintenance of innovations in the face of individual unpredictability.

Clustered neighborhoods thus act as social incubators that protect new ideas from being swamped early on by countervailing influences from the rest of the population. Contrary to the lessons learned from decades of research on the diffusion of simple contagions, incubator neighborhoods accelerate the diffusion of a contested innovation precisely because they limit early adopters' exposure to the rest of the network.[12]

The diffusion of a contested innovation in a hostile environment bears an interesting similarity to the spread of cooperative behavior in a population of defectors. For instance, when altruists are clustered together in social networks, the mutual benefits that they provide each other can allow them to outcompete the surrounding defectors, eventually transforming a population mired in mutual defection into a cooperative social regime. For both contested innovations and cooperative behaviors, the same logic applies.[13] Network clustering allows social innovators to work together to reinforce each other's behavior, while protecting them from the countervailing influences of the rest of the population. This process falls apart, however, when there are too may long ties in the network. The less clustering there is in the neighborhood, the more exposed social innovators become to the countervailing influences around them, and the harder it is for them to coordinate their efforts to challenge entrenched social norms.

A transformation in the capacity for social change takes place when the social topology moves from a network composed of long ties to one composed of interlocking chains of wide bridges. All of sudden, a small group of social innovators who previously faced impossible odds—who would have been outcompeted, taken advantage of, and eliminated—find themselves embedded within incubator neighborhoods. Reinforcing support from clustered ties protects innovators from the influences of entrenched opposition. By limiting early adopters' exposure to the rest of the population, a clustered social topology organizes the social innovators into a local critical mass, whose efforts can grow into a social movement that transforms the normative landscape of a population.[14]

The promising finding in this chapter is that the reasonable expectation that people will resist behavior change does not mean that diffusion will fail. Instead, this expectation reveals the strategies that can be used to improve the flow of behavioral contagions through a population. Chapter 7 shows how the ideas developed here can be applied to the challenge of organizational change, where managers must make decisions about how to structure organizational networks to promote the diffusion of innovative ideas and complex knowledge.

CHAPTER 7

Diffusing Change in Organizations

Perhaps the most influential application of network theory to organizational performance comes from Ronald Burt's theory of structural holes.[1] Burt defines a structural hole as a gap between two diverse social clusters that prevents access to nonredundant information. Figure 7.1 shows an example. Groups A, B, and C have lots of internal structure but no bridges between them. Information, ideas, and new opportunities available to members of Group A are unknown to members of Groups B and C.

Thousands of articles have been published on structural holes and their implications for everything from innovation diffusion to the growth of philosophical schools of thought.[2] The major focus of this literature is on the advantages that can be gained by individual managers, entrepreneurs, and innovators who "bridge" structural holes. For instance, figure 7.2 shows that if Robert forms weak ties to Elizabeth and Emily, these links establish bridges that close the structural holes and permit novel information to flow between the groups. As Burt put it,

> Robert's bridge connections to other groups give him an advantage with respect to information access. He reaches a higher volume of information because he reaches more people indirectly. Further, the diversity of his contacts across the three separate groups means that his higher volume of information contains fewer redundant bits of information. Further still, Robert is positioned at the cross-roads of social organization so he is early to learn about activities in the three groups. He corresponds to the 'opinion leaders' proposed in the early diffusion literature as the individuals responsible for the spread of new ideas and behaviors (Burt 1999). Also, Robert's more diverse contacts mean that he is more likely to be a candidate discussed for inclusion in new opportunities. And there is a feedback loop in which benefits beget more benefits: Robert's early access to diverse information [makes] him more attractive to other people as a contact in their own networks."[3]

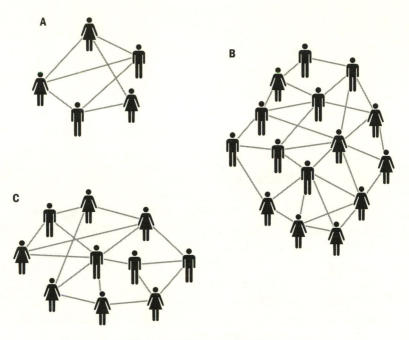

Figure 7.1 Structural Holes

The strategic benefits for individuals who bridge structural holes are enormous. In turn, the individual benefits for brokers also translate into collective value for an organization. Without brokers, information would fail to diffuse, and opportunities for collaboration, exchange, and innovation would be lost. Bridges that span structural holes have thus been argued to play an essential role in promoting innovation diffusion within organizations and creating novel opportunities for cultural exchange and knowledge transfer across firms.[4]

Nevertheless, a central implication of the results on complex contagions is the need to circumscribe carefully the scope of Burt's claims about the organizational value of brokers for diffusion. While Burt's theory of structural holes is not explicitly concerned with diffusion, it is a theory of information transfer and therefore has implications for the spread of ideas, knowledge, and norms through organizational networks. The implication that I wish to draw out here is that although narrow bridges across structural holes may facilitate the spread of information, they are unlikely to transmit innovative practices or workplace norms that require social reinforcement.

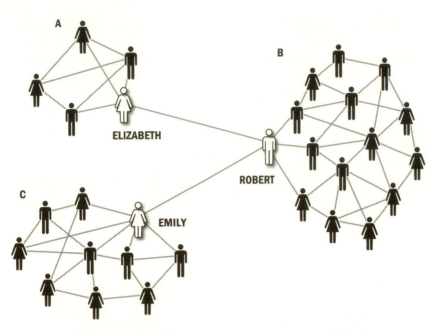

Figure 7.2 Information Brokers Bridging Structural Holes

In chapter 6, I focused on settings in which complexity in a diffusion process arises from people's opposition to an innovative behavior. Here, I focus instead on situations in which the source of complexity is not opposition but, rather, the requirement that colleagues coordinate with each other in order to adopt innovative practices or new workplace norms.

For instance, one highly studied workplace innovation is Total Quality Management, or TQM: a management paradigm that emphasizes customer satisfaction at every stage of an organizational process, integrating feedback from all members of an organization to improve business practices. This management innovation was designed to be applicable to any industry, from superconductor manufacturers to real estate agencies, and was expected to diffuse widely across several markets.

However, while TQM was adopted in many firms, it failed to spread to a surprising number of organizations that had external contact with it. To explain this, several studies of how external contacts and brokerage relations between groups affect the spread and adoption of organizational practices have emphasized the importance of strong intergroup connections for innovation diffusion. Morten Hansen observed that "weak interunit ties help a project team search for useful knowledge in other subunits but impede the useful transfer of complex knowledge." Similarly, Deborah Ancona and David Caldwell found that a high frequency of "lateral communications" is one of the primary indicators of when effective workplace practices will be adopted: "In all the cases we reviewed, successful teams were deeply engaged in communications with outsiders."[5] In other words, wide bridges, not weak ties, were the key to effective organizational exchange.

For structural holes research, these observations suggest that there may be a tension between what is good for the individual broker and what is good for the organization. Because an information broker controls the flow of information between two groups, she is in a position to exploit both groups in order to extract resources for herself. If coworkers attempt to create additional links across groups, it is in the broker's interest to prevent these ties from forming. Her individual gains are maximized when she is the only channel through which information can flow. The more additional channels of communication there are to outside groups, the less structural advantage she has.

Figure 7.3 shows a situation in which additional ties create a wide bridge between Groups A and B. Robert still has an advantaged position because he is the unique connector between all three groups. However, his strategic power is diminished by the fact that other members of Group B can now exchange information and form partnerships with members of Group A. From Robert's point of view, the situation in figure 7.2 is better than the situation in figure 7.3. But, what is best for diffusion across the organization?

To find out, I constructed a model of organizational networks with varying degrees of brokerage and studied which conditions were most favorable for the diffusion of complex innovations.[6] Figure 7.4 shows three networks along the continuum of structural holes. The network in panel A has no structural holes. It is a random topology in which every node has equal access to the entire network. There are no groups for bridges to form between, so brokerage opportunities are minimized. At the other extreme, panel C shows a network with abundant brokerage opportunities. There are lots of structural holes and only a few brokers who span them. Each broker is in a unique position to transmit information between groups and, in turn, to reap the rewards of structural advantage.

Between these two extremes, there is a third option. In panel B, every individual has memberships in multiple groups. Individuals have a

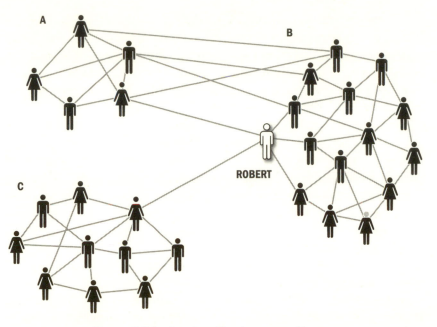

Figure 7.3 Redundant Ties between Clusters

primary membership in the group where they have the most internal ties; however they also share overlapping connections to other groups.[7] These overlapping connections create wide bridges across the organization. In these kinds of organizational networks, there are only modest opportunities for individuals to gain the advantages of brokerage. Nevertheless, the successful spread of an innovative practice throughout the organization still requires that it diffuse across several distinct clusters.

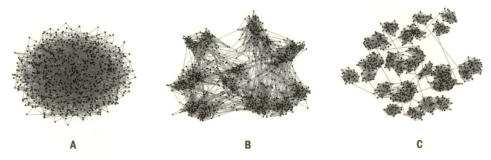

Figure 7.4 Networks with Different Levels of Brokerage

To see how effective each of these organizational networks is for the diffusion of a novel business practice, I ran computational experiments on each one using a "minimally complex" innovation. An innovation with minimal complexity has a threshold of two, such that individuals need to receive confirmation from two colleagues in order to be convinced to adopt.[8]

Unlike a complex innovation, a simple innovation, such as self-explanatory software for computer-aided design, may require no coordination with anyone else in order for a team member to adopt it. A person simply needs to download it in order to start using it. Thus, informational exposure from a single colleague can be sufficient to transmit the innovation. By contrast, a minimally complex innovation would require an adopter to coordinate with a small number of colleagues in order for the innovation to be useful.

An example of this kind of innovation is project management software that is easy to learn but requires two or three members of a work team to coordinate with each other to determine their times for logging into the software and updating their progress on a project. Failures to coordinate might result in lost data or scheduling conflicts. So, teammates would have to work together to use the system. Adoption by one person would be dependent upon adoption by a few other members of the team.

A more complex innovation would be project-management software that takes a long time to learn and requires all the members of a large team to coordinate with each other to determine who has priority for editing, saving, and deleting files when using the software. An individual's decision to adopt this technology requires having all the other members of the team collectively agree that they will integrate it into their work routines and will establish shared norms for using the software. As the need for social coordination increases, so does the complexity of the innovation. Given this range of complexity in organizational diffusion, it is useful to start small—by seeing how minimal complexity would affect the dynamics of spreading for an organizational innovation.

I began by seeding the innovation into a single neighborhood in each network (that is, approximately 1% of the population in each case) and observing the extent of integration on the behavior that followed. Unexpectedly, the results showed an inverted U-shaped effect of network structure on diffusion. The networks that were the farthest away from each other in terms of brokerage potential—that is, the one with no

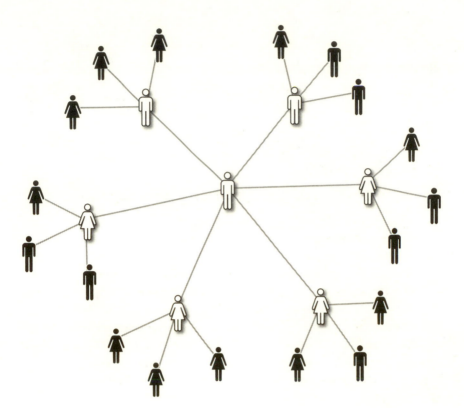

Figure 7.5 Seed Neighborhood in the Low-Brokerage Network

brokerage (panel A) and with high brokerage (panel C)—both performed the same. In both cases, integration of the behavior failed.

In the low-brokerage network (panel A), the results resembled the
random seeding experiments described in chapter 6. In this case, however, instead of seeding randomly all over the network, all the seeds
were in the same neighborhood. However, because the network was
random, none of the seeds shared neighbors in common, so they could
not provide their neighbors with any confirmatory support to coordinate on their adoption of the innovation. Figure 7.5 shows a closer view
of the seed neighborhood in the low-brokerage network. The nodes
shown in white are the seeds, and the black nodes are their neighbors
who have not yet adopted. Each seed sends a signal to its neighbors that
arrives without any peer support. This lack of support prevented the
innovation from spreading beyond the initial 1% of the organization
that was seeded.

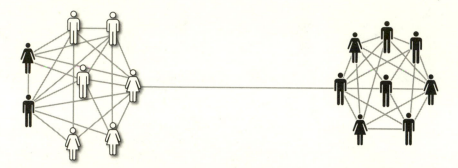

Figure 7.6 Seed Neighborhood in the High-Brokerage Network

At the other extreme, figure 7.6 shows the seed neighborhood in the high-brokerage network (panel C). The seeds, shown in white, are all within a single cluster. A few remaining members of this cluster, shown in black, are connected to the seeds. The members of another cluster are connected to the seed neighborhood by a brokerage tie. These individuals are also unactivated and shown in black. In this network, the innovation quickly reached everyone within the initial seed cluster, but it did not spread beyond that. The bridges across the clusters were long ties and therefore too narrow to provide the reinforcement required to spread the new practice. Consequently, the innovation only reached individuals within the original seed cluster (5% of the population).

By contrast, in the "goldilocks" network between the two extremes (panel B), the innovation reached 95% of the population. The seed neighborhood in this network, which is depicted in figure 7.7, shows that the seed nodes, in white, are all within a single cluster. As in panel C, the seeds have reinforcing ties to a small number of unactivated individuals within their cluster, shown in black. However, in figure 7.7 the members of the seed cluster also have overlapping ties that create a wide bridge to another cluster, in which everyone is unactivated.

When the innovation began to spread in this network, clustering within the seed neighborhood allowed rapid coordination on the innovation within the seed group. From there, wide bridges across clusters then carried the innovation to neighboring groups. These cross-cutting ties ensured that the innovation reached each new group while accompanied by reinforcing signals from several peer adopters, allowing it to spread from group to group, across the network. Compared to the network in panel C—where individual brokers have a lot of strategic advantage within the network—in panel B, the individual benefits for

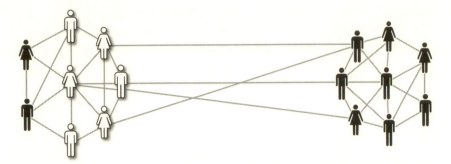

Figure 7.7 Seed Neighborhood in the Wide-Bridges Network

brokers are reduced by the redundant contacts across groups. However, in return, these networks of wide bridges create significant organizational benefits for achieving network-wide adoption of an innovation.

Wide bridges have three important advantages over brokerage ties for spreading complex innovations through an organization. First, a major weakness of brokerage ties is that they are often weak ties. A single individual who spans a structural hole is not necessarily trustworthy. As Burt elaborated, "The holes between [Robert's] contacts mean that he can broker communication while displaying different beliefs and identities to each contact. Simmel and Merton introduced the sociology of people who derive 'control benefits' from structural holes: the ideal type is the *tertius gaudens* (literally, 'the third who benefits')." A broker across a structural hole can exploit both sides for her individual advantage. This advantage comes from the fact that both sides know that she is the unique link between two disconnected groups. This may not have any consequences for simple information diffusion, but for the spread of a new business practice or a costly innovation, the sincerity and trustworthiness of the messenger may be just as important as the message.[9]

As shown in figure 7.7, one advantage of wide bridges is that individuals on both sides of the bridge have multiple contacts in common. Thus, the potential for reputation effects at both ends puts constraints on the actions of the bridge members.[10] Careless or exploitative behavior by a bridging individual is likely to be detected and is therefore less likely to happen. Wide bridges between groups thereby increase the trustworthiness of messages coming from other parts of an organization.

A second advantage of wide bridges over brokerage ties has to do with the fact that an innovation that diffuses across multiple groups may come from members of the organization who do not necessarily share the same concerns or needs as other groups. In other words, one group's innovation is not necessarily useful to the members of another group. Even if a broker has good intentions, the interests and goals of an innovating group may be too different from those of a receiving group to merit integrating their innovations.[11] A wide bridge between groups can change this.

If multiple members of a receiving group share contacts in common with members of an innovating group, the credibility of the innovation increases. For instance, when the members of a receiving group have multiple contacts with colleagues who have adopted a new kind of project management software, it allows them to observe how easily the members of the innovating group work together to use the new software and how effective it is for improving their performance. These reinforcing exposures increase the likelihood that the receiving group will be willing to coordinate on adopting it.[12] Moreover, the transfer of a complex practice across groups can rely on the ability of members of the receiving group to work together to integrate it. When members of the receiving group share bridging contacts with each other, they can confirm each other's beliefs about the value of the innovation. Team members who all have contacts with the innovating group may therefore have social incentives to work together to integrate the new practice into their group's routines.

Finally, a third advantage of wide bridges over brokerage ties for organizational diffusion is that they make cross-group channels of exchange robust to attrition. A single broker between two groups is a fragile bridge. Indeed, the power that an individual gains from holding this structural position is due in part to the costs an organization will face if she leaves. Redundancy eliminates this advantage. Wide bridges are stable features of an organizational environment that endure even as individuals come and go.

These three advantages of wide bridges over brokerage ties within an organization apply equally to brokerage networks across organizations. The wider the bridges are between organizations, the more reliable and enduring these relationships are likely to be, and the more influence they are likely to have over each other's business culture, norms of conduct, and the adoption of innovative practices.[13]

By contrast, the very feature of brokerage ties that makes them so desirable for individuals—namely, their exclusivity—can be their Achilles' heel for supporting diffusion across organizations. The fewer ties there are between organizations, the fewer incentives there are for firms to have compatible organizational structures, similar norms of conduct, or shared standards of evaluation. Wide bridges, by contrast, increase institutional isomorphism, making it more likely that organizations will share similar values and internal structures.[14] A single brokerage tie, on the other hand, has very little influence over the internal practices that govern a peer institution. Therefore, the narrower the bridges are between organizations, the more challenging it can be to spread innovative practices between them.

These organizational implications of complexity are as applicable to science as they are to business. Brokers across academic disciplines have historically faced many of the same challenges of knowledge transfer that firms face. Disciplinary norms of authorship credit, contribution expectations, and publication outlets vary enormously across academic disciplines. For a sociologist, a first authorship is a meaningful signal of contribution; however, for an economist it is not. For a physicist, last authorship is often a strong signal of contribution, whereas for an anthropologist it is not. For a physician, dozens of researchers may be coauthors on a paper, while for a philosopher, only the scholar who actually writes the paper will be the author. And for a political scientist, journal publications and books are the only valid forms of academic currency, whereas for a computer scientist, tenure review may consist entirely of conference papers.

These differences have historically been a tremendous barrier to the transmission of ideas across disciplines. Only a small number of individuals could afford to pay the "costs" of publishing in an outlet that their disciplinary colleagues would not value or of including dozens of coauthors on a paper that they wrote. Consequently, through much of the 1950s, '60s, and '70s, academic networks resembled the structure shown in panel C of figure 7.4. Several well-known scholars played the role of disciplinary brokers, and they were individually rewarded for it, but very little collective headway was made in the form of interdisciplinary research.

It was not until newly formed subdisciplines created overlapping ties across several departments that the broad pattern of academic networks could be restructured, allowing new research ideas to diffuse and blossom much faster than before. Wide bridges between fields that previously seemed to have no relevance to one another—such as philosophy and neuroscience—sparked the diffusion of new scientific ideas, the formation of new degree programs, and the productive exploration of new areas of research. These changes helped to produce the new field of cognitive science, which emerged through increasingly wide bridges between neuroscience, philosophy, linguistics, and psychology—fields that historically did not have much to say to one another. A more recent example comes from the field of network science, which has prospered through wide bridges that have formed between sociology, physics, biology, and computer science. And, most recently, the emerging fields of computational social science and data science have cast an even wider net across computer science, information science, communication, political science, economics, sociology, and even anthropology. The resulting network of disciplinary interactions is now much closer to the network shown in panel B in figure 7.4. Disciplinary structures still exist, but most departments have several faculty who are cross-listed with other departments and share multiple, overlapping affiliations.

The main lesson from Burt's work on structural holes is that broker-age ties can be essential for creating new channels of information diffusion where none previously existed.[15] When this happens, brokers' interests are aligned with the interests of the organization. But the main lesson from this study of complexity is that the structural advantage that individual brokers enjoy can come at the cost of reducing the spread of innovative practices across firms, industries, and disciplines. The successful transfer of complex knowledge typically requires wide bridges to broker the transmission of influence and expertise across organizational boundaries.

STRUCTURING ORGANIZATIONAL NETWORKS

A reasonable question at this point is, how can someone create wide bridges for diffusion in their organization? It seems like a tall order. First of all, people already have social ties to colleagues and friends. And, second, everyone has an interest in preserving their existing channels of influence and exchange. Is it really practical to think that social ties can be manipulated to create better organizational networks? In part 3 of this book, I will discuss strategies for doing this by constructing social networks online. These strategies can be quite powerful for improving diffusion in virtual settings, but we would also like to know if it is possible to do this kind of thing within face-to-face settings. The rest of this chapter is dedicated to showing how managers can use these ideas to control the structure of the social networks that naturally emerge in such contexts.

The main idea is as old as sociology itself: social relations do not appear out of nowhere. Rather, they emerge from the social contexts that we inhabit in our neighborhoods, schools, and workplaces. In its most basic articulation, this means that for people to form ties, there must be a social setting where they can meet one another.[16] For instance, a software programmer and a graphic designer who work in different divisions of Microsoft might never have an occasion to meet. If they are both asked to participate in a joint working group between the two divisions, however, they will have a context in which they can interact. As a result of their interactions in that setting, they might find that they like working together, and form a new tie within Microsoft's social network. This link may become a pathway for the designer and the programmer to coordinate on future activities across their respective divisions. An analogous situation is two students at the Massachusetts Institute of Technology (MIT) who have different majors and are in different years. While they may never meet each other in their classes or in their dormitory hallways, if they both sign up for an indoor soccer league and wind up playing on the same team, the sports league may offer a context for them to establish a friendship. Playing on the team together, these students may not only become friends, they may also discover complementary research interests, which may give rise to an innovative project that integrates ideas from one student's work in mechanical engineering with the other student's research in neuroscience.

These are familiar kinds of examples. We intuitively understand that work ties, friendship ties, and acquaintance ties form through social contexts. The new idea that I want to discuss here is how managers can use these social contexts *strategically* to shape the social network within an organization, or within any community more broadly.[17] By changing the set of opportunities that people have to meet one another (for instance, on intramural teams, on working groups, and even in their hallways), managers can restructure the resulting pattern of social ties within an organization to meet specific organizational goals. We have already seen how the structure of social networks affects the flow of new ideas and behaviors throughout an organization. The next step here is to show how managers can use the social contexts within an organization—as the foundation for social networks—to design organizational networks that improve institutional capacities for innovation and adaptation.[18]

This idea has substantial practical value because, unlike social networks, which are very hard to manipulate directly in face-to-face settings, social contexts can be more easily calibrated to shape the channels of influence and exchange within an organization. Thus, if the variety or composition of the social contexts within an organization are altered—for instance, by reorganizing the number of working groups at Microsoft Research in Redmond, or by changing the hallway assignments of the faculty offices at the Los Alamos National Laboratories, or by introducing a new Ultimate Frisbee intramural league for the undergraduate community at MIT—then, within a reasonable period of time, the pattern of social connectedness in the population can be expected to endogenously reform into a new configuration. Some existing ties will be dropped, some new ties will be added, and the resulting width and length of the bridges across the organization will be altered. As a direct consequence of specific changes to the number and size of social contexts, an organization's capacity for informational and cultural diffusion can be changed, and with it the organization's ability to adapt to, and produce, innovations.

To take control of this process of network formation, we need to look "under the hood" of people's existing social networks. How did those networks come about in first place? What features of people's identities determined how people made their connections? For instance, in some organizations a person's job title may be a defining feature of their identity that determines how they form social ties. In these kinds of organizations, members of the maintenance staff may interact almost exclusively with one another, while they may never have opportunities to interact with the C-level executives. Thus, although Joseph the Janitor and Carlos the Chief Operating Officer (COO) may work in the same building with one another, they may never meet. For each of the members of this organization, such as Joe and Carlos, their roles within the firm determine the set of social interactions that they are likely to have.

Unbeknown to either Joe or Carlos, from a bird's-eye perspective these individual patterns of interaction produce an emergent network topology for the entire organization. Just like the networks shown in figure 7.4, this emergent (and unseen) topology can affect the speed at which information, ideas, and behaviors spread across the organization. The key to creating social contexts that can optimize this organizational network, and produce an innovative and adaptive organizational culture, is to understand people's organizational identities.

ORGANIZATIONAL IDENTITIES

To see how this works, let's consider a large organization with several different in-house divisions, such as research, production, design, and sales. Intuitively, there are several different kinds of social contexts in which the members of an organization like this are likely to meet each other and form ties. First, geographical location is important. Convenience is a big factor in communication networks, and the people who work in the same building, or in the same hallway, will tend to know each other and talk about their work together.[19] In some organizations, these effects are so pervasive that even within a single building there can be strong patterns of social stratification corresponding to the floor that someone works on. For instance, people within a certain group, such as finance, might never be seen outside of a particular floor; conversely, people who are not part of the finance group might never be seen on that floor and may be regarded as (unwelcome) aliens if they are ever caught walking those hallways. This kind of strong identification between place and position is the hallmark of an organization in which a person's social identity at work is tied very strongly to their professional role within the organization. Naturally, we would expect the social networks that form in this kind of organization to reflect this.

In addition to geography, members of an organization are often assigned to participate in working groups or project teams. Like hallways, these are settings in which people are colocated in the same social space on a regular basis—perhaps for weekly or biweekly meetings. However, unlike hallways, the members of a team can be drawn from geographically distant parts of an organization, which means that teams can be explicitly designed to encourage people to develop ties with colleagues who are far away geographically. Although these colleagues might never meet in the hallways near their respective offices, they may still get to know each other as members of the same working group.

Another familiar context for social interactions is meals. People have to eat, and where they eat tells a lot about an organization, the identities of the people there, and the flow of ideas and behaviors between them. Many large organizations have several different kinds of lunch options that differ in both the tier of service that they offer and in the kind of food they serve. Some organizations, like the Central Intelligence Agency, stratify their cafeterias, such that one dining hall permits only high-level staff to enter, while other cafeterias permit all to enter (but the highest-level employees would rarely, if ever, deign to visit them). In other kinds of organizations, like Facebook and Google, dining spaces are intentionally open to all, so personal preferences play a more important role in determining who dines together. Members of those organizations can find themselves eating lunch with colleagues based more on dietary interests rather than based on their professional roles.

One example of this kind of social context comes from the lunchtime culture at MIT, where (weather permitting) most lunch conversations take place around the food trucks along the streets in Kendall Square. Interactions among the intermingling throngs of graduate students, postdocs, and faculty are determined more by whether people have a taste for Momogoose, Clover, or the Falafel Guys than by people's departmental affiliations or professional ranks. From these random interactions, the conversations that arise may give birth to new friendships, advising relationships, and research collaborations.

However an organization structures its lunchtime routines—either by executive status or through dietary preferences—these simple routines are the invisible structures that give rise to the interpersonal networks of informational and ideational exchange that define the social web within an organization.

With a little thought, we can think of several other social contexts that help to play a similar role in structuring social interactions. A regular cocktail hour can do this. For instance, the towering social science building at Harvard University, William James Hall, hosts a monthly sherry hour, which provides an informal setting for the faculty to meet new students, postdocs, and visiting researchers in sociology, psychology, and social studies.

A similar kind of informal social context is offered by research organizations that host seminars with guest speakers. These events can be a vehicle for individuals in an organization to discover common interests and form new social ties. For instance, Microsoft Research hosts regular seminars in which scholars from a wide range of disciplines—from sociology to computer science—are invited to give lectures to the Microsoft community. These events are open to the entire campus, and although the speaker's ideas may not be directly related to everyone's work, the seminar provides a context for social interaction. A provocative speaker can catalyze a conversation between people from different parts of the organization who may thereby discover new topics of mutual interest and collaboration.

There are many other examples of social contexts that we can think of, but for now, let's take a step back and look at the landscape.

Considering the large variety of contexts for social interaction—from working groups to cocktail hours—let's imagine looking at an organization from a bird's-eye perspective. Taking an overview of all of the different social contexts in which people may interact with each other, we can begin to characterize the set of contexts to which each person in the organization is likely to belong. Does Joe the Janitor go to the cocktail hour? What about the working groups? What about Carlos the COO? It is surprisingly easy, even in a large organization, to get a fairly clear picture of the social contexts that each individual is likely to inhabit.

Looking at things this way, we can see that each person in an organization "belongs to" a particular set of social contexts. If we look at each person in terms of these memberships—for example, everyone has a hallway, a set of working groups, a lunchtime routine, and so forth—then the social web of the entire organization can be roughly mapped in terms of the overlapping affiliations among its members. From this viewpoint, we can already begin to see what these memberships might mean for the social networks that will emerge and, in turn, what they mean for the flow of information and behavior through the organization.

For instance, Carlos the COO is in the Bethesda, Maryland, office, and sits on the forty-fifth floor. He works with a small set of administrators and high-level assistants to run the operations for the organization and is a member of the Energy and Efficiency Working Group. He attends the weekly cocktail hour, routinely eats lunch in the executive cafeteria, and plays basketball in the company's intramural league. This information gives us a very clear sense of the social contexts that Carlos inhabits at work and therefore the people that he is likely to interact with regularly. For each person in an organization, we can construct a corresponding profile of the social contexts they inhabit—that is, the hallway where their office is, the working groups they are on, the typical places they eat lunch, the intramural teams they are on, and so forth. This profile defines each person's organizational identity.

Unlike social network data, which are often difficult to collect with a high degree of accuracy, it is easy to collect these profile data with a great deal of precision. Most of these features of a person's organizational identity are already known. A person's hallway, working groups, teams, and so on, are all part of their organizational record. Other features, such as their preferred lunch venues, can be easily collected from surveys.

With these profiles in hand, things get very interesting. If we assemble the entire collection of profiles for every member of an organization and combine them, it creates a map of people's patterns of association. In other words, these profiles reveal the web of network ties in an organization. From there, it becomes possible to start exploring how changes in people's affiliations can be used to redesign the large-scale structure of an organization's social network. The results of these counterfactual explorations can reveal the best ways of altering an organization's social contexts in order to increase its capacity for innovation.[20]

The next few pages show how to do this. In particular, I show how an organization can actively shape its social network by changing specific features of the organizational identities of its members. Although there are many ways that this might be done—and organizations attempt to do this kind of thing all the time—there is one factor, above all else, that is the primary determinant for how an organizational network will take shape. This controlling factor is the degree to which organizational identities are either *focused* or *expansive*.[21]

FOCUSED ORGANIZATIONAL IDENTITIES

Consider a pharmaceutical company in which all of the members the research division are in the same building and where all of the subunits for research, like drug delivery, cancer treatments, pharmaceutical cell biology, embryo cloning, medicinal chemistry, and so forth, are on separate floors. The office hallways on each floor are social contexts where people interact almost exclusively with colleagues from the same subunit. Consequently, ties made within this setting tend to be homophilous; for instance, people who work on drug delivery tend to have hallway interactions only with other people who work on drug delivery. That seems intuitive enough. The question of interest here is what happens when we look beyond their hallways.

Consider the lunch routines of these individuals. If people in a given hallway all tend to go to lunch together, then their opportunities for social interactions at lunch are also limited to people in their same subunit. Now, consider their working groups. If members of each subunit also tend to be in working groups with each other—dealing with problems that only people in their hallway can understand—then those groups will be composed of the same people that they would find in their hallways and at their lunch tables. It soon becomes clear that if we look at the profile of any member of, for instance, the embryo cloning subunit, their organizational identity (that is, the set of social contexts that they inhabit) would look identical to the profiles of everyone else in their subunit.[22] The implication for the social network is that the members of each of the research subunits interact almost exclusively with other members of their subunit.

This simple example highlights the main value of collecting these identity profiles. They provide a litmus test for characterizing the entire structure of an organization's social network. This is the test: if I know a person's membership in one social context, can I accurately predict the other social contexts to which they belong? For instance, if I know what hallway a person is in, can I predict where they go to lunch? And, if I know where they go to lunch, can I predict what working groups they are on? The more correlated the features of a person's profile are, the easier it is to know everywhere they will be, and everyone they will come into contact with, just by knowing one feature of their organizational identity.

When organizational identities are *highly focused*, it is trivially easy to predict the social contexts that people will inhabit and who they will meet there. The organizational map tells us who each person is likely to interact with at lunch, who they are likely to interact with in their working groups, and who they are likely to see in their hallways. From there, it is straightforward to calculate the ego networks that each person within an organization is expected to have. If the members of each subunit belong to social contexts that are inhabited exclusively by other members of their subunit, then the structure of the organizational network is likely to resemble tightly clustered, highly exclusive, cliques.

EXPANSIVE ORGANIZATIONAL IDENTITIES

At the other extreme, consider an organization in which individuals' profiles are *highly expansive*. In this kind of organization, knowing one part of a person's profile does not give any insight into their other memberships. Knowing what hallway a person is in tells you nothing about the working groups they are part of. And knowing where they eat lunch tells you nothing about the division of the organization they work in. There is no correlation between participation in one social context and the likelihood of participating in other contexts. When organizational identities are highly expansive, people mix unpredictably across the organizational space. Every social context creates opportunities for people to meet colleagues from every hallway and subunit of the organization.[23]

Considering these two extremes—highly focused and highly expansive organizational identities—there are some obvious implications for organizational culture. Organizations with highly focused identities tend to be fairly hierarchal, with rigid boundaries that may limit the acceptability of cross-group interactions.[24] In this kind of organization, an individual's organizational identity may be determined by a single feature of their role in the organization (like being a C-level executive), and this may define all of the other contexts in which it is appropriate or inappropriate for them to interact with their colleagues. For instance, in an organization with highly focused identities, it would be inappropriate for a C-level executive like Carlos to play pick-up basketball with a member of the maintenance staff, like Joseph.

By contrast, expansive organizational identities are typically found in flat organizations. In these settings, individuals can float from context to context, forming ties with people in every part of the organization. Social ties would be expected to form across all divisions, and it would not only be appropriate but also socially encouraged to have members from all roles within the organization participate on sports teams with one another. These organizations intentionally build their social contexts, such as open office spaces with no doors, to disrupt traditional norms of social stratification and network segregation in the workplace.

EMERGENT NETWORKS

Intuitively, we can see what these organizational identities might mean from a networks perspective. Expansive organizational identities create lots of opportunities for cross-cutting ties to form, generating a random pattern of highly diverse social connections throughout an organization. By contrast, highly focused identities limit the opportunities for interaction across an organization, producing tightly clustered cliques.

To make these ideas more precise, we can map these descriptions of emergent organizational networks directly onto the brokerage networks shown in figure 7.4. In fact, using a simple computational model it is possible to exactly reproduce the network structures shown in panels A, B, and C of figure 7.4 by varying the degree of expansiveness in actors' organizational identities.[25]

In the model that I used, the network in panel A was reproduced by giving individuals *highly expansive* organizational identities, in which there was zero predictability in people's organizational profiles. Because individuals in a setting like this have contact with people from every part of the organization, knowing a person's hallway or working group does not give any insight into the other contexts that they belong to. The network that emerges is essentially random. Intuitively, this makes it very easy for information to spread. However, the Achilles' heel of this organizational structure is that individuals' identities are not focused enough to allow them to coordinate with one another if they need to organize a change in organizational norms.

At the other end of the spectrum, the network shown in panel C of figure 7.4 was created by giving individuals *highly focused* organizational identities. In the model that I used, about 90% of people's social contexts could be predicted by knowing only one of their affiliations. As shown in figure 7.4, this produced a large number of fairly dense cliques with only a few brokerage ties between them. One advantage of this kind of organizational structure is that individuals within each cluster can easily coordinate with one another. However, the corresponding problem is that coordination across groups can be difficult because there are only weak ties between them. As a result, organizational behavior may be highly Balkanized. Strong reinforcement of local norms within each group makes it difficult to integrate new ideas or innovations across groups.

A compromise between these two extremes can be found by altering the structure of the social contexts to create *balanced organizational identities*—approximately 70% focused and 30% expansive. This ratio gives rise to the network shown in panel B of figure 7.4, a network composed of overlapping groups with wide bridges between them. In this kind of organization, individuals' memberships can be predicted about 70% of the time. However, about 30% of the time people participate in social functions, join working groups, or have office locations that would not be predicted by their other patterns of association. As shown in panel B of figure 7.4, this creates a network in which most of people's ties are located within a focused cluster of colleagues, making coordination within groups fairly easy. At the same time, coordination across groups is facilitated by the moderate fraction of reinforcing ties that individuals have to other groups. These overlapping memberships create wide bridges across the organization, permitting new ideas and innovative practices that emerge inside one group, to spread effectively to the others.

The question I turn to now is how these insights into organizational identity and network structure can be used to increase an organization's capacity for coordination, innovation, and adaptation.[26] There are four implications of these ideas for managers who want to use social networks to improve organizational performance: (1) measuring social networks, (2) changing social networks, (3) initiating critical mass, and (4) making adaptive organizations.

Measuring social networks

Measuring social networks is often challenging. Things would be much easier if we could just ask people who they are connected to, but most of the time people cannot remember who they talk to in a given day, let alone in a given year.[27] By contrast, people do know where their offices are located, what working groups they are part of, and what their favorite lunchtime spots are. In other words, it is a lot easier to collect data on people's identities than it is to collect data on their networks. The main implication of the foregoing discussion is that knowing people's organizational identities can give a good picture of the overall structure of their social networks. This approach can be very powerful because it connects decades of research on the demography and sociology of organizations with contemporary methods of network science. Traditional sociological methods have been refined over nearly half a century of research to provide insight into the distributions of individuals' characteristics and affiliations within organizations. The approach here shows that these methods can be used to gain new insight into the structure and dynamics of an organization's social network.[28]

Changing social networks

Once organizational networks can be measured, they can be controlled.[29] A simple example of how to do this is to use working groups. The number and composition of working groups within an organization is often decided by managers. At any given time there may be dozens (or even hundreds, depending on the size of the organization) of active working groups, each of which provides opportunities for colleagues to form connections with one another. Varying the number, size, and diversity of groups across an organization changes the contours of the social space. New opportunities for social interaction are created, and thereby people who might otherwise never meet one another may form new connections. Moreover, the strength of ties may also be controlled. For instance, if two people share several social contexts in common, the tie between them is likely to become stronger. There are many ways to rearrange the social structure of an organization. Changing the assignment of people to working groups, hallway locations, and intramural teams can all be used to shape people's organizational identities and thereby their patterns of social interaction. As discussed below, these ideas can be used strategically to structure an organization's social network in order to improve the spread of innovative practices.

Initiating critical mass

The most important implication here is that managers can design organizational networks to provide a structural foundation for accelerating the dynamics of change. Consider, for instance, a social change initiative to reduce an organization's carbon footprint. We can imagine that a few environmentally aware members of an engineering research group want to spearhead a policy that would reduce the consumption of nonrecyclable paper products within the organization's daily activities. This "greening" of the organization is often hard to do because it requires disrupting people's routines. It often requires changing relationships with established vendors and may even require altering budgets that have already been approved. Asking people to accommodate a green initiative may not only be inconvenient but may also involve asking them to do a lot of extra work. Thus, the challenge of mobilizing change within an organization may have less to do with convincing people that the idea has merit and more to do with the challenge of getting everyone to agree to do the extra work of implementing it.

We can imagine that this green initiative starts small—beginning with several members of a research group who ask their colleagues to use electronic documents instead of paper handouts in their weekly project meetings. It is a fairly minor change, but if the initiative catches on in a large organization, it could significantly reduce the organization's overall carbon footprint. So, how does the structure of organizational identities facilitate, or hinder, the spread of this initiative?

In an organization with *highly expansive* identities, it would be easy for people to find out about the initiative. However, as we have seen, telling people about an initiative is not the same thing as getting them to adopt it. There may be lots of procedures to figure out in order to make the initiative work. Successful implementation may depend on solving several coordination problems, such as developing strategies for distributing files, agreeing on a common file format, agreeing on which viewing devices and software to use, and so on. To make this kind of initiative work, a critical mass of colleagues must work together to develop these procedures and come up with a way to implement them.

This process requires considerable coordination. In the network shown in panel A of figure 7.4—without reinforcing ties among coworkers—coordination will be impossible, and the initiative will be a nonstarter.[30]

By contrast, an organization with *highly focused* identities—as shown in panel C of figure 7.4—faces an opposite but equally fatal problem. Within a single, tightly knit organizational cluster, colleagues are likely to be able to coordinate with each other to come up with procedures for paperless meetings. However, without reinforcing ties to other groups, the procedures will not spread from the initial group to other parts of the organization.

A solution to both of these problems comes from organizations with *balanced* identities. In the network shown in panel B of figure 7.4, an initial group of engineers would have enough reinforcing ties with each other to coordinate on the design of new procedures for their weekly meetings. Wide bridges across clusters would then make it easy to spread the initiative to other parts of the organization.

To see how this would work, imagine that several people from the design and marketing teams are members of the working group where the engineering team spearheads the green initiative. The overlapping ties between design, marketing, and engineering provide two key advantages for spreading the paperless meeting procedures. First, the individuals from the design and marketing divisions can observe just how efficient and cost-saving the engineers' procedures are for running their meetings. Second, the overlapping ties between engineering, design, and marketing act as pathways for social learning. The marketers and designers who see the initiative at work in the engineering meetings can then coordinate with one another to adapt the new procedures for use in their project meetings in the design and marketing departments, creating a flow of social learning from the activist group to other parts of the organization.

From there, the process of social learning can become self-reinforcing as it spreads from group to group. Each additional group that adopts the new procedures expands the set of overlapping pathways for social learning in the rest of the organization. The more widely adopted the initiative becomes, the more opportunities there are for the new procedures to be reinforced elsewhere. As the initiative spreads, ever wider segments of the organization can learn how to adapt their weekly meeting procedures to the growing office norm of paperless meetings.

Making adaptive organizations

The final implication of using organizational identities to manage social networks is that this approach offers managers a structural way of thinking about how to make their organizations more adaptive. Organizations that are *highly expansive* may miss opportunities for innovation because they cannot muster the social reinforcement necessary to sustain changes in organizational behavior. Conversely, *highly focused* organizations may have local success adapting to new ideas, but the organization's culture may be so Balkanized that widespread integration becomes difficult, as different groups converge on different local conventions. By contrast, *balanced* organizational identities create organizational networks that act as a filter for testing innovative ideas. For an idea to gain momentum in this kind of organization, it must win support within several overlapping groups. If an innovation passes this test of local integration, wide bridges in the network can then facilitate the spread of the new practice throughout the rest of the community. On a longer time scale, wide bridges between groups create stable interpersonal channels of ideational exchange, social learning, and mutual cooperation. While individuals may come and go, these enduring pathways can establish norms of social coordination across groups that sustain an organization's capacity for change.[31]

The next part of this book builds on these ideas by considering the more general implications of how social identity can be used to design networks that improve diffusion. The discussion in part 3 widens our gaze to look at how relational features of social ties work together with network structure to influence the spread of behavior. In particular, I show how social identity and relational context can determine how people will activate their network ties and what this means for the success of behavior-change initiatives. The purpose of chapters 8 and 9 is to make the results on complex contagions useful for applied researchers, practitioners, and entrepreneurs who are interested in finding ways to increase the diffusion of innovative behaviors in applied online settings. To this end, the approach in these chapters differs from the previous chapters in this book in that they take the hands-on perspective of someone who wants to build an online community with the goal of spreading a new behavior. The most innovative, challenging, and difficult behaviors require the greatest levels of social reinforcement. The question turned to next is how new forms of online social capital might be designed in order to make these behaviors spread most effectively.

PART III

Social Design

The Internet will not automatically offset the decline in
more conventional forms of social capital, but it has
that potential. In fact, it is hard to imagine solving
our contemporary civic dilemmas without it.
—Robert Putnam, *Bowling Alone*

INTRODUCTION TO PART III

By far the widest-reaching implications of the results on complex contagions are what they show for the future of cultural change. As the world becomes smaller, the ratio of weak ties to strong ties in people's social networks will increase. This change in the composition of people's contacts may be imperceptible at the individual level, but it is nevertheless consequential for society. The smaller the world becomes, the more likely it is that the signals that people receive through their social networks will be simple contagions—fast spreading, easily digested bits of information. Simple contagions are easy to absorb and easy to propagate; as ties become longer and narrower, simple contagions are likely to become an increasingly common currency in social interactions.[1]

Bandwidth constraints on the number of messages people can receive each hour, day, or week mean that people need to make choices about what to pay attention to.[2] As the fraction of weak ties increases, simple contagions are more likely to be represented in the stream of social content. Moreover, as the world becomes smaller, complex contagions spread with less ease. Thus, as the structure of social networks becomes ever more conducive to simple contagions, complex contagions are likely to become less common in the economy of behaviors and ideas.

As complex contagions become less represented in the stream of social consciousness, a society may begin to suffer a form of cultural amnesia. As the composition of social content becomes simpler, expectations about interactions are likely to change. People may no longer come in contact with cooperative practices, shared cultural norms, or complex ideas that require social reinforcement in order to stay in circulation. The less frequent these artifacts of cultural discourse are, the more easily they can fail to pass to the next generation. The everyday memory of how people interact and the kinds of gestures or civic-minded behaviors they are expected to display may be transformed by the kinds of cultural items that can spread through weak ties.

Social research can be an unwitting accomplice to this amnesia. As the world becomes smaller and simple contagions become more frequent, observational studies of large-scale communication networks and social media diffusion are more likely to find that contagions benefit from the presence of long ties. The easier it is to collect network data with a small-world structure, the more prevalent these observations will become and the greater the consensus will be about the value of weak ties for diffusion.

What these data will not show is what is not spreading through these networks. Because the transmission of cultural practices relies on social reinforcement, the diffusion of rules, norms, and values that require time to understand and discipline to follow will be less frequent in the data. The more common it becomes to study weak-tie communication networks, the less common complex contagions will be in the empirical terrain.

At the individual level, these subtle shifts in the cultural landscape are likely to go unnoticed. As the volume and simplicity of the content that diffuses across social networks increases, the tumult of new material to which people are exposed can eclipse thoughts of what is not spreading. The abundance of simple contagions can easily encroach on the social space that was once reserved for complex contagions. Members of an increasingly connected, weak-tie society will likely not experience fewer complex contagions passing by, nor will they experience a conspicuous lack of social contact. Instead, the contagions they see, and the normative practices that they engage in, will slowly, invisibly devolve into patterns of behavior that are easily transmitted through weak-tie networks, which is to say, they will be behaviors that are easy, simple, and familiar.[3]

As natural as this cultural process seems, it also has a consequence. While simple contagions may be conspicuously better spreaders, they typically are not very effective for changing behaviors or transmitting new ideas that will improve the common welfare.[4]

* * *

Ralph Waldo Emerson offered an inspiring view of American innovation: "If a man has good corn or wood, or boards, or pigs, to sell, or can make better chairs or knives, crucibles or church organs, than anybody else, you will find a broad, hard-beaten road to his house, though it be in the woods."[5] More colloquially, "if you build a better mousetrap, the world will beat a path to your door." It is as inspiring as it is false.

Emerson's Panglossian vision of American entrepreneurship has been falsified several times over. The market has often rewarded a poorer technology with greater success. The QWERTY and Dvorak keyboards, VHS and Beta video recorders, and heavy-water versus light-water nuclear reactors are all examples of failures of the market to select the option that was clearly the better choice. The reason for this is that what determines whether one product wins or loses can have less to do with the product itself than with the network effects that can allow a product to spread more quickly, thereby gaining greater traction in the population and drive its competition to extinction.[6]

In the diverse realms of ideas, political opinions, and consumer products, the drivers of success are often the same. In all of these domains, there is competition for survival. In a broad sense, these are evolutionary systems in which innovation is encouraged because it improves the likelihood of success. However, industry competition, like political competition, and even genetic competition, does not thrive on pure innovation, but only on those innovations that benefit survival, growth, and reproduction.[7] Sometimes these innovations are the result of meticulous engineering, and sometimes they are discovered by accident. Either way, innovations are continuously emerging, putting constant pressure on the incumbents to keep innovating in order to maintain their foothold in the environment.

This principle of feverish competition has been dubbed the Red Queen Effect, and it has specific implications for how the dynamics of network diffusion may evolve over the next decade. Borrowed from Lewis Carroll's *Through the Looking Glass*, the term was first used by the evolutionary biologist Leigh Van Valen to explain why species extinction is so prevalent in the historical and fossil record.[8] In *Through the Looking Glass*, the Red Queen had to keep running just to stay in the same place. As she put it, "Now, here, you see, it takes all the running you can do just to keep in the same place. If you want to get somewhere else, you must run at least twice as fast!"[9]

In evolutionary systems, the idea is the same. A member of a species is only as fit as its closest competitor. If a more fit mutation emerges, then an individual that was considered fit in the previous generation might quickly become obsolete—and therefore die out. To stay competitive, genetic lines must keep innovating, constantly staying ahead of the next great adaptation. Everyone needs to keep running just to stay in the same place.

In a networked world where diffusion equals success, there is unabating pressure to innovate. Survival requires discovering more-effective strategies for spreading products, ideas, and influence. The easiest way to do this is to make the contagions simpler. An arms race may inevitably follow, as everyone competing to spread their messages strives to find increasingly effective ways to reach the population. But the arms race may in fact be a race to the bottom.

In an increasingly small world, the competitive environment favors options with fewer complexities. For marketers trying to sell new products and ideas, the challenge becomes reducible to one goal: make contagions simple. This same conclusion extends to the democratic process. In a world with increasing numbers of long-distance links, actors striving for popularity and power are encouraged to cultivate messages that are best suited to diffuse quickly through weak ties. The process of selection can eventually eliminate complex contagions from the strategic space altogether. The result is a political and intellectual world that is entirely composed of simple contagions. The resulting ecology of memes and behaviors passing by a consumer or a voter inevitably becomes an ever-denser stream of content that is as digestible as it is familiar.[10]

Fortunately, foreshadowing the implications of an increasingly small world does not make them inevitable. Nor does it mean that complex contagions are any less important for understanding social change. While simple contagions propagate easily in small worlds, they are likely to have very little impact on behaviors that are difficult, costly, or unfamiliar. Simple contagions offer attractions for our attention that are more familiar and less costly than complex contagions, but which are often less useful for improving our lives.

So, what do people do when they need to change behaviors but lack the social support to do it? Increasing numbers of people are turning to the Internet to find a solution. The maturation of social life online has given rise to a trend in which people actively seek out new kinds of social networks that can directly support their goals of behavior change.[11] Online workout groups, peer counselors, and even investment forums create cohesive support networks that provide a social infrastructure that helps to counterbalance the constant stream of signals that are received through long ties. While these communities constitute only a very small fraction of activity online, they present a promising trend—and a valuable opportunity.

As the social resources that are available online have become more diverse, so, too, have the people who seek them out. A widening cross-section of users worldwide have chosen to embed themselves into rich communities that provide online social support for finding jobs, joining activist groups, and discovering new health resources.[12] The more people who join online networks, the more opportunities there are to discover peers who can provide social reinforcement for complex behaviors. The result is a new infrastructure for social capital.

Thus, a hopeful assessment of the expansion of social connectivity online is that complex contagions will not disappear from the cultural landscape. Rather, they will be less likely to spread through networks composed of increasingly long and narrow channels of communication. However, even as the forces of global communication seem to make these topological changes inevitable, people have instinctively found, and in many cases created, clustered networks of social reinforcement that can sustain real changes in behavior. And in the unlikeliest of places—the unbounded virtual spaces of the Internet.[13]

To show how to make use of these new forms of social capital, the next two chapters take a hands-on approach to social networks. Chapters 8 and 9 take the Olympian perspective of a social planner whose job it is to construct social capital among the members of an online community in order to diffuse innovative behaviors. The most challenging behaviors require the greatest amounts of social reinforcement. The topic turned to now is how to create online communities that can spread these behaviors effectively.

CHAPTER 8

Designing Social Networks for Diffusion

Let's take a new perspective. Let's shift the focus from understanding how diffusion works to take a more hands-on approach to improving diffusion in specific settings. Is it possible to give people social capital that will encourage them to change their behaviors? For example, if you wanted to build an online social network to promote the spread of healthy behaviors, how would you do it? How would you build the website? How would you connect people to create influential ties? And how would you control which kinds of behaviors become popular?

Robert Putnam argued that the "anonymity and fluidity [of] the virtual world encourage 'easy in, easy out,' 'drive-by' relationships . . . which discourages the creation of social capital." He continued, "If entry and exit are too easy, commitment, trustworthiness and reciprocity will not develop."[1] I present a contrasting view that suggests that the anonymity and fluidity of the virtual world empower organizations to offer new forms of social capital to individuals who might otherwise suffer from social isolation, exclusion, and disempowerment in traditional face-to-face settings. My guiding principle is this: the rarer social capital is, the more valuable it becomes. As I will describe below, if online settings are able to create rare and valuable forms of social capital for their members, then online networks will not only be enduring, they will be influential as well.

If I put on the hat of a social planner, I can use the ideas developed in this book to show how these new forms of social capital might be constructed. To be concrete, I will focus on the example of building a website to spread health-related behaviors. It should be clear, however, that a health setting is not the only context in which these ideas may be applied. Nevertheless, this example is helpful because health is one of the domains in which these ideas may be very quickly made productive.

Today, thousands of anonymous web communities and online discussion groups provide millions of participants worldwide with social resources for making medical decisions. For any health-care organization interested in promoting the spread of health-related behaviors, these online resources for health present both an opportunity and a problem. The opportunity is that online interactions can be very effective for influencing people's behavior.[2] Of course, this is also the problem. Online communities provide access to a limitless variety of opinions, with very few constraints on the kinds of influences that members are exposed to or the resulting behaviors that are propagated. There is no way of knowing what behaviors or beliefs will emerge in these settings, or what kinds of individual or collective outcomes will result. There is a temptation to see only danger in these possibilities.

My approach, however, is not to resist the tide but instead to catch the wave. Organizations that embrace the expanding world of emerging social resources for health may be able to create and manage social settings that can be quite useful for providing healthcare for hard-to-reach populations, as well as for improving the general quality of patient care. Beyond the rudimentary goal of offering a portal for digital records,[3] provider organizations can use online settings to facilitate collective learning, emotional support, and the spread of lifestyle-improving behaviors through structured patient networks. This chapter shows how this can be done.

WHY STRANGERS ARE INFLUENTIAL—REINFORCEMENT AND RELEVANCE

The main insight from the previous chapters is that networks with wide bridges of social reinforcement can improve the spread of complex contagions. Is this all we need to know—put people into clustered networks and things will spread? That's a surprisingly large part of the story. But it is not the whole story.

To build networks that promote diffusion in real-world settings, we need to move beyond network topology to consider the other features of social networks that affect social influence. Particularly in an anonymous online setting, reinforcing signals are probably not going to improve diffusion significantly unless they come from people who are seen as relevant. This is where *homophily* comes into play. The transmission of complex contagions often requires that social contacts should be similar to one another.

This is not the case for simple contagions. For disease transmission, strangers can infect each other on subways and in airplanes without even noticing one another. A network tie is simply a pathway for transmission, nothing more. The same is true for learning about the score of the game or finding out about a flight delay. Information can pass from strangers to you, and from you to other strangers, with only superficial contact.

Not so for most complex contagions. Consider, for instance, the decision to try an innovative, but still experimental, medical treatment for a chronic health condition—say an autoimmune disease such as rheumatoid arthritis or asthma. You, the patient, may be exposed to several people who have used this treatment for other conditions. However, as friendly or likable as those people may be, if their medical conditions bear no resemblance to yours, their treatment choices will have no impact on whether you choose that treatment too. In this regard, their behavior is irrelevant to your medical decision-making.

Now imagine that some patients with conditions that are more similar to your own begin to use the treatment. The more reinforcement you get from these individuals, the more likely you may be to begin considering the treatment for yourself. However, in most medical situations (particularly ones in which the treatment has side effects), these testimonials will probably not be enough to get you to actually adopt it. Instead, you may find yourself trying to find people whose conditions are even closer to your own. It is to these people you are likely to give greater attention when thinking about what to do.

This is where the process gets interesting. If you begin to consider the treatment in earnest, you are likely to seek out patients who have your specific condition to see whether any of them have adopted the treatment. This is the kind of situation in which social design can be effective. If you can be provided with access to the right group of relevant patients in a network structure that creates the right kinds of social reinforcement, you may decide to adopt a treatment that you would not have tried otherwise. By designing peer networks that provide people with relevant sources of social reinforcement, innovative behaviors can be diffused through online populations to reach people who otherwise would never have used them.

In the abstract, this seems straightforward enough; however, there is an important wrinkle in the real world. Not all forms of similarity create relevance. Your spouse is relevant for some decisions and irrelevant for others.[4] Your parents are relevant for some decisions and irrelevant for others, as is your college roommate, as are the people who live on your block. Whether or not a contact is seen as relevant is largely determined by the social context.

In a fitness setting, health characteristics are likely to determine who is seen as a relevant source of advice and influence. In a professional setting, intellectual and educational characteristics are more likely to determine who a relevant source of social influence is. In other words, even if people are nestled into clustered online networks with plenty of reinforcement, if they are surrounded by irrelevant social contacts there is not likely to be much behavior change. While all of this seems clear, the wrinkle comes from the fact that what makes online strangers into relevant sources of social influence is largely determined by which personal characteristics are made salient by the features of the online setting.

So, how do we know ahead of time which traits will be relevant for social influence? Even within a particular context, such as health, there are hundreds of possible traits to choose from. The challenge is to identify which of the hundreds of characteristics that people *might* have in common are the right ones for creating influential ties.

To find an answer to this question we can look at a real world example of how social influence emerges within a successful online health community. The website Patients Like Me (PLM) was founded in 2006,[5] and it has since grown into a social and medical community for nearly 200,000 patients being treated for over 3,500 diseases, with a primary focus on the chronic care of rare diseases—specifically amyotrophic lateral sclerosis (also known as ALS, or Lou Gehrig's Disease). Members of the platform are anonymous, yet they are able to communicate with one another by posting comments directly on each other's profile pages, which can be seen by every member of the community. Profile pages consist of structured and unstructured information about a patient, including their medical histories, treatments, symptoms, health events, personal diaries, and medications.

When initiating interactions with one another, members typically reach out to others who have similar conditions and treatment histories as themselves. While these interactions are anonymous, they have resulted in members starting and stopping new medications, adopting new medical devices, and joining medical trials for experimental treatments.[6] The most popular form of engagement is for users to ask questions of one another. For instance, a member considering adopting a new treatment asks another member:

> *I notice you are using ginger root and you believe it is slowing your progression. I'm very interested in this. Can you tell me more about how it's working for you?*

Another participant gives a more thorough inquiry:

I see you are using Glyconutrients. What are the exact ones that you're using, how long have you been using them for, and what benefits if any have you seen. I have heard a lot of encouraging things about them, but I have yet to hear anything about their use by ALS patients. Are they helping with a particular symptom? Please let me know what you have learned by taking these supplements.

In another instance, a member reaches out to a fellow patient to share some concerns that were raised after talking with his physician. He asks the patient to share her experience with a new device since it might change his mind about using it.

[Jen], I'm a new member of PLM like yourself. I notice you have had a tube for about 8 months. I'm having difficulty eating, so the neurologist suggested I look into getting one. My meeting with the gastroenterologist did not leave me with desire to get one. It would help me if you would send me a message about your experience, pro and con, with your feeding tube.

A more sophisticated participant cross-references the treatment and progress records of another patient and then inquires about the implied effectiveness of a new breathing assistance device, abbreviated BIPAP.

Hi [D] I am [Adam] in the PLM web site. My ALS was like yours breathing onset. I see your FRS improved a bit after you went onto BIPAP in april 06. Did it in fact make that much difference.?? [Adam]

Instead of seeking advice, some participants volunteer it. For instance, one patient who came across a profile in which a member discussed his difficulties with a symptom takes the time to offer his experience with a helpful treatment:

I see you note emotional lability. I had that very bad, but now I take a compound of dextromethorphan and quinidine that controls it beautifully.

In another instance, a member sees that another member is struggling with a symptom and offers news about a new randomized controlled trial for a treatment that might help.

[Joanne], I see you are legs onset; have you heard about the new diaphragm implants they are doing at Case-Western and Johns Hopkins? It means you don't have to vent to breathe. [George]

Members of PLM also initiate contact with the more basic goal of establishing an empathetic connection to someone who understands their situation. Here a patient reaches out by listing his similarities and then offering details about his condition that might lead to a conversation.

> *Hi [Michael], I see we are pretty similar. I am 62 dx 11/06 with leg onset. I need a walker to help me walk. I move slower and have had a few recent falls due to my leg dragging. I would like to be available if you want to compare progress. I started noticing symptoms a year ago, but just dx this month.*

Intuitively, what makes members of PLM relevant to one another are their experiences with specific ALS symptoms. In some cases, people who differ from one another on every obvious demographic and socio-economic indicator (such as race, gender, income, and occupation) may nevertheless discover that they are highly relevant to each another because they suffer from similar kinds of ailments. Within the social world created by PLM, these strangers can become important sources of social capital for each other.[7]

Unlike health-advocacy websites where patients consult medical professionals or expert advisors, patients in PLM take advice from other patients. The members giving the advice are not medical experts, nor are they vetted, nor even qualitatively rated. Nevertheless, informal relationships in PLM may be more influential than the physician-patient relationships found in more formalized settings. Thus, contrary to Putnam's notion that anonymous online interactions lead to "depersonalization," the reason that members of PLM are so influential is that they offer one another a rare and valuable form of social capital that cannot be found in face-to-face settings.

For patients with rare and debilitating diseases, contact with other patients does not happen often. For them, PLM is a setting in which they can actively seek out interactions with each other. Social agency is restored to their lives. Unlike the vast majority of social and medical interactions that these patients have, in PLM they can find others who must overcome familiar challenges in managing their daily routines, who understand when a solution is useful and when it is not, and who have experienced the same difficulties finding social and medical resources for managing their care. In other words, they can find people with whom they can exchange both information and empathy. The members of PLM are thereby immediately valuable to each other because they offer one another an all-too-rare network of relevant social contacts. The rarity of this network makes it easy for participants to recognize the value of the social capital that they offer each other—turning anonymous online interactions among strangers into stable pathways for social influence.

SOCIAL DESIGN 101—SELECTION AND INFLUENCE

From the perspective of a social planner, the goal is to derive lessons from everything that we have seen so far in order to devise a general strategy for constructing online networks that will bring about real-world changes in health behavior. Obviously, the specific traits that are effective in PLM will not be useful in most other situations. However, two observations from PLM offer guidance for how to proceed.

1. *Selection.* The first observation is that participants in PLM are highly selective in their interactions. Out of a sea of almost 200,000 members, individuals choose to interact with only a small fraction of participants.
2. *Influence.* The second observation is that the selections that people make often create influential relationships. In other words, the factors that determine how people choose their network ties are also the factors that determine who influences their behavior.[8]

These observations provide a useful starting point. They suggest that if it is possible to identify the traits that define attraction, then it may also be possible to use those traits to control the flow of influence.

The main problem with this idea is that it is not easy to implement. How can you identify people's selection preferences? As Paul Lazarsfeld and Robert Merton observed more than half a century ago,[9] while patterns of selection can give rise to networks of social influence, people's selection preferences are not fixed. Preferences vary from situation to situation, making it hard to determine exactly which traits will be selected in which contexts. This makes it very hard to come up with a general strategy for determining which characteristics will be useful for creating influential networks. Fortunately, this kind of problem is one for which the online domain may offer a solution that is not available in face-to-face settings.

Online, the simplest approach to this problem is to narrow our focus to the design of a specific social setting.[10] To make headway on the task of creating an effective website for spreading healthy behaviors, it makes sense to select a fairly specific health context—for instance, an online fitness program—and then to observe how people choose to form social ties there. If a general pattern of social selection emerges, we can then try to use those characteristics as the basis for structuring relationships among the participants in that setting. This "selection-and-influence" strategy may then provide a way of designing networks that make anonymous strangers into relevant sources of social influence.

DESIGNING NETWORKS FOR DIFFUSION

To see if this approach might work, I partnered with an online fitness program run by the Medical Office at the Massachusetts Institute of Technology (MIT).[11] The MIT fitness program was an impressive feat of social design in its own right. For three months out of the year, thousands of participants were recruited from MIT, and affiliated university campuses around the world, to voluntarily record their daily exercise activity in an attempt to reach their weekly goals. Regardless of whether participants succeeded or failed in a given week, when the next week started everyone was back at it, recording their daily minutes. Given this impressive level of engagement in the program, I wanted to see whether there might be a general pattern in how the participants would choose to form connections with each other.

Identifying selection

To study participants' selection preferences, 432 members of MIT's fitness program were recruited to join a health-buddy community. To register for the community, participants provided informed consent and completed a detailed profile that included their age, body mass index (BMI), gender, race, exercise interests, dietary preferences, and overall level of fitness. Each participant was provided with a home page that contained a detailed online dashboard with a real-time chart that kept track of their daily activities, exercise intensity levels, and exercise minutes. Members in the program were also assigned anonymous health buddies, who were other members of the fitness program. On the home page, participants could see the complete profile information and exercise records for each of their health buddies.

Much like the Healthy Lifestyle Network, which was discussed in chapter 4, participants in this fitness community were embedded within online social networks. The basic design of the study was similar to the one used in chapter 4. The network topologies were created before any of the subjects arrived, and each participant was randomly assigned to occupy a single node in one of the network communities. However, this time there only were six independent communities in total, and every network had an identical structure: each one was a clustered spatial lattice in which everyone had six neighbors. Each member's immediate neighbors in the social network constituted their health buddies. The size of the networks in this study was smaller than before. Each network contained 72 participants.

Also, unlike the previous study, this time the goal was to see how people would choose to connect themselves to other people in the program. In chapter 4, people's health buddies were fixed for the entire study, but here the network structure could change as people made new contacts. As soon as people started changing their network ties—adding new health buddies and dropping old ones—the network structure began to "evolve" into a new social topology.

Over the course of five weeks, participants in the program were permitted to drop their assigned health buddies and choose new ones from a list of other members of their network community. Social exclusion was not possible. Participants could not prevent other members of the network from linking to them. This design made it possible to identify pure selection preferences since anyone who wanted new neighbors could simply choose them. Members could also drop ties to whomever they wanted. A complete record was kept of tie addition and removal, which made it easy to identify which characteristics were most attractive and which were most likely to be dropped.

This process of social selection ran concurrently in all six independent network communities during the same five-week period. This setup provided six independent observations of the same process of network evolution. This replication was useful because it ensured that any patterns that emerged were not an idiosyncratic result of a particular network's evolutionary path, but a reproducible process of peer selection across all six social worlds.

Strikingly, all six networks exhibited the same general pattern of social selection. In every case, health buddies were selected predominantly on the basis of similarities in age and BMI, along with preferences for same gender ties. Older people preferred to connect with older people, and less-fit people typically chose less-fit people. Other relevant characteristics, such as race, favorite exercise, dietary preferences, exercise intensity, typical exercise minutes, and exercise experience, were not significant factors for tie selection. Homophilous social selection was prominent along just three traits: age, gender, and BMI.[12]

Constructing influence

Having identified a clear pattern of social selection, our next goal is to use these selection preferences to design influential social networks. The hope is that these constructed relationships might increase the spread of a health innovation through the member community. To see if this would work, I ran a diffusion study within the same fitness program.

The basic setup and registration process for the diffusion study were the same as for the selection study. This time, ten independent network communities were created. As described above, every network had the same clustered-lattice network structure and the same population size as used in the selection study. However, in this study, participants could not alter their network ties, so the network structure remained fixed in every community for the duration of the diffusion experiment.[13]

After participants were assigned to their networks, the experimental conditions were created by randomly choosing five of the ten networks to undergo a homophilous social design process.[14] While all ten network topologies remained the same, in the five "homophilous networks," individuals were relocated in the network until each person was optimally matched with six health buddies who had the greatest similarities in age, gender, and BMI. Figure 8.1 illustrates this by showing fixed network topologies in which individuals with varying traits (indicated by shade) are randomly distributed (on the left) or homophilously arranged (on the right).

In the five non-homophilous networks, participants were randomly matched with their buddies, who had varying age, gender, and BMI. In these networks, less-fit individuals were often directly connected to more-fit individuals. Consequently, less-fit individuals typically had exposure to the interests and activities of healthier members of the community. By contrast, in the homophilous networks, participants typically had buddies with similar ages and BMIs as themselves. All ten networks had a topological structure that was favorable for diffusion, but only the five homophilous networks were designed to create relevant relationships.

The behavior being studied in this experiment was the adoption of a new dieting tool, called the Diet Diary. The Diet Diary was an online dietary journal that used an interactive commercial database to instantly look up the caloric and nutritional content of more than fifty thousand brand-name and generic foods. It provided participants with

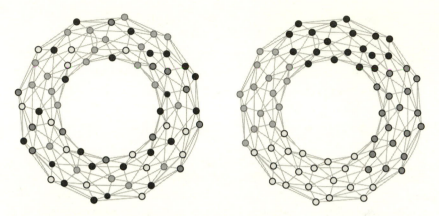

Figure 8.1 Non-homophilous and Homophilous Social Networks

an easy way to compare their caloric and nutritional intake with their exercise levels over the duration of their participation in the fitness program. As in the Healthy Lifestyle Network study, this health innovation was constructed exclusively for use with this study, which made it possible to observe the real-time diffusion of the innovation through the member networks.

The diffusion process was simultaneously initiated in all ten networks by activating a seed node in each network, who posted messages to their health buddies' home pages. In every network, these messages notified the seeds' buddies that one of their neighbors had adopted the Diet Diary and invited them to adopt it, too. Each time a new member adopted the innovation, a notification would appear on their health buddies' home pages inviting them to adopt, as well. Diffusion processes ran concurrently in all ten communities for a seven-week period, at which point the effects of social design were clear.

Homophilously designed networks significantly increased the uptake of the dieting tool, producing a 200% increase in overall adoption. This effect was consistent across all communities, as each of the five homophilous networks produced greater levels of adoption than each of the non-homophilous networks. These effects of homophily were most prominent among the least healthy members of the community. Participants who were obese received the same amount of exposure to the innovation in both network conditions. Yet, in the non-homophilous networks not a single obese participant adopted the innovation. By contrast, in the homophilously designed networks, nearly half of all obese individuals who were exposed to the innovation adopted it. By the end of the study, the number of *obese* adopters in the homophilous networks was equivalent to the number of *total* adopters in the non-homophilous networks.[15]

While both networks offered reinforcing neighborhood structures, the homophilously designed networks provided social reinforcement that came from relevant peers. One implication of the increase in adoption rates among participants in the homophilous networks is that aligning relationships based on social identity may increase participants' susceptibility to behavior change.[16] In other words, homophilously structured social ties may be able to shape the social context in which individual decisions are made in order to allow an innovation to spread farther into a population than it might otherwise.

These observations suggest a useful parallel between the dynamics of complex contagions in network diffusion and recent work in behavioral economics, which has emphasized the importance of *choice architecture* in determining how people make financial and health-related decisions. Findings on choice architecture have shown that the choices that people make can be altered simply by controlling the way that the options are presented to them. Deceptively simple changes to the choice setting can improve the healthiness and financial savvy of the options that people select. Similarly, the results here suggest that by changing the social context in which people make decisions, their choices may be altered. An innovation that was previously ignored may instead be adopted as a result of a person being in a network of relevant social contacts.

In thinking about these implications, I found it useful to consider how the findings here would have been interpreted if the non-homophilous condition had been observed by itself. Without comparison to the results in the homophilous networks, the fact that there was zero adoption among obese members in the non-homophilous networks might suggest that the dieting technology was not well suited for obese individuals.

From a product engineering point of view, those results might suggest that the innovation needed to be redesigned to make it more attractive for the obese subpopulation.[17] However, by using the social network, rather than the features of the product, as the engine for diffusion, it was possible to transform the way that the innovation was received. Increased uptake did not require that the technology be reengineered, only that the social networks be structured to create the right kind of social relevance.

In other kinds of online settings, the particular traits that would be effective for creating influential relationships would be different. In PLM, for instance, specific ailments are a much stronger basis for social connection than age, gender, or BMI. Similarly, in other kinds of online settings, such as the art-sharing community DeviantArt or the physician networking community Doximity, the characteristics that will be effective for creating relevant peer networks will have more to do, respectively, with individuals' artistic orientation or their type of medical practice than with their health characteristics.

In any online setting, homophilous networks need to be designed with characteristics that are salient in that social context. While the details of these characteristics are expected to differ across settings, the procedures that were used in this study are expected to be effective for creating influential networks in a variety of contexts. Selection preferences can be identified using controlled observations, and those preferences can then be used to design online relationships that turn strangers into valuable, and influential, sources of social capital.

The more general implication of these results is that the influence of online relationships can be increased by matching people based on relevant features of social identity. The more similar people are to their contacts, the more natural it is for them to imagine what life is like in their shoes. In other words, homophily creates empathy. The right kind of homophily makes it easier for people to understand how their peers' decisions might be applicable to their own, which can make it more likely that they will adopt their peers' behaviors. For individuals for whom finding relevant peers is difficult, online contacts who offer this kind of relevance may be highly valued, and highly influential, sources of social capital.

Chapter 9 extends these findings to consider how the relational context of network ties can be designed to shape social relevance. There are several ways that relational factors may influence network diffusion.[18] I focus on how the contextual features of a social situation can mold the expectations that people have of their online contacts, thereby determining how they are likely to be influenced by them. The topic turned to next is how the quality of the relationships in an online setting can be just as important as the structure of the ties for controlling the flow of behavior.

CHAPTER 9

Creating Social Contexts for Behavior Change

Chapter 8 showed how homophily can be used to create social relevance. Now, let's take our thinking a step further. Where does the perception of relevance come from? What features of a social setting determine how people will use their social ties? And, are there choices we can make when designing a social setting that determine the kinds of behaviors that will emerge? This chapter is dedicated to answering these questions.

To start, it is useful to think of online settings as institutions.[1] In other words, online settings use rules, rewards, and punishments to create expectations for behavior. The rules that define how people interact with each other in an online setting also do the powerful and subtle work of shaping perceptions of relevance. What we would like to know now is: how does the design of a social setting determine the way that social relevance is created among strangers, and what implications does this have for how people will influence each other's behavior?

A useful approach to this comes from Simmel's observation that people's "social worlds" shape the meaning of their relationships:

> Among officers, church members, employees, scholars, or members of a family, every member regards the other with the unquestioned assumption that he is a member of 'my group.' ... We see the other not simply as an individual but as a colleague or a comrade or a fellow party member—in short as a cohabitant of the same specific world.[2]

On this view, society is only possible because people experience each other as members of a social world in which they have interests, commitments, and beliefs. Instead of seeing others as unfathomable individuals, we experience one another as intelligible actors with specific goals. Because of this, we have expectations for the intentions and behaviors that others will exhibit, which determine the intelligibility of other people, and ourselves, as social actors. These social worlds are what make society possible.[3]

Online, these social worlds are explicitly designed. Online settings establish the rules and expectations that define social interdependence. For instance, is Felicia a mother, an ALS patient, a divorcee, or a physician? The identity that is selected for her by a social setting determines how she is able to productively interact with others. The more narrowly specified an online context is, the less relevant every other feature of a person becomes until only a few features, or perhaps even one feature, defines who she is, how she behaves, and why she seeks social interaction.

For social design, this suggests that an important advantage of online settings is that information about people's attributes can be omitted in order to increase interpersonal relevance. Status characteristics such as age, class, race, and gender have an unavoidable influence over offline interactions. While they can establish relevance, they can also create implicit barriers to social exchange when expectations for behavior are heavily shaped by these factors. By eliminating these features from a social setting, people who differ on nearly every important status characteristic may nonetheless establish meaningful relationships. In more rarified online spaces like PLM, where only pertinent information may be available, the omission of status characteristics can be a useful ally for increasing the salience of particular kinds of social capital.[4]

These ideas suggest that whom people choose to interact with and how those interactions affect their behavior are not solely determined by the individual actors. They are determined by the structure of the social world they inhabit, the identities it activates, and the interdependence that it creates. Online, all of this can be controlled. While this control often goes unused, the contextual features of an online setting may nevertheless implicitly shape the dynamics of social interaction. My interest here is to show how this control can be used to alter the trajectory of collective behavior.

An important limitation of this book up until now is that it has focused almost exclusively on diffusion processes in which an exogenously seeded behavior spreads through a population. One imagines dropping a pebble into a pond and watching the wave front ripple across the water's surface. This idealization can be a useful approximation of how diffusion processes work, particularly for behaviors that are one-and-done. Vaccination behavior, for instance, can spread in this fashion, cascading through peer-to-peer networks.

However, there are also many times when this diffusion metaphor breaks down. In these situations, behaviors are not seeded exogenously but instead emerge endogenously through people's interactions with each other. For instance, although the decision to start dieting can be treated as a behavioral contagion, dieting itself is a complex behavior that comprises the times and places where people eat, the number of times a day they eat, and the sizes of their meals. Referring to changes in these eating practices as "the diffusion of dieting behavior" can easily understate the complexity of the social process that it alludes to, and can thereby overlook the importance of the social context in which people interact and how it mediates the social process of coordinating on dieting routines.

In these situations, diffusion is not analogous to an expanding wave front but is more akin to the interference pattern that emerges when raindrops speckle the water's surface. Instead of a single behavior spreading through a population, a collective change in behavior emerges from the interdependent interactions of many individuals. This chapter shows how the network dynamics of behavior change function in these more complex settings. In what follows, I present an example from a policy study that demonstrates how the relational context in which social networks are embedded can shape the way that social reinforcement and social relevance operate to influence behavior—in some cases creating desirable behavior change and in other cases suppressing it.

Consistent with the previous chapters, the example that I provide comes from an online health community.[5] However, to take up the task of social design in earnest, this application is not an intervention deployed within an existing health program. Rather, with a team of social scientists at the University of Pennsylvania, I constructed a fitness program from the ground up. The goal was to design every aspect of the fitness program so that it would be possible to detect whether a minimal intervention within an online health-buddy network might directly influence participants' offline exercise behaviors (in particular, attendance at fitness classes). In order to do this, we hired fitness instructors, designed the class schedules, rented out exercise rooms, and recorded each person's class attendance. Doing all of this ourselves ensured that we would be able to detect with the greatest level of precision whether small changes in online networks would have a direct effect on people's levels of physical activity.

The results were much stronger than anticipated. There were predictable and sizable effects of participants' online networks on their offline behaviors. Moreover, the relational features of these networks directly controlled the kinds of social influences people had over each other—that is, the rules of the social world determined whether people's physical activity levels increased or whether they declined. The description of this study that follows highlights several popular predictions for how artificially constructed online relationships might impact offline changes in behavior. Some of these predictions are borne out, while others fail. With this in mind, readers are invited to make their own predictions about how relational contexts used in the design of health buddy networks might alter the collective dynamics of behavior change.

DESIGNING SOCIAL WORLDS TO INDUCE BEHAVIOR CHANGE

The PennShape program was conducted as an eleven-week fitness initiative in partnership with the Graduate Student Association at the University of Pennsylvania. Funding from the Annenberg Foundation and the National Institutes of Health allowed us to offer more than 90 weekly exercise classes to nearly 800 graduate students. We constructed an online social community for the participants, which doubled as the main program website. This site was the only way for participants to sign up for fitness classes. Prizes for participation were awarded to the members who attended the greatest number of fitness classes over the eleven-week program. Class instructors provided us with complete data on all participants' attendance and activities in the classes, which included yoga, pilates, strength training, cardiovascular exercises, flexibility training, and resistance training.

We focused on two ways in which an online setting might be designed to create useful social capital for participants: supportive relationships and competitive relationships. In the first type of setting, the value of anonymous contacts came in the form of supportive interactions, social encouragements, exercise advice, and opportunities to meet up offline. In this setting, health buddies had incentives to interact with each other and help each other increase their participation levels. By contrast, in the competitive setting, participants did not have any communication tools or supportive incentives. The value of health-buddy networks came in the form of providing competitive sources of social comparison.

We constructed four different online communities for the program. Each one was its own self-contained social world. As such, each one provided participants with a different kind of social setting, and each

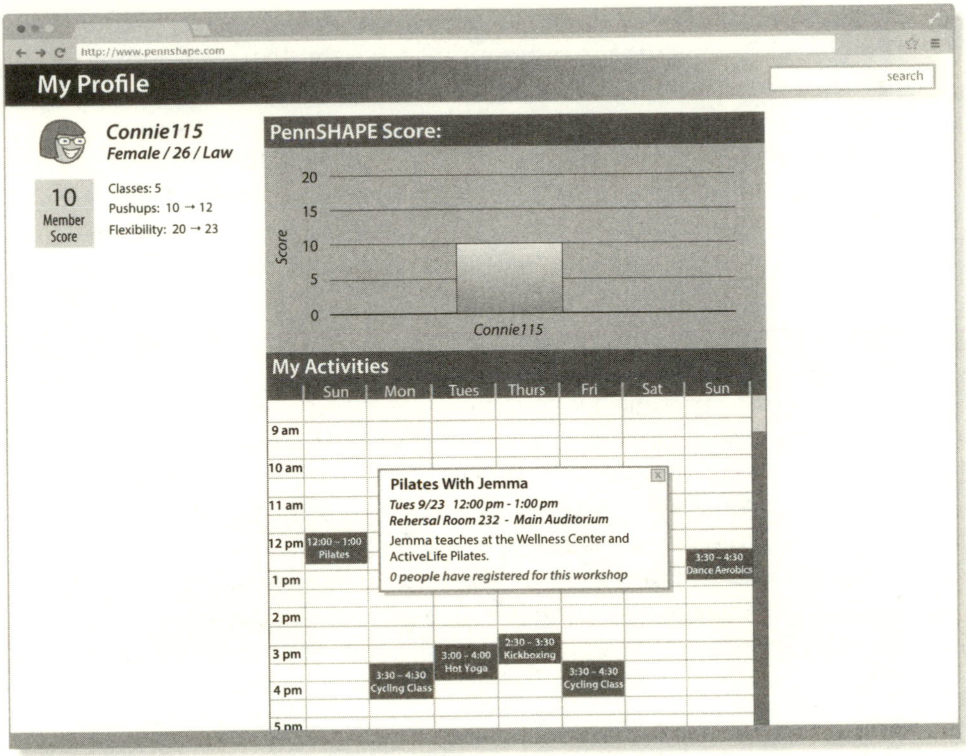

Figure 9.1 Control Condition

one was also a unique experimental condition. The four conditions were: a Control Condition, a Social Comparison Condition, a Social Support Condition, and a Group Comparison Condition.

The most basic community was the Control Condition, shown in figure 9.1, which was not really a community at all. This provided participants with basic access to the fitness program via the web portal. In figure 9.1, the class registration tool is shown in the lower part of the web page. The upper left-hand part of the page shows the focal individual's profile information. Her cumulative progress in the program is shown by the bar chart in the center of the page. This condition had no social network. Thus, it provided a baseline for evaluating the expected level of fitness-class participation among program members in the absence of any social reinforcement from online health buddies.

Scientifically, the Control Condition is especially useful because it allows us to establish the "null hypothesis" for this experiment. For this study, the null hypothesis is that participation will be incentivized by the monetary rewards for progress in program (that is, the prizes participants can win for attending the most classes). The baseline expectation is that participants will not be influenced by social incentives from anonymous health buddies. Thus, according to the null hypothesis, there should be no difference at all in exercise levels across the different experimental conditions. All of the social worlds should produce the same overall levels of participation as the Control Condition. We can refer to this hypothesis as the Economist's Prediction since it assumes that people are only motivated by financial rewards and not by social incentives.[6]

The second experimental condition, which is shown in figure 9.2, was a competitive social setting, called the Social Comparison Condition. In this condition, participants had access to the same generic web portal for signing up for classes that participants had in the Control Condition. However, in addition, the left-hand panel of the screen shows the profile information for the focal individual along with the profiles of five anonymous health buddies. Health-buddy connections were designed using the network principles from the previous chapters of this book, namely social reinforcement and social relevance. In other words, health buddies were embedded in clustered social networks and matched with each other based on their similarities along relevant health characteristics.[7]

In this social setting, individuals could not interact or communicate with one another. Their usernames and avatars were blinded, which meant that individuals could not identify each other if they attended the same exercise classes. The only value of the social capital from these health buddies was to provide competitive standards of social comparison for one another. In other words, health buddies provided each other with reference points for personal goal setting and for evaluating their own progress in the program. The guiding hypothesis for this experimental condition is that anonymous reinforcement from relevant peers will increase individuals' aspirations and thereby improve members' engagement in exercise classes. We can call this the Social Comparison Prediction.

In the first two experimental conditions—that is, *control* and *comparison*—the rewards for program participation were based on individual performance. Prizes were given to participants according to the number of classes that they attended in the program. By contrast, in the second two conditions—that is, *social support* and *group*

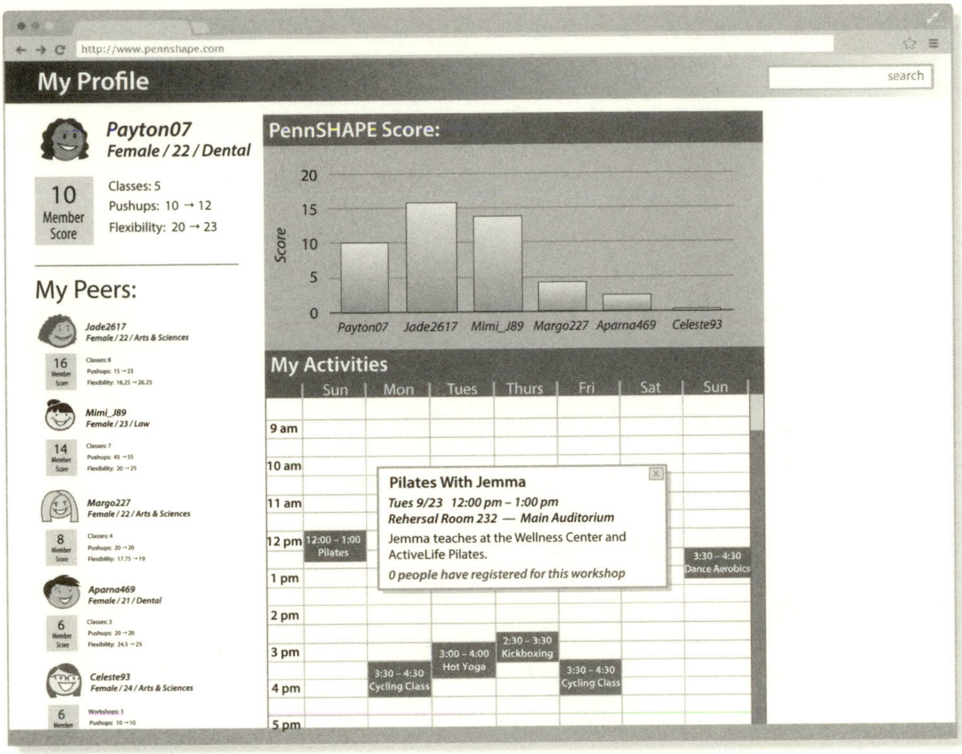

My Profile

search

Payton07
Female / 22 / Dental

10 Member Score

Classes: 5
Pushups: 10 → 12
Flexibility: 20 → 23

PennSHAPE Score:

Score: Payton07, Jade2617, Mimi_J89, Margo227, Aparna469, Celeste93

My Peers:

Jade2617
Female / 22 / Arts & Sciences
16 Member Score
Classes: 8
Pushups: 15 → 23
Flexibility: 16.25 → 26.25

Mimi_J89
Female / 23 / Law
14 Member Score
Classes: 7
Pushups: 45 → 55
Flexibility: 20 → 25

Margo227
Female / 22 / Arts & Sciences
8 Member Score
Classes: 4
Pushups: 20 → 20
Flexibility: 17.75 → 19

Aparna469
Female / 21 / Dental
6 Member Score
Classes: 3
Pushups: 20 → 20
Flexibility: 24.5 → 25

Celeste93
Female / 24 / Arts & Sciences
6 Member
Workshops: 1
Pushups: 10 → 10

My Activities

	Sun	Mon	Tues	Thurs	Fri	Sat	Sun
9 am							
10 am							
11 am							
12 pm	12:00 – 1:00 Pilates						3:30 – 4:30 Dance Aerobics
1 pm							
2 pm							
3 pm				2:30 – 3:30 Kickboxing			
4 pm	3:30 – 4:30 Cycling Class		3:00 – 4:00 Hot Yoga	3:30 – 4:30 Cycling Class			
5 pm							

Pilates With Jemma
Tues 9/23 12:00 pm – 1:00 pm
Rehersal Room 232 — Main Auditorium
Jemma teaches at the Wellness Center and ActiveLife Pilates.
0 people have registered for this workshop

Figure 9.2 Social Comparison Condition

comparison—rewards for participation were based on team performance instead of individual performance. Prizes were given to teams based on the total participation of all the team members.

Do team incentives help or hurt individual performance? When considering the possible outcomes of this study, it is worth thinking about how the relational differences between settings based on individual incentives versus collective incentives may interact with the dynamics of social reinforcement. For instance, team-based rewards can create free rider effects, in which some people do all the work for the team, while others do nothing. The free riders gain all of the rewards of a successful team effort without having to put in any of the individual work. Using this logic, one prediction is that team-based incentives will ruin group performance. In fact, the Economist's Prediction from above can be extended to suggest that an unintended consequence of team-based incentives is that they will induce free riding by everyone in a group,

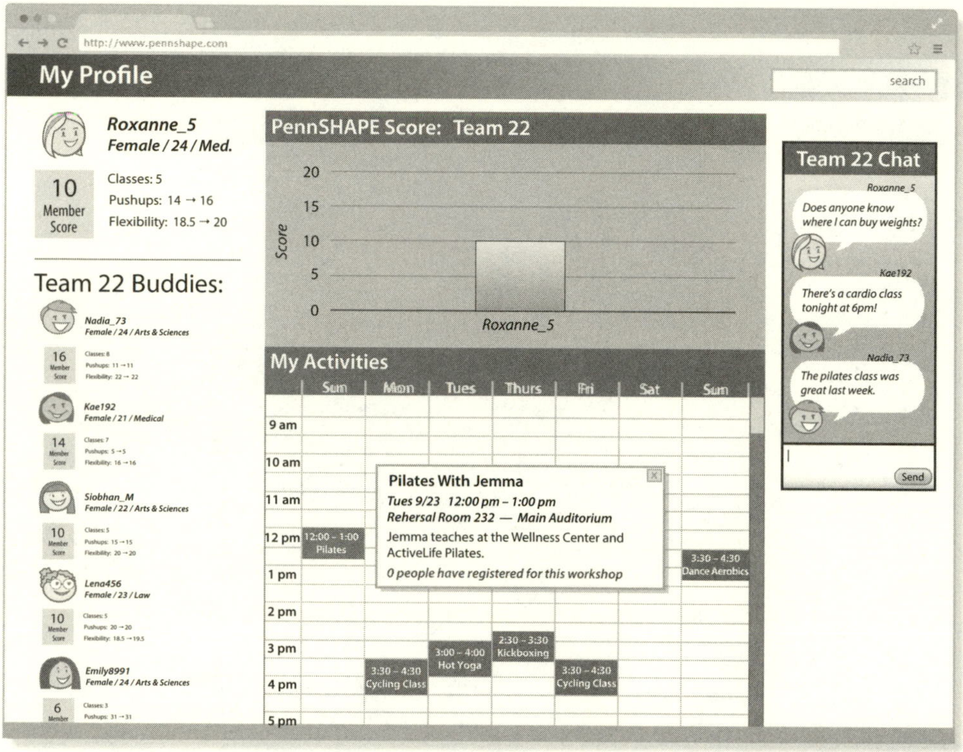

Figure 9.3 Social Support Condition

significantly reducing both individual and team performance. However, there is also a competing prediction. Contrary to the Economist's Prediction, this view suggests that the value of team-based incentives is that they give participants a reason to interact with each other and to support each other's participation in the program. On this view, shared incentives can strengthen the dynamics of social reinforcement, giving an important advantage to groups with team-based rewards.

To see whether this happens, the third experimental condition, shown in figure 9.3, created a supportive social setting in which individuals were assigned to a team and were collectively rewarded for participation based on their team's progress in the program.

As in the first two conditions, participants in the Social Support Condition had access to the web portal for signing up for classes. As in the Social Comparison Condition, the left-hand panel of the screen shows the five program members who were assigned to be teammates with the focal individual. As before, these health buddies were embedded in a clustered social network and shared relevant health characteristics. In all of these ways, the Social Comparison Condition and the Social Support Condition were identical; however, there were two important differences between them.

First, participants in the Social Comparison Condition were given individual rewards for making progress in the program, whereas in the Social Support Condition participants were rewarded based on team performance. Consequently, in the *supportive* setting, health buddies were not only social resources for advice and encouragement but also partners in achieving a collective goal.

The second difference between the competitive setting and the supportive setting was that in the Social Comparison Condition health buddies could not communicate with one another. By contrast, in the Social Support Condition, participants were able to interact directly with one another using an online chat tool that was provided in the website interface. In figure 9.3, the right-hand side of the screen shows the chat window that participants could use to talk with the other members of their team. Communication was unrestricted. Participants could share workout tips, motivate each other to sign up for fitness classes, de-anonymize themselves, arrange to meet up offline, and plan to go to their fitness classes together.

Although participants in both settings were embedded in networks that were *structurally* identical (that is, with the same topology and the same level of homophily), these conditions were *relationally* different. Participants in the Social Support Condition had more reasons to be invested in their health buddies. They had more channels of communication and greater interdependence in terms of their shared goals. The guiding hypothesis for this experimental condition was that collective incentives and rich communication technologies would encourage participants to establish stronger affective attachments with their health buddies. Doing so would increase social influence, create stronger norms for increased physical activity, and produce greater social incentives to maintain high levels of participation. This expectation can be called the Social Support Prediction.

Finally, since the Social Support Condition used collective rewards, while the Social Comparison Condition used individual rewards, the final experimental condition was devised to complete the symmetry of the experimental design. This condition was designed to see what would happen if a relational context based on social comparison was

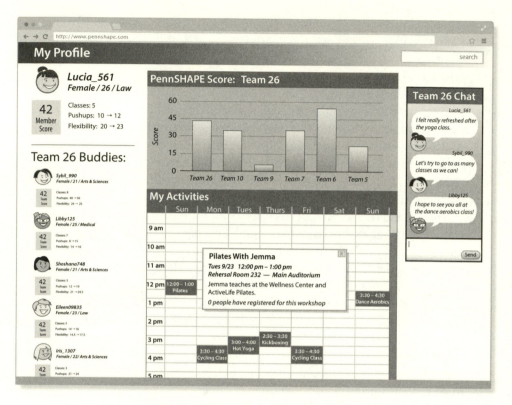

Figure 9.4 Group Comparison Condition

combined with collective rewards. The Group Comparison Condition, which is shown in Figure 9.4, placed people onto teams with shared rewards and then provided information about the performance of other teams.

The Group Competition Condition closely resembles the Social Support Condition. The left panel shows the focal individual and the list of five teammates. As before, all of the teammates were embedded in a clustered network and shared relevant health characteristics. The right-hand panel shows an unrestricted chat window for team members to interact with one another, and the bottom part of the screen shows the calendar tool used for signing up for fitness classes.

The only difference between the Social Support Condition and the Group Comparison Condition is that the latter condition also shows the scores of five other teams. In other words, the Group Comparison Condition introduces out-group competition into the social support framework. The hypothesis for this condition is that competition with other groups will induce social comparison effects between teams. Much like the Social Comparison Prediction, the prediction for this condition is that competition will create increased expectations for performance by team members and increase participants' overall levels of exercise. The Group Comparison Prediction differs only slightly from the Social Comparison Prediction by emphasizing the relational importance of out-group competition as the motivation for strong in-group performance.

Overall, there were 186 participants in each experimental condition (744 participants in total). The retention rate was above 95% for participants in every condition, with no significant differences in attrition across them. So, how did each of the predictions fare?

THE DIVERGING PATHS OF SOCIAL SUPPORT AND SOCIAL COMPARISON

Health-buddy networks had a sizable impact on physical activity. As shown in figure 9.5, participants in each of the three social conditions had significantly different rates of class attendance than participants in the Control Condition. This means that we can reject the Economist's Prediction that participants would ignore social influences from their anonymous health buddies and respond exclusively to program incentives.

To make things even worse for the Economist's Prediction, the two conditions that significantly outperformed the Control Condition were the Social Comparison Condition (with individual incentives) and the Group Comparison Condition (with collective incentives). Contrary to the Economist's Prediction, collective incentives did not create free-rider effects or in any way reduce individuals' engagement with the program. In fact, subjects in the Group Comparison Condition attended the most classes of anyone in the program, performing better than either of the conditions with individual incentives.

The results were most unexpected in the Social Support Condition. Social support produced the lowest levels of physical activity in the entire program. Participants in this condition were significantly less likely to go to the gym than people in the Control Condition. They would have been better off without any health buddies.

The good news came from the competitive conditions. Adding competitive influences to the social setting turned the negative effects of

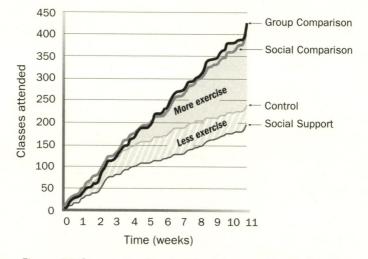

Figure 9.5 Cumulative Physical Activity over Eleven Weeks

social support into strong positive effects of group comparison. From a social planner's perspective, these results are illuminating. They show that the relational context of network ties can indeed influence the collective dynamics of group behavior. The important thing now is to understand why this happened. From the results in chapter 8, we know that health buddies were influential because they were relevant sources of social reinforcement. What we do not know yet is why competitive reinforcement was so helpful, and why supportive reinforcement was so harmful. Once we know this, it may be possible to identify general lessons for how to design social settings that encourage desirable changes in behavior.

PITFALLS AND SOLUTIONS FOR SOCIAL DESIGN

An important difference between supportive settings and competitive settings is that they create social relevance in different ways. In a competitive social setting, participants often use their contacts as reference points for establishing their own aspirations. Social capital takes the form of social comparison. If the most active members in the group become the most salient individuals in each person's network, this draws attention toward positive reinforcement for increased activity.[8] By contrast, in a supportive online setting, the value of online contacts often comes from peer support and encouragement. The benefit of this kind of setting is that people can motivate their less engaged peers to keep up with the team, so no one will be left behind. However, the downside of this way of creating relevance is that it can make individuals who are less engaged in the program into focal points for their neighbors' attention. In other words, a supportive setting can create the social expectation that members will be attentive to all of their contacts. This can backfire if the poor performers create social inertia that pulls the entire group toward inactivity. If a few people stop exercising, it can give permission for others to do so as well.[9]

We saw a similar effect of social inertia in chapter 6, where the simulation results on seeding a public health intervention revealed that non-adopters could act as countervailing influences that reduced the ability of seed individuals to spread an innovation. Something similar happened in the Social Support Condition. Individuals who were less engaged in the program acted as countervailing influences that pulled against the positive signals from their more engaged peers. As a result, the daily exercise rate for participants in the supportive setting was 17% less than in the Control Condition, while in the social comparison setting the daily exercise rate was increased by 90%.

These diverging effects of social comparison and social support may offer useful insight into recent intervention studies that have suggested that supportive social-media environments can be helpful for promoting healthy diets, smoking cessation, and physical activity.[10] There are some cases in which this is certainly true. However, a closer look at many of these intervention studies shows that they typically incorporate some level of social comparison into the online setting. For instance, in addition to providing subjects with chat tools and incentives for social engagement, smoking interventions show participants the number of days that others have gone without smoking. Dieting interventions show changes in peers' caloric intake. And fitness interventions show the number of exercise classes attended, or fitness goals completed, among peers in the program. In other words, while the obvious explanation for an intervention's success may be its online tools for social support, its impact may nevertheless come from features of social comparison that are implicit within the design of the social setting.

An example of this in the PennShape study can be seen by looking at the successful growth of physical activity in the Group Comparison Condition. Consider how these results would have been interpreted if there had been no other experimental conditions in this study. If we just compared the results from the Group Comparison Condition to those from the Control Condition, an intuitive conclusion would have been that the reason for the success of the Group Comparison Condition was that group members were on teams where they could actively receive social support from one another. However, when we compare these results to the other experimental conditions, we can see that this explanation does not work. The Social Comparison Condition performed almost exactly the same as the Group Comparison Condition, but it did not have any of these tools for social support. Moreover, the Social Support Condition, which had the exact same team structure and supportive online tools as the Group Comparison Condition, performed the worst of all.

Social support is an intuitive explanation for why people can influence each other online. Indeed, if you were to ask the participants in the Group Comparison Condition, they may even tell you that social support was the reason for their success. However, once we are able to tease apart the dynamics of behavior change more carefully, it becomes clear that this intuitive idea does not necessarily work as we would hope.

The point here is not that social competition is always beneficial while social support is harmful.[11] There are plenty of social settings where constructing a relational context based on social support would be a valuable way to create the right kind of social relevance. Rather, the lesson for social design is that seemingly intuitive decisions about how relationships are designed within an online setting can affect the social expectations that people have about their online contacts and, therefore, how they will be influenced by them.

A useful insight for social design is that sometimes *less is more*. In the Social Comparison Condition, participants were given a bare minimum of social contact—mere exposure to what others were doing—and yet participation levels skyrocketed. By contrast, the Social Support Condition gave participants chat tools with real-time updating and live social connectivity. Ironically, the result was that performance in this condition was worse than in the Control Condition. Social technologies did not just fail, they backfired. When it comes to social design, providing people with the right kind of social capital is far more important than providing them with more social technologies.

This lesson is particularly important in light of the fact that the social technologies that were provided to participants in the Social Support Condition were exactly the ones that people had requested. Before designing the PennShape study, we had asked participants from an ear-lier fitness study if there was anything that they felt was missing from their online experience. Was there anything we could add that would make them more engaged in exercising? By far, the most popular re-sponse was that people wanted to be able to interact with their health buddies: they wanted more online tools for social support. However, when we implemented these tools in exactly the way that people had requested (that is, in the Social Support Condition), the effect was disastrous.

A useful take-home lesson from this study concerns the dangers of using people's self-reported preferences as a guide for social design. It would certainly be great if this worked, but if we have learned anything so far it is that what will be effective for changing people's behavior often has very little to do with what is intuitive. Thus, a cautionary con-clusion from this study is that our intuitive ideas can lead us astray. However, the more important finding is the good news that comes from seeing just how easy it can be to solve this problem. A small change to the relational context can make a big difference in the network dynam-ics of group behavior. In particular, the Group Comparison Condition had a remarkably different outcome than the Social Support Condition, yet the only difference between the two was the introduction of a com-petitive element into the social setting. It seems like a small change to make, but it had a large impact on how people used their social ties—transforming the social dynamics from actively limiting people's en-gagement with physical activity, to dramatically increasing it.

Whether this kind of transformation in social dynamics ultimately happens in an online setting is determined by how social relevance is created among the participants. The preceding chapters have shown that the lessons of this book are cumulative. Successful diffusion de-pends on having all of the pieces in place. Without social reinforcement from clustered networks, challenging behaviors are unlikely to spread. Moreover, without social relevance among network contacts, people are unlikely to be influenced by their peers. Building on these findings, the results here show that when social networks are structured to cre-ate influential relationships, the relational context of the network ties can determine whether these social influences will help to spread de-sirable behavior change or whether they will instead suppress it.

These findings have implications for several domains of application, ranging from energy consumption to voting behavior. For instance, some energy companies have begun to notify their customers about the consumption practices of their neighbors. The goal of these social noti-fications is to employ many of the same dynamics described in this chapter to promote more responsible energy use. However, whether these efforts will ultimately succeed, or whether they will instead back-fire, may depend upon how they activate the dynamics of social rein-forcement. Successfully implemented, social influences may generate desirable norms of responsible energy use; however, without proper at-tention to the way that social relevance is created, these same social influences may have the unwanted effect of creating increased compla-cency. The useful lesson here is that if relational contexts are designed to create the right kind of social relevance—in this case through social comparison—they may be used to provide people with new sources of social capital that can successfully activate the network dynamics of desirable behavior change.

PART IV

Conclusions

It is not the consciousness of [persons] that determines their existence, but, on the contrary, their social existence that determines their consciousness.

—Karl Marx, *A Contribution to the Critique of Political Economy*

CHAPTER 10

Conclusion

The findings from these chapters are encouraging. The results have shown that social diffusion can get started and spread in diverse environments and that diffusion can create a stable behavioral norm once it gets established. But what is most helpful is how little had to be assumed about the individuals or the social setting in order to find these results. The individuals do not need to be rational: social reinforcement promotes the spread of behaviors even if the actors do not know why social reinforcement is important. Nor do people have to provide reasons or commitments: their actions speak for themselves. Likewise, there is no need to assume that people have complex emotional histories together, or even that there is trust between them: the normative and informational signals from social reinforcement can be enough to encourage people to change their behavior. People do not need to be early adopters in order to get swept up in a process of social change: social reinforcement can elicit participation even from initially resistant individuals. Finally, support from established institutions is not necessary in order for social change to take place. Nor is peer-sanctioning a requirement. People do not need to be policed or coerced into adopting new behaviors. The minimal requirement is only that individuals are embedded in social networks that provide them with relevant sources of social reinforcement.

The science of complex contagions is still a long way from fulfilling the promise of understanding how the patterns of social influence in a population govern the often-mercurial movements of its collective behavior, to say nothing of how institutions may be designed to promote desirable collective outcomes. The modest progress here is to show that our understanding of these social processes is advanced considerably by shedding the convenience of classic epidemiological tropes and adopting a set of new theoretical and methodological approaches that help to uncover the complex dynamics of social life.

One of the main implications of these chapters is that the traditional network categories of strong and weak ties bundle together several concepts—both relational and structural—that can easily be conflated in studies of network diffusion. Strong ties tend to be structurally clustered, but they are also relationally proximate, homophilous, affect-laden, and higher frequency. By contrast, weak ties are structurally long, but they are also relationally distal, heterophilous, low affect, and low frequency. From this list of attributes, it is challenging to decipher the key features that affect diffusion. This makes it difficult to see how the theoretical notions of strong and weak ties might be applied to specific contexts in order to promote the spread of behavior.

To find a way of bridging this divide, this book employs several different approaches to social research. Part 1 demonstrates new theoretical results on network diffusion and then tests these findings experimentally. The experimental results show that network clustering can improve both the speed and the success of diffusion. The results also show that reinforcing signals from multiple contacts can increase the likelihood that people will be committed to a new behavior once they have adopted it. Part 2 then examines the practical implications that follow from these findings. For innovations that face opposition, the main insight is that diffusion can be improved by clustering early adopters together—the reach of their influence is expanded by limiting their exposure to the population. Applying these findings to organizational settings, wide bridges were found to be more effective than information brokers for transmitting innovations. The results also show that organizational identities can be used to shape social networks in ways that improve the diffusion of complex knowledge and innovative practices. The pervading conclusion throughout all of these chapters is that wide bridges of social reinforcement can be used to improve the spread of complex social contagions.

Part 3 then explores how the relational features of social networks may be used in combination with network structure to improve the effectiveness of online policy applications. The results show that empathy is an important part of how social networks control diffusion in these settings. Empathy does not depend on people having a long interpersonal history, strong affect, or even a shared shadow of the future. Rather, the right kind of homophily can create empathy between strangers, providing a rare and valuable form of social capital. The more similar someone is to their alters—in the relevant ways—the easier it is for them to understand how their alters' interests and motivations might be applicable to their own and the more likely it is that their alters' behaviors will be adopted. The lessons from these chapters also show how the relational context in which network ties are embedded can shape the way that social capital is used and thereby influence the kinds of collective behaviors that are likely to spread.

A consistent finding throughout these chapters is that social inertia can impede a diffusion process. A few different strategies are offered to help solve this problem. In chapter 3, theoretical results on degree heterogeneity showed that hubs in a social network can unintentionally block the spread of innovations. This is because hubs have so many contacts that countervailing signals from non-adopters can prevent highly connected individuals from adopting novel behaviors. Chapter 5 showed examples of this phenomenon in the diffusion of political hashtags on Twitter and the spread of normative behaviors in Second Life. In both cases, peripheral networks of clustered peers were able to provide more-effective channels of diffusion than central individuals. In chapter 6, another challenge of social inertia arose in the analysis of viral strategies for seeding public health interventions. The random seeding strategy failed because countervailing influences from untreated neighbors pressured the seeds to abandon the treatment behavior. There it was found that a clustered seeding strategy was more effective because it harnessed social inertia, putting the weight of neighborhood activity in favor of the innovation instead of against it. Finally, in chapter 9, the problem of inertia again emerged in the guise of resistance to physical activity. The results of that study found that relationships based on social support led to decreasing activity levels as a result of participants giving greater attention to countervailing influences. However, those results also offered a solution. They showed that designing relationships based on social comparison could draw attention away from countervailing influences by focusing participants' attention on social signals coming from peers who were engaged in the desired behavior.

There is exciting new territory to explore here. With increased understanding of the complex dynamics of social contagions, new solutions may be found to age-old problems of diffusion. The findings from these pages show that both *reinforcement* and *relevance* are key factors for any such solution. The findings also show that much more work needs to be done. Little is yet known about the diverse ways in which reinforcement and relevance emerge in different social contexts. For instance, in some behavioral contexts, such as fraternity settings, high levels of homogeneity among reinforcing contacts may be necessary to establish the social relevance necessary to induce compliance with ritualistic behaviors. However, in other settings, such as political mobilization, diversity among adopters may instead increase the relevance of reinforcing signals by demonstrating the broad legitimacy of a political movement. A fruitful direction for future research will be to investigate how different mechanisms of complexity (such as emotional contagion versus legitimacy) can shape the ways in which social relevance is determined.

To begin this exploration, the experimental approach developed in this book offers several new ways of studying the collective dynamics of crowd behavior. These developments will hopefully serve not only to offer greater empirical insight into the dynamics of social complexity but also to advance our theoretical understanding of the diversity of social forces that underlie unanticipated changes in collective activity.

As this book draws to a close, it is only appropriate that I return to the theme of scientific intuitions with which I began. Chapter 2 demonstrated the powerful intuition that sits behind decades of work on the strength of weak ties and small world networks: long-distance ties speed up diffusion in just about every setting where contagions spread. This intuition is compelling and pervasive. However, this book has been dedicated to demonstrating the general principles that circumscribe its application.

Beyond the scope of this book, there are many relevant domains in which the findings on complex contagions may be applied. Intuitions from simple contagions can be found in every arena of scientific research and policy application. Chapter 3 showed that many of the most intuitive ways to solve problems of diffusion—such as focusing on hubs, turning to high-status opinion leaders, or increasing the density of the social network—can worsen the problem of diffusion. Similarly, chapters 6 through 9 showed that in many of the practical settings where there is an interest in promoting diffusion—such as the development of seeding strategies for public health interventions, the use of information brokers for spreading innovations, and the design of social media applications to induce behavior change—the most intuitive ways to spread simple contagions can backfire when it comes to spreading complex contagions.

It is understandable that diffusion efforts often fail. The dream of virality does not take context into account. To appreciate social context is to appreciate that the socially embedded nature of human behavior typically makes diffusion processes just as susceptible to countervailing influences as they are to positive reinforcement. To understand this is to change the way that we think about social diffusion, transforming our intuitions from those based on simple contagions to ones that are based on complex contagions.

The implications for social policy that arise from these findings suggest that social capital may be designed to improve institutional capacities for spreading beneficial behaviors. There is a useful parallel here with recent developments in behavioral economics and their applications to public policy. A rapidly growing literature has identified how forces outside of people's control, such as exposure to regular violence, extreme poverty, and lack of education, limit an individual's capacity to make the same kinds of choices as people who do not face these structural challenges. Thanks to the efforts of behavioral scientists, governments are now increasingly receptive to the idea that behavioral economics can be used to mitigate structural limitations on individual freedom. Deceptively simple design interventions that change the "architecture" of a choice setting can be used to increase people's capacity for good decision-making. These policies are based on the idea that individual freedom can be increased through intelligently and fairly designed choice environments.

This study of social networks and diffusion suggests an analogous idea for the "architecture" of social capital. When people do not have adequate social capital to help them make the decisions that they want to make, their capacity for individual choice is limited. These limitations may affect everything from a person's choice of vocation, to their ability to identify a healthy body weight, to their decision to drop out of school. Each of these decisions may be guided by the social influences that steer people's expectations for themselves and others. The ideas described in this book suggest that social design—much like the role of choice architecture in behavioral economics—may be used to enhance individuals' capacity for choice. Improving the social resources that are available to people whose networks do not offer them adequate support—and so providing them with rare and valuable sources of social capital—can improve their individual capacity for choice and thereby their individual freedom.

The most pressing social problems today concern the ability of people to find the resources they need to make good decisions about health, sustainability, and civic participation. Perhaps if we give greater attention to the network structure of social reinforcement that is available within their existing social networks, it will become easier to provide people with the social capital they require to encourage the adoption of beneficial behaviors. The most innovative, challenging, and difficult behaviors require the greatest levels of social reinforcement. The findings on complex contagions offer structural insight into how social networks may be used to spread these behaviors more effectively.

Experimental Sociology

Is it possible to study society the same way that we study a school of fish? Scientists can conduct controlled experiments in an aquarium on how predatory signals, environmental changes, and physical barriers affect complex schooling behavior.[1] If the fish are instead studied individually, the same number of individuals examined one at a time in isolation cannot explain how the group will behave. The school is a collective phenomenon. To understand how schooling works—when it functions properly, and when it breaks down—it needs to be studied as a whole. It may be the same with society.

Consider a traffic jam. Interviewed individually, drivers seem to be self-interested actors who are not concerned with producing a collective pattern of driving behavior. Nevertheless, when these same myopic individuals are put onto a highway together, it is difficult to believe the complex patterns that they produce—emergent waves of collective behavior that extend for miles.[2] Could these patterns ever be deduced by studying drivers individually? Or, in order to understand how traffic jams work—and what can be done to stop them—do we need to study traffic jams the same way we would study a school of fish—collectively?

What about revolutions? Can we study them person by person, or are they fundamentally collective? What about electoral outcomes? Individuals vote, but populations make choices—often completely contrary to what any individual expects.[3] What about fads? Can the reasons for the success or failure of a fad be deduced from individual reports? What about organizational performance, or the emergence of new social norms, or the distribution of wealth in a society? Can any of these be understood by sampling a large number of individuals and then guessing at how they might have interacted to produce the collective phenomenon?

For generations, we have proceeded as if it were possible to study society this way because the available data have encouraged it.

Collective phenomena are easy to observe. We see traffic jams recorded from helicopters; we can count the number of people who show up at a protest rally; we can observe social norms in people's customary behaviors; and we can track national distributions of wealth in Internal Revenue Service data. The collective facts are known. Similarly, it is easy to observe individuals. We can interview them, survey them, experiment on them, and secretly monitor them. There are lots of data on what people do. With these two things in hand, we have tried to make sense of the rest. However, what is not known is the dynamics. How do individuals interact to produce these collective phenomena—and what might be done to alter the outcomes?

The stock market is a great example of a situation for which we have an unfathomable expanse of data on both the individual choices that people make and on the collective market trends that they produce. Yet we know far less about the dynamics that lead from one to the other.[4] Indeed, after more than a century of dedicated research on this topic and many Nobel Prizes later, the 2008 near collapse of the global financial system came without warning. Despite the best efforts of economists to synthesize micro and macro theories of market dynamics, there is no predictive science that explains how they interact, and there is no way to foretell the emergence of a market crash, to say nothing of how to prevent it.

The question that we must confront is whether the crowd is fundamentally unpredictable, or whether there is a way for social science to inspect the mysterious system of gears and ratchets that lead from individual choices to collective behaviors, and back. The experimental approach developed in this book offers an answer.[5]

FROM A CLOCKWORK UNIVERSE TO A CLOCKWORK CROWD

It is a bromide in the philosophy of science that there is an analogy to be made between the history of physics and that of social science.[6] I do not want to take issue here with the proponents of this view or their critics. Rather, my interest is in a recent incarnation of this idea that has attempted to offer an historical interpretation of the web-based approach to social research that I have presented in this book.

It has been suggested that the availability of new sources of big data—that is, the abundant digital traces of social life online—may be analogous to the revolutionary astronomical data set collected by Tycho

Brahe in the late sixteenth century. Brahe dedicated his entire life to collecting a massive, obsessively precise record of the movements of the heavenly bodies. Brahe's data were the gold standard in the physical sciences for centuries—establishing the empirical foundation for the work of Kepler and Newton. The analogy, of course, is that the Internet will provide an equivalently massive, coherent, and precise account of social life—and, in turn, a modern physics of society may follow.[7]

This analogy is deeply flawed, however, by its adherence to an equally antiquated notion—that progress in science comes from simply "looking and seeing". As if all one needs is a big enough telescope to stare through, and the mysteries of the big bang will be revealed. It is a view that philosophers of science aptly call naïve empiricism.[8]

For a quick counterexample to this view, look above at the history of the stock market, and notice the incredible volume of data that we have collected on it. Brahe's data were Lilliputian by comparison. Although we have been looking over these market data for more than a century, we have little clue as to how they work.

The crucial thing left out of this look-and-see view of scientific progress is that, in addition to being historically inaccurate, it mischaracterizes the nature of scientific discovery. Brahe dedicated his life to collecting those remarkable data as guided by Ptolemy's and Copernicus's theories of celestial mechanics. In other words, useful data are governed, in their collection and analysis, by a theoretical view of how the system underlying the data is expected to work. Brahe had Ptolemy and Copernicus to guide his efforts, as did each of the advances that followed from Brahe's work, from Kepler to Newton. Each step was predicated on revisions to the Ptolemaic/Copernican theoretical lineage, which coordinated and focused their cumulative efforts.[9]

This highlights what is most useful for us. The most important empirical advance to set modern mechanics onto its Newtonian footing was the combination of Brahe's remarkable data with the ability to conduct experiments on gravitational force. Newton's elegant formulation of the system of planetary motion came from the fact that he could experimentally test his ideas by studying how pendula behaved under different complex configurations. It was this ability to manipulate forces—that is, to ask counterfactual questions about gravity and the centripetal and centrifugal forces of motion—that allowed him to formulate a single logic of mechanics that described both the system of the planets and the behavior of objects on Earth. In other words, Newton's laws of celestial mechanics were derived from his unique insight that the experimental dynamics of pendula reveal the same underlying forces that govern the motions of the planets.[10]

If there is any analogy to be made between a revolutionary moment in physics and the contemporary path of social science, I believe this is where it lies. The ability to experiment—to ask counterfactual questions about the mechanics of collective behavior—gives social scientists the ability, for the first time, to see into the unfolding machinery of invisible forces that animates the process of social change.

Good data on individual behaviors are increasingly easy to come by. There are also lots of good data on collective activity. What has been missing are data on the dynamics that connect them. The revolutionary advance offered by Internet experiments is that we now have the ability to establish a direct connection between the collective behaviors that emerge "in the wild"—that is, the movements of populations within the massive and uncontrolled world of social life online—and the systematic and reproducible collective behaviors that can be studied in online experimental settings. Like latter-day Newtons, we are now in a position to study how the astronomical forces that govern large-scale social dynamics also operate at close range, experimentally, and to finally see whether there just may be a single logic of social mechanics that can describe social life at both scales.

A NEW WAY OF "DOING SOCIOLOGY" AND SOME EXAMPLES OF HOW TO DO IT

Institutional scholars and social theorists alike have hypothesized for centuries that it might be possible to alter the collective outcomes of society by manipulating features of its structure. For instance, Emile Durkheim posited that the frequency of suicides in a society could be directly controlled by its level of social integration. Karl Marx argued that people's beliefs and attitudes about everything from government to morality could be altered by changing the system of economic relations. And Max Weber argued, contrary to Marx, that the system of religious beliefs and cultural values in a society could control the pattern of economic relations that emerged.[11] Each of these theories posits a counterfactual hypothesis about society—that is, they each suggest that specific changes in social structure can produce predictable changes in population behavior.

The problem with these theories has always been that they are difficult to test and impossible to falsify.[12] However, contemporary social research has remedied this problem by shifting its orientation to target more manageable, "middle range" theories of social change. This work tends to focus on the problem of social emergence—in particular, how changes in institutional rules or social structures can have unintended consequences for changes in collective behaviors—such as the emergence of riots, racial segregation, innovation diffusion, corruption, crime, collective action, team productivity, gender inequality, and health disparities, to name just a few.[13]

Similar to the way that a traffic jam might emerge as an unforeseen collective consequence of drivers' individual behaviors, each of these theories articulates a hypothesis about what *could have happened*, or indeed what *could happen*, if a specific feature of a population's structure were to be altered. For instance, one theory predicts that had the ratio of women to men been slightly higher in an organization, discrimination practices would not have emerged as part of its culture. These are compelling ideas. They suggest that specific, often simple policies might result in surprising changes to seemingly unavoidable collective outcomes.[14] Decades of progress in developing formal and empirical predictions in this tradition has produced several important conjectures about the role of structural variables in social change. But further progress has been halted by the empirical problem that confronts all work on the emergence of collective behavior—it has been impossible to put any of these theories to a direct experimental test.

The experimental approach developed in this book offers a way out of this bind. The approach here is to study these collective phenomena as whole systems. To borrow an apt metaphor from biology, online worlds are petri dishes that can be used to grow "cultures." Under some conditions, we may not see any collective pattern emerge, whereas under others we may see collective patterns emerge predictably.[15] This method of "experimental sociology" is a necessary next step in order for the cumulative science of collective behavior to progress. The motivating conceit of this approach is that the same process of social emergence that governs the complex dynamics of collective behaviors in the wild can also be replicated and studied under controlled, counterfactual scenarios in online laboratories.

This idea has already been put into practice in dozens of research labs across the world. Internet experiments have been used to study a variety of topics, including the popularity of songs in cultural markets, the accuracy of online recommendation systems, and the growth of inequality in cooperative interactions.[16] For some, the value of this approach is its sheer practicality. A growing number of scholars have come to realize that, dollar for dollar, the volume of data that can be collected using web-based approaches can make online studies a much more efficient way to collect data than traditional paper-based methods.[17] These practical advantages are indeed significant. However, my interest here is to shift our focus from the practical advantages of web-based research to the new kinds of theoretical advances that may be possible with this approach.

The topic of this book—that is, how behavior spreads through social networks—is just one example of the kind of problem that can be tackled with this method. Web-based social experiments are useful for studying a wide range of scholarly topics—including gender scholarship, race scholarship, social epidemiology, theories of scientific discovery, and studies of organizational behavior, among others.[18] To make these possibilities concrete, I will briefly sketch four ideas for new studies that I think could easily be conducted by making only minor changes to the studies that I have described above. These examples range across several domains of social research; however, they share a family resemblance in the sense that each one is concerned with identifying how specific changes in the structural features of a population can have important consequences for its collective behavior.

Heterogeneity and inequality

One possible study concerns Peter Blau's theory of heterogeneity and inequality.[19] Blau hypothesized that systematic patterns of inequality can be generated by changing the number of different groups in a population and varying the relative sizes of those groups. Re-stated in fairly abstract terms, Blau argued that, regardless of who the group members are, systematic differences in the number and sizes of groups will generate predictable patterns of inequality between them. It is a striking prediction about how the social structure of society can produce significant consequences for people's welfare. Given the studies that I have described so far, it is not hard to imagine how this idea might be tested using a web-based experiment. A sketch of it is as follows.

To test Blau's hypothesis, a study of team-based activities could be used to assign people to groups of different sizes and then to observe their relations to one another while they performed reward-based tasks. In each experimental condition, a different distribution of group sizes would be used. Experimental conditions could also vary the information that is available to people about their group size, their group membership, and their peers' characteristics. Each of these experimental conditions would, of course, need to be replicated to ensure that the distribution of rewards across groups would be reproducible. With such a design, it would be easy to see whether the overall distribution of rewards that emerges would be—as Blau predicted—a direct result of the number and sizes of groups in the population. The study could then be elaborated to incorporate other relevant factors into the structural design. How would the observed effects of the distribution of group sizes interact with the composition of the groups in terms of people's race, gender, socioeconomic status, education, and so forth? Would it matter if the groups were homogeneous or mixed? How would the findings differ based on whether information about peers' characteristics was shared with the participants? There have already been many interesting theoretical and empirical studies conducted on these topics. Now they can be evaluated experimentally.

Emergence of status

A related topic that could also be explored in a similar way is Cecilia Ridgeway's theory of status construction. She argues that specific patterns of social interaction between the members of a population can create an emergent status hierarchy between people based on arbitrary, nominal characteristics (such as eye color). According to this theory, controllable features of social structure, such as a modest correlation between nominal characteristics and financial resources, or the pattern of mixing among different groups in a population, can determine whether arbitrary characteristics become meaningful status differences between groups.[20]

Previous studies of this topic have shown that in settings where expectations about individual value involve judgments about identity and performance, individuals with arbitrarily chosen characteristics can come to be seen as higher status.[21] Ridgeway and Shelley Correll argued that slight changes in the structure of the interactions between subjects can alter these social dynamics of status formation, thereby affecting which characteristics emerges as higher status, and even controlling whether status differences emerge at all. Extending the very interesting work that they have already done on two-person and three-person interactions, online studies could be conducted to test how these structural hypotheses translate into the emergence of status differences within large groups of people. In particular, one untested but very provocative conjecture to come out of their research is that while many of the people in a large population may never come into direct contact with one another, they may nevertheless all come to form shared beliefs about one another's status.[22]

A web-based experiment that places subjects into task groups could study this process by controlling the pattern of interactions among people while selectively revealing information about their identities and their resources. Would reproducible patterns of status emerge? Imagine, for instance, that a social setting was constructed in which people had repeated exposures to a small subset of individuals who had a particular nominal characteristic and a high level of wealth, for example in an online stock-trading environment. Would this pattern of interaction generate population-wide expectations about the status of every person who happened to have that particular characteristic? Could specific features of the social structure control whether people treat complete strangers as higher or lower status? What implications might this have for the design of stock trading websites, dating websites and employment websites?

Structural holes

A different kind of structural theory that could also be tested using an Internet experiment is Ron Burt's theory of structural holes.[23] As discussed in chapter 7, Burt argues that individuals who are located in particular positions of structural advantage within an organizational network will be more successful (that is, they will get faster promotions and higher salaries) than individuals of comparable professional skill who happen to be located in less advantaged structural positions. It is a compelling thesis; however, it requires being able to distinguish the effects of selection from those of treatment.

The selection effect that might explain Burt's important observation is that people who are professionally skilled enough to be deserving of higher salaries might naturally gravitate to good structural positions— that is, they "select into" those network positions. That may offer one reason why people in structurally advantaged positions tend to have greater success: they are more skilled at their jobs. The competing "treatment" explanation is that any person of average skill who is put into a good structural position will have more success because of the opportunity and power that the structural position affords.

An Internet experiment could be used to test these competing hypotheses about network structure and individual performance by observing the performance and productivity of individuals who were assigned to occupy various structural positions within team-based networks in an online task system. At the outset, all individuals in the study might be given a pretest that evaluates their baseline level of skill and strategic ability related to the online task. A study might then assign individuals at random into network positions with high and low structural advantage and then evaluate the rewards that different subjects receive based on their performance and productivity.

A good design would replicate this study across many independent trials using different populations. The results would then be able to identify whether the structural position of actors was the primary determinant of success or whether, regardless of network position, the more skilled actors always performed better. A nice follow-up to this study could then allow actors to change their network ties to see whether network evolution follows the path predicted by Vincent Buskens and Arnout van de Rijt and whether the most skilled individuals from the pretest would indeed gravitate to the most structurally advantageous positions.[24]

Simulacra and simulation: Using bots to study polarization

Finally, there are lots of new experiments to be run on the burgeoning topic of simulated social interactions. Here I will discuss a few examples that concern how Internet experiments can be used to explore the peculiar social dynamics of influence and conformity in the online domain.

In Solomon Asch's classic study of conformity effects, he placed subjects into experimental groups that were secretly composed of members of the research team (that is, "confederates") who pretended to be other subjects in the study. Asch found that when his research confederates exhibited an unusual behavior, such as guessing the wrong answer to an easy question, experimental subjects would often conform to the confederates' behavior and even become confused about whether the wrong answer was in fact correct. In the many decades since Asch's pioneering work, researchers have developed hundreds of ways of replicating this design. Today, the inevitable extension of this idea into the digital domain is to use computer programs—or "bots"—as experimental confederates.[25] One provocative question this approach raises is whether computer programs online are really any different from human confederates offline.

Beyond the practical novelty of using bots for social experimentation, the theoretical value of this idea has recently been amplified by the increasing prevalence of bots in the online social landscape. Bots have emerged as a common element in online political discourse. Hundreds of thousands of bots were used during the most recent (2016) presidential election, both to advocate for certain candidates and to launch vitriolic attacks against others. The increasing presence of bots in the online social ecology suggests that their scientific value may not only be their practical use, as simulated confederates, but may also come from their substantive and theoretical importance as a topic of study in their own right. As manipulable features of the social environment, bots may have significant implications for altering the trajectory of human collective behaviors, ranging from the social norms of "trolling behavior" to their impact on electoral outcomes.[26]

An apt extension of experimentation with bots is to use them to study the political polarization process. Some theories of deliberative democracy have argued that polarizing speech will increase overall participation levels in democratic debates and is therefore beneficial for the overall quality of the political discourse. Contrasting views argue that polarizing speech reduces participation and hurts the quality of discourse by engendering a spiral of silence in which certain groups withhold their opinions for fear of confrontation.[27] These causal theories are hard to evaluate in observational data. However, a properly designed experiment could identify the causal effect of polarizing speech on political discourse by using bots to vary the levels of polarization within online political discussion groups.

For instance, if we construct a set of political discussion groups—in which each group has the same number of people from each political party and each begins with equivalent levels of participation by all of the subjects—"polarizing bots" could then be introduced into the groups to see whether a reproducible change in the level and quality of group discourse emerges. Experimental conditions might vary the number of bots as well as whether bots were programmed to be polarizing or consensus building. A control condition would contain the same number of groups and be run for the same duration, but without including any bots. Replicating this design across several independent groups, it would be possible to evaluate the effects of polarizing bots on the quantity and quality of the resulting political discourse across experimental conditions.

How might the bots' level of vitriol affect participation? Would subjects who share the same political orientation as the bots be affected by the strength of the bots' messages? Would these subjects be emboldened by the force of the bots' language, becoming even more aggressive in their discourse and more entrenched in their opinions? Or would seeing their own views articulated so strongly give them pause and encourage them to adopt more moderate positions?[28] What if the bots played a moderating role, helping to soften the views articulated by the members of each party? Would this exacerbate conflict or promote more amicable discussions? And if the results reveal ways that bots might be used to enhance the quality of deliberation between political groups, what could this mean for the future design of social media platforms?

This brief set of examples suggests a much larger universe of studies that can be conducted using online social experimentation. Internet experiments, like counterfactual models, are not the right method for every problem, but for social scientists interested in understanding how the structural features of society may create unexpected patterns of collective behavior, the methods developed here provide a powerful new way of studying the complex dynamics of social change.

APPENDIX A

The Ethics of Social Design

What are the ethical implications that arise when we can design social networks to influence behavior change? This important question deserves serious treatment alongside the scientific content presented in the foregoing chapters. I have reserved this discussion for the appendix because what is offered here is not a comprehensive treatment of the ethics of sociological interventions, nor is it a philosophical analysis of the implications of social planning. Rather, this discussion is intended to open a conversation about how social technologies for behavior change might impact social welfare.

My approach is to begin with the implications that arise when scientific insights into the network dynamics of collective behavior can easily be turned into practical technologies for altering patterns of social influence. The aim of this discussion is to address both the dangers and the opportunities that this presents.

THE DISTINCTION BETWEEN THE "PRACTICE" OF SCIENCE AND THE "USES" OF SCIENCE

There is a necessary distinction to make here between ethical considerations that address the "practice" of science—for instance, how research is conducted, how subjects are treated, what information is used, what rights subjects have, and so forth—and the ethical considerations that govern the "uses" of science after studies have been conducted and published.

With regard to the former, discussions of ethics in the practice of science have been primarily concerned with three issues in sociological research:

1. *Institutional Review Board (IRB) procedures*—ensuring that social scientific studies conducted by federally funded researchers follow proper ethical guidelines.

2. *Informed Consent*—the rights of individuals to be informed about their participation in any kind of scientific study.
3. *Privacy*—the rights of individuals to prevent their personal information or behavioral records from being shared with, or used by, research organizations.

These issues have been topics of active debate ever since the National Research Act of 1974 and the Belmont Report of 1978,[1] which codified standards of ethical conduct in scientific research on human subjects. As a result of documented abuses of human subjects during and after World War II, IRB certification and ethical review of scientific studies using human subjects have become requirements for federally supported research organizations.

Computational social science poses several new challenges for these guidelines. The discovery of new ways to monitor and report people's activities with unprecedented detail, and at an unimaginable scale, has made it possible to reveal personal, medical, and even criminal behavior among unwitting subjects. Consequently, new computational tools for data collection and analysis have raised entirely new ethical issues about the responsibilities of scientists conducting research on human subjects, the need for informed consent, and the protection of privacy.

Unfortunately, the literature on these topics does not provide much guidance about how scientific research should be used once it has been published. The question that motivates me here is whether social scientists have any ethical responsibilities to society other than following the right procedures when collecting their data.[2] If social science research is conducted in an ethical fashion, does that end the researcher's responsibility? Or do scientists also have a responsibility to consider how their research will be used? My answer is that there are ethical considerations that govern both the obligation to use scientific discoveries to improve human welfare and the proper regulation of new social technologies to prevent them from being used for exploitative ends.

ARE THERE REALLY ETHICAL IMPLICATIONS?

For theoretical social science, ethical problems have been rare. Since the majority of ink dedicated to ethics has been spilt on the topic of human subjects research, theorists have typically had a free pass when it comes to the ethics of their work. However, in some of the most enduring areas of theoretical research, such as topics in collective action and social cooperation, there are long-standing ethical conundrums that now draw the spotlight as these theories move closer to the world of empirical application.

One classic paradox stems from the fact that research on social cooperation is typically framed in terms of solving an essential human problem: how can social scientists discover ways to overcome individual selfishness in order to secure the collective benefits of social cooperation? It is an important question and is relevant to a large number of situations. However, there are also quite a few situations in which cooperation is not a public good, but instead is a very large public bad.

For instance, this happens in situations in which actors overcome their selfish interests and collude with one another to fix oil prices or rig a securities market or alter the standards of risk assessment for mortgage-backed securities. The small groups of actors who manage to cooperate with one another do indeed benefit, but everyone else suffers. The social problem in this case is not how to create cooperation, but how to create individual incentives to prevent it.[3]

A collective action theorist will eventually be confronted with the paradox that her theoretical efforts to identify the special conditions under which cooperation will succeed can equally be used to identify the special conditions where collusion and exploitation will thrive. A relevant question for the theorist is what she can do to ensure that her ideas will be used for good and not for ill.

Unfortunately, general models of cooperation may be applied to a wide variety of situations for a wide variety of ends without regard for normative ethics. The policy paradox of cooperation theory—that is, that efforts to solve the problem of public goods may also discover ways to create public bads—does not have a good resolution. It is a paradox that theorists typically accept as a matter of course.[4]

This kind of problem becomes more poignant when studies move from theory to data. And it becomes urgent when the discussion moves from empirical research to the design of policy applications. It then becomes essential for theoretical researchers to consider how their work might be applied and what future ethical implications may arise. In this light, the results in this book highlight the need for theoretical and empirical researchers who study social diffusion to consider the broader implications of how their work might be used; these results demonstrate the importance of a more general discussion about the ethical concerns that may arise from new theoretical and empirical insights into the social dynamics that govern collective behavior.

In Part 3 of this book, I demonstrated how social networks could be designed to produce measurable changes in people's behaviors. In particular, chapter 9 showed that even small changes to the social setting in an online health community could effectively "switch on" and "switch off" people's willingness to exercise. While exercising can seem like a trivial example of how behavior change can be induced, we should not be deceived by the apparent simplicity of that context. It is only a small illustration. And even there, simple manipulations to the website altered the way that participants related to their online contacts, generating very different trajectories in their collective behaviors.

The ethical implications become more palpable when other examples are considered. Individuals' susceptibility to social influence is typically greater in situations having greater uncertainty, such as social settings for online investing, or where the stakes are higher, such as online settings in which peers offer each other medical advice. The more attention that people give to their online contacts, because they are rare and valuable sources of social capital, the more powerful those social influences may be. A social planner who can even slightly manipulate the flow of these influences through a population may be in a position to significantly alter the course of its behavior.

The consequences of this new capacity for intervention may be to change collective patterns of energy consumption, increase the use of new vaccines, alter the adoption of new consumer products, control the growth of radical political beliefs, change the spread of ethical business practices, influence the flow of immigration, spread moral and religious doctrines, change the acceptability of bullying behavior, affect the prevalence of teen suicides, alter patterns of voting behavior, and influence a vast array of other collective behaviors that we care deeply about.[5]

Each of these topics deserves to be treated in far greater depth than I can offer in this brief appendix. Other scholars have already begun to explore some of these issues with regard to policies that guide individual decision making, for instance in the field of behavioral economics.[6] By contrast, the discussion here takes a social perspective. Here I give attention to the general ethical implications of social technologies for behavior change and what we might do to appropriately manage this growing area of scientific research and application.

PREVENTING POLICIES THAT HARM

The findings in this book suggest that people's interests in cultivating social relationships with like-minded peers can be harnessed to provide them with useful social capital that can improve their lives. From this perspective, social design offers an inspiring opportunity to use social technologies to advance the collective welfare. But this opportunity also comes with a caveat.

In any field of scientific discovery, new insights into the mechanics of how the world works also create new opportunities for exploitation. Physics, chemistry, biology, and economics have all been used at various points in the last century to develop industrial technologies and social policies that have amplified social ills. One implication of this book is that sociology is no different; as with other scientific disciplines, it has the capacity to develop technologies that may be used for exploitation.

Consequently, one concern that has surfaced in the last couple of years is that the rapidly growing field of research on social design is itself a source of danger. The concern is that the development of new online technologies may give rise to destructive new capacities for manipulating population behavior. Attention is certainly warranted; however it is incorrect to assume that the danger of exploitation arises primarily from the practice of scientific discovery. Quite the opposite. The best protection against the threat of exploitation comes from scientific discovery itself. The reason for this is that once the underlying social mechanisms that make exploitation possible are discovered and understood, they can be monitored and regulated. But until this happens, they present a latent danger that is available for use by any exploitative organization that happens upon them.

A useful illustration of this point comes from early discoveries in the field of cognitive and perceptual psychology, which showed that visual and auditory messages that are broadcast at rapid intervals may be undetectable by an audience but can nevertheless induce them to choose certain products or behaviors. In the decades since, the dangers of subliminal messages have been a topic of active debate. Some researchers argue that the effects of subliminal messages are inconsequential for behavior, others that argue that subliminal messages can only induce behaviors that would have taken place anyway, and still others that argue these messages can in fact induce behaviors that subjects would not have chosen otherwise.[7]

My interest here is not to detail these debates but to highlight the opportunity for social exploitation on a mass scale that this kind of the scientific discovery creates when it is coupled with emerging technologies for broadcast communication. During the same decades when broadcast television was becoming a viable tool for mass communication, advertising firms were exploring new ways to use these broadcast technologies to influence behaviors. Much of the early work in cognitive and perceptual psychology followed these explorations closely to understand why certain advertising techniques were more effective than others.

During the last several decades, research into cognitive and perceptual psychology, and more recently neuroscience,[8] has identified the exact broadcast frequencies at which subliminal messages may be effective for activating cognitive and behavioral responses. The ethical implication that I want to highlight here is how these scientific discoveries were used to identify and regulate exploitative practices, rather than to promote them. These findings enabled agencies to monitor the use of subliminal techniques, leading to well-known federal protections that govern the legality of subliminal messaging in advertising practices today. Using these guidelines, both the Federal Trade Commission and the Federal Communications Commission of the United States issued policy statements prohibiting the use of these techniques in advertising, and in the United Kingdom these messaging techniques have been banned entirely.

The expansion of social media technologies presents an analogous situation. Even more than television, the Internet and World Wide Web offer an unprecedented scale of media access to vast numbers of people. The worldwide growth of these technologies and their associated industries has given rise to a corresponding growth in systematic research on how social interactions online may be used to produce changes in individual and collective behavior. This research may offer new insights into how these technologies can be used to address social ills; however, its value also comes from the ability to identify how to monitor and regulate new opportunities for social exploitation that arise from these channels of communication. One of the central findings of this book is that imperceptible changes to the social structure of an online population may have direct and sizable effects on its patterns of behavior. Research into these effects is the only way to anticipate and monitor the inevitable attempts at exploitation that are likely to occur.

It thus falls to theoretical researchers, empirical scientists, and policy researchers to identify the best ways to regulate the activities of social media organizations that may engage in social design without participants' consent.[9] Researchers may also offer useful support to watchdog groups and federal organizations to improve their capacity to identify situations in which manipulation or exploitation may be taking place— there is an essential role for scientific researchers to play in informing policy decisions in the virtual domain. By understanding the basic mechanics of how online social systems may be used for exploitation, there is a greater capacity to develop policies to ensure that they are not.

UNINTENDED CONSEQUENCES

Scientific research into social design may also be used to improve social welfare by identifying the unintended consequences of well-intentioned policies. A recent, well-publicized example of such a policy that backfired comes from the Securities and Exchange Commission's attempt to limit skyrocketing salaries of chief executive officers (CEOs) by requiring companies to disclose their compensation packages. Motivated by the expectation that transparency in salaries would create incentives for executives to demand lower levels of compensation, the intended effect of the policy was to stem the growth of CEO wages. However, the actual effect was to inflate them.[10] Rather than using the published figures to reign in CEO paychecks, boards of directors instead used the published salaries as reference points for evaluating their own compensation levels against that of their competitors. Similar to the findings in chapter 9, the dynamics of social comparison among firms led to a ratcheting-up effect. The highest salaries became the benchmarks for future offers, leading to further increases in CEO compensation.

This kind of unintended consequence can emerge whenever a policy that is designed to trigger a change in individual behavior instead engages a social feedback process. When this happens, the outcome can often be the opposite of what the policy was trying to achieve. Another striking example of this phenomenon comes from a study of an Israeli day-care center that instituted financial incentives (in the form of fines for parents) to reduce tardiness by parents picking up their children. The result of implementing these fines for tardiness was an immediate increase in the number of parents who were tardy. The reason for this unexpected outcome is that parents were initially responding to social and normative pressures to be on time. The introduction of financial incentives changed the behavior from a socially controlled activity into a financial transaction. Once this happened, it became normatively acceptable to show up late.[11]

In both cases, the failure of these deterrence policies came from their reliance on individual incentives to produce collective behavior change. Although individual incentives may work when people act in isolation, this approach to incentivizing behavior change does not account for the social feedback dynamics that underlie changes in group behavior. As a result, even well-intentioned individual-based policies can lead to collective outcomes that most people would find undesirable (such as a disregard for day-care policy), if not unethical (such as increasing CEO salaries).

The theoretical and experimental approach developed in this book may be of use in these situations. The studies presented in chapters 8 and 9 illustrate how researchers might use small-scale, experimentally designed policy tests to explore social feedback processes in realistic behavioral contexts. These kinds of tests can be used to offer new insight into the unanticipated outcomes that may arise from well-intentioned policies. The method of using web experiments to test policy ideas suggests a general strategy for anticipating the complex social dynamics that can emerge when individual incentives interact with social feedback. Beyond the goal of anticipating when policies might go astray, this approach may also offer the novel opportunity to develop policies that are specifically designed to *harness* the social dynamics of complexity, rather than being foiled by it.

APPENDIX B

Methods of Computational Social Science

The approach to computational social science used in this book is based on the idea of causality as "counterfactual intervention." On this view, causal insight comes from understanding whether things could have gone differently than they did, and from identifying whether there are general, reproducible mechanisms that control the trajectory of these alternative outcomes. This idea frames my approach to both theoretical and empirical research.

Importantly, this approach is not based on a prescriptive model of how one ought to do science. Rather, it is guided by a few simple principles that have been useful for steering my work toward a cumulative, collective effort to develop a stable foundation for scientific progress. The three principles that define my approach are counterfactuals, robustness, and replication.

1. *Counterfactuals*: testing what would have happened in situations that differ from actual events.
2. *Robustness*: testing the ability of a mechanism to produce consistent collective behaviors under varying assumptions about social structure and individual decision rules.
3. *Replication*: evaluating the empirical reproducibility of a social mechanism by studying collective dynamics across multiple independent populations.

I think that our best chance of gaining causal insight into how a social system operates—and, thereby, into how interventions might be used to change social outcomes—is to understand how things might have gone otherwise if the system had been designed differently, and to show that these alternative trajectories are robust under a wide variety of conditions. There are two main benefits of this approach. First, it offers a reliable foundation for basic science because it generates reproducible insights into the mechanisms that underlie collective behavior. Second, it creates a sound basis for public policy because it identifies a broad set of real-world circumstances in which specific social mechanisms can reasonably be expected to produce changes in group behavior.

Although there are many ways that the three principles of counterfactuals, robustness, and replication might be employed, my approach is to start with theory. Counterfactual models are useful for *identifying* the social mechanisms that can generate changes in collective behavior. They are also useful for *testing* the robustness of those mechanisms under a wide range of realistic conditions. My approach is always to start very abstractly, identifying the precise mechanism that governs a system's behavior, and then to incrementally increase the realism of the model. This has been a reliable way both of demonstrating the generality of a mechanism under various conditions, and of identifying the boundary conditions past which the identified mechanism no longer governs the system's behavior.

Both of these considerations—generality and boundary conditions—are important for moving theoretical research into the empirical domain. Together they provide guidance for finding empirical settings in which collective behaviors can be expected to be governed by a particular social mechanism. In other words, by first identifying the general range of empirical situations in which a social mechanism is expected to operate, it becomes easier to design empirical studies where theories can be tested. Importantly, this not only makes it possible to marshal support for a theory, but also makes the theory vulnerable to confrontation with conflicting evidence. This capacity to evaluate theory has two useful implications. First, if the predicted dynamics do indeed occur, we can confidently generalize the findings from the particular empirical setting where the study was conducted to other settings that fall within the boundary conditions of the model. Second, if the predicted dynamics do not occur, we are then confronted with convincing evidence that forces us to acknowledge that we need to revise our theory.

This last point is something that theoretical social science has been in search of for decades. Instead of theorizing in a vacuum, theories can now be tested and refined. In contrast to the simplistic logical positivist notion of verifying theories, the more exciting implication is that recalcitrant data can be used to motivate the development of new ideas, the discovery of new mechanisms, and the improvement of our approaches to theoretical modeling. Our theoretical models today are probably not as sophisticated as they will ultimately need to be to truly understand the governing dynamics of social behavior, but they are a start. And, hopefully, the ability to test theoretical models, using both observational and experimental data will offer an opportunity for a powerful cumulative dialectic between theory and data to emerge.

When it comes to conducting empirical research on collective behavior, I think that replication at the population level is essential. As discussed in chapter 4, the unit of observation for a collective social process is not the individual, but the population. Theoretical models typically study collective behavior by replicating trials at the population level (for instance, by averaging across multiple independent realizations of a given network configuration). Today, we are able to evaluate those theories using empirical data that offer the same level of resolution on group activity. This ability offers two important advantages over previous approaches to studying collective dynamics. First, and most simply, replication at the group level allows the dynamics of collective behavior to be identified with much greater precision than was possible previously, making it easier to evaluate causal theories of collective behavior. Second, it offers the exciting opportunity to discover new kinds of variation at the population level that would be impossible to detect without multiple, independent observations of the same collective process.

EXTERNAL VALIDITY

For the experimental approach used in this book, the question that is most commonly raised is about external validity. Can the conclusions drawn from the relatively pristine world of a controlled experiment be generalized to the "real world"? There are two concerns that are implicit in this question. The first, most obvious concern is whether an outcome that occurs within an experimental setting would also occur in more natural settings, once the noise and confounding factors that are excluded from an experimental study are allowed back in. Let's call this the problem of *validity*. The second question is whether the results that are found in one empirical setting will generalize to other settings. Let's call this the problem of *generality*.

Even if we can solve the problem of validity for an empirical study, the problem of generality will always remain. The data from any empirical setting are necessarily limited by the features of that setting. This is true for both observational and experimental data. Unfortunately, the problem of generality cannot be solved simply by collecting more data. It can only be addressed by identifying the theoretical mechanism that operates to produce an empirical finding and by demonstrating that this mechanism is also operating in other settings. Experiments may have an advantage here, because they are particularly useful for identifying whether a specific mechanism is in fact able to produce an empirical outcome. Moreover, experiments can also be replicated multiple times—in different settings with different subjects. In this regard, an experimental approach provides a good foundation for producing empirical evidence that offers support for generality.

This brings us back to the question of validity. How can we know that the empirical findings within an experimental setting will be applicable to a world filled with noise and confounding influences? This question is essential. My belief is that this question needs to be answered before the first data point is ever collected. In other words, before an experiment is ever conducted, the question of validity needs to be explicitly addressed. I have found that the best way to do this is through the robustness of the counterfactual model and the fidelity of the experimental design.

First, the robustness of a model shows that the theoretical mechanism of interest can be expected to generate consistent effects despite many variations in parameter values and the inclusion of confounding influences that can be expected to occur in the natural world. Robustness provides a foundation for establishing the validity of an experimental result. While it is impossible to empirically explore all of the possible (present and future) variations that can arise in the natural world, a lot of progress can be made computationally toward ensuring the validity and generality of an experimental study by first establishing the robustness of the mechanism that it is testing. The simpler and more abstract a model is, the easier it is to explore the variety of conditions under which a finding may be robust. This is because simple models have clearly identifiable mechanisms, making it possible to evaluate a wide range of empirically relevant parameter variations while still being able to identify whether the mechanism of interest is operative.

Second, while models benefit from abstractness, when it comes to experimental design, experiments benefit from fidelity to the natural world. The more that an experimental design embodies the natural situations in which a theoretical mechanism is believed to operate, the more likely it is to produce results that are externally valid. To start, I have found it helpful to identify a specific setting where the behavioral dynamics that we want to study are expected to emerge. If such a setting cannot be identified, then the experiment is not likely to have much validity. Indeed, it is not clear what we would be studying in that case.

Once a setting is identified, I have found that a good way to ensure the validity of a study is to set up an experiment within that very setting. This can be done by partnering with an existing social environment or by creating a new one. Either way, the validity of an experiment is markedly improved by studying the behavior of interest within a context where it naturally occurs. By studying behavioral dynamics in natural social settings, the validity of the findings is made self-evident. In this sense, designing embodied experiments, particularly on the Internet, bears a strong resemblance to field experiments. If we can experimentally study people in natural habitats, surrounded by natural influences, then we can identify how theoretical mechanisms can be used to control the dynamics of human behavior in the natural world.

Once the validity of a study is established within a given setting, the broader problem of external validity then reverts back to the question of generality. As discussed above, this can then be addressed through robustness and replication.

OBSERVATIONAL DATA

To conclude this methodological appendix, it may be useful to contrast my approach with a different kind of guiding principle that is often used to steer contemporary empirical work in computational social science, namely prediction. Powerful new computational techniques, such as machine learning, are increasingly being applied to massive online data to derive new predictive insights. These data-driven approaches have allowed scientists to reveal previously unseen correlations at unprecedented scales.

Broadly conceived, data-driven approaches such as machine learning fall within the purview of observational research. Observational methods have long had an important symbiotic relationship with theoretical and experimental methods in social science. All three ways of studying the social world—theoretical models, experimental tests, and observational exploration—can, and do, work well together to advance the cause of scientific knowledge.

If there is any problem with big data, it comes from the fact that at a massive scale, it is hard to know whether the regularities that emerge are simply an effect of the fact that we do not yet know how to properly evaluate significant effects at very large scales or whether there are actually new kinds of structures that emerge at these scales that we can detect only with massive data sets. I do not see any advantage in turning a blind eye to these approaches but instead have found it useful try to integrate their insights into computational simulations and experimental designs as a means of understanding and replicating their results. There are many fascinating new domains to be explored, and we should certainly explore them—if for no other reason than we have no idea what kinds of new methodological and substantive insights may arise.

If I were to caution against anything, it would be the movement of science in any one methodological direction without concomitant movement in the other two. Today, observational research on big data has grown so quickly that it has threatened to dwarf progress in theoretical and experimental social science. However, it is useful to note that two decades ago an analogous situation emerged when theoretical models were proliferating, but there were no available data for testing them. It was the same kind of problem—one method of social research was going so far ahead of the others that there was no way of knowing how important or relevant any of the findings were since none of them could be tested. Today, the pendulum has swung in the other direction, and now it is data that are exploding. Yet, the guiding idea remains the same. All three approaches—theory, experiment, and observation—need to grow in tandem,[1] or else we run the risk of generating lots of competing results without having any way of arbitrating between them.

APPENDIX C

Technical Appendix for Models

This technical appendix provides a brief summary for each of the models that appears in this book, arranged by chapter. The material in this appendix is derived from the referenced publications, which provide more detailed information for the advanced reader.

CHAPTER 2*
Small-world network model

The small-world network model uses a random rewiring procedure based on the one developed by Duncan Watts and Steven Strogatz,[1] in which randomly selected ties in the spatial network are broken and then reattached to randomly selected members of the population, creating "shortcuts" across the lattice. The rewiring model uses the parameter q $(0 \leq q \leq 1)$ to determine the probability that ties will be randomly rewired. For $q = 0$, no ties are rewired and the network is a regular lattice with uniform neighborhoods, while for $q = 1$, every tie is rewired, making the social network into a random graph. As the parameter q increases, there are more weak ties in the social network, which reduces local structure and transforms the social topology into a small world network.

Mark Newman and Duncan Watts showed that adding ties to a regular lattice is a more robust method of network permutation than the Watts and Strogatz rewiring method because it eliminates the possibility of multiple components forming at high levels of randomization.[2] However, the Newman and Watts method simultaneously increases the network density while also changing the structure of the topology. Additionally, both the Newman and Watts tie-addition algorithm and the Watts and Strogatz rewiring algorithm create degree heterogeneity as a result of randomization, which is not present in the lattice. Sergei

* From Centola and Macy, "Complex Contagions" and Centola, "Homophily, Networks and Critical Mass."

Maslov and Kim Sneppen address these problems by proposing a pair-wise permutation rewiring method, which prevents the network from breaking into multiple components while also keeping the network at a constant density (like the Watts and Strogatz rewiring algorithm) and preserving a constant degree distribution at all levels of randomization.[3] The Maslov and Sneppen rewiring procedure is used here. For all rewiring simulations (chapters 2 and 3) and rewiring experiments (chapter 4), and at all levels of randomization, networks are connected in a single component with a fixed degree distribution, constant size, and constant density.

Simple-contagion diffusion model

A "threshold" is the number of activated contacts required to activate a target individual. A threshold t is represented as a fraction $t = a/z$, where a is the number of activated nodes and z is the number of neighbors. The simple-contagion model of diffusion assumes that $t = 1/z$.

In this model, diffusion is initiated by exogenously activated "seed nodes." Every round of the model iterates through all agents in random order. In each round, each agent evaluates whether or not to become activated based on whether any of their contacts are activated. If they have contact with an activated agent, they become activated. The model iterates until there are no further changes in activation.

CHAPTER 3*

Complex-contagion diffusion model

From above, a threshold t is represented as a fraction $t = a/z$, where a is the number of activated nodes and z is the number of neighbors. The notation used here distinguishes,[4] for example, between $t = 1/8$ and $t = 6/48$. Both thresholds require an identical proportion of activated neighbors, but the former is a simple contagion and the latter is complex. One of the main findings of this study is that there is a qualitative difference between $a = 1$ and $a > 1$, even when the proportions are identical. The complex-contagion model of diffusion assumes that $a > 1$.

Thresholds can be expressed in two ways—as the *number*[5] or the *fraction*[6] of neighbors that need to be activated. The conceptual distinction reflects an underlying (and often hidden) assumption about the influence of non-adopters. Fractional thresholds model contagions in which

---

* From Centola and Macy, "Complex Contagions."

both adopters and non-adopters exert influence, but in opposite directions.

As above, diffusion is initiated by exogenously activated seed nodes. Every round of the model iterates through all agents in random order. In each round, each agent evaluates whether or not to become activated based on whether a sufficient number of their contacts are activated to trigger their threshold. If they have contact with a sufficient number of activated agents to trigger their threshold, they become activated. The model iterates until there are no further changes in activation.

Bridge width

Figure C.1 illustrates the width of the bridge between two neighborhoods (I and L) on a ring lattice with $z=4$. Neighborhood I is the ego network containing focal node i and all of i's neighbors $[g,k]$ (black and gray/black nodes). Neighborhood L contains $[j,n]$ (gray and gray/black nodes), where $[l,n] \notin I$. These two neighborhoods have two common members (gray/black nodes). C_{IL} is the set of all common members of both I and L, hence $C_{IL}=[j,k]$. The disjoint set D_{IL} contains the remaining members of L that are not in I, or $D_{IL}=[l,n]$. A bridge from I to L is then the set of ties between C_{IL} and D_{IL}, where the width of the bridge, W_{IL}, is the size of this set. In figure C.1, the bridge consists of the three ties jl, kl, and km (shown as bold lines), making $W_{IL}=3$.

The overlap between the neighborhoods is the number of nodes in C_{IL} (i.e., $|C_{IL}|$). In figure C.1, the neighborhoods I and L have the maximum possible overlap. Neighborhood M containing $[k,o]$ is one step farther from I, so only node k is shared between them ($|C_{IM}| = 1$), and there is only a single tie (km) between I and M, making the width of the bridge $W_{IM}=1$.

More generally, on a ring lattice of degree z, $0 \le |C| \le z/2$. The widest bridge on the ring is limited by the maximum overlap $|C_{max}| = z/2$. There will be $z/2$ ties from I to the member of L closest to I, $z/2-1$ ties to the next closest member of L, and so on, giving

$$W_{max}=z/2+(z/2-1)+(z/2-2)+\cdots+1 \tag{1}$$

$$W_{max}=z(z+2)/8 \tag{2}$$

The bridge from I to L is therefore the maximum possible width for $z = 4$, giving $W_{max}=3$.

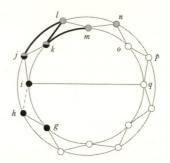

Figure C.1 Bridge Width between Neighborhoods on a Lattice

The width of the bridge between neighborhoods determines the upper bound on the threshold at which a contagion can pass. In figure C.1, $W_{IL} = 3$, which imposes an upper bound of $a = 2$. So long as $a \leq 2$, the two ties from j and k will be sufficient to activate l, and l and k can then activate m, and so on.

Conversely, thresholds determine the *critical width* (W_c) of the bridges, defined as the minimum number of nonredundant ties required for a contagion to propagate from an activated to an unactivated neighborhood.[7] For simple contagions, $W_c = 1$, regardless of network topology. On a ring lattice, for minimally complex contagions ($a = 2$), $W_c = 3$. For example, in figure C.1, the three ties between C_{IL} and D_{IL} (two to activate l and one to activate m once l is active) allow the contagion to spread from I to L.

More generally,

$$W_c = a + (a-1) + (a-2) + \cdots + 1 \tag{3}$$

$$W_c = a(a+1)/2, \tag{4}$$

giving $W_c = 3$ as the critical width for a minimally complex contagion ($a = 2$). A contagion can propagate around the ring so long as $W_c \leq W_{max}$.

The critical width also determines the minimum number of ties that need to be rewired to create a shortcut across the ring. Figure C.1 shows how a single random tie is sufficient to increase the rate of propagation of a simple contagion. Suppose we were to randomly select tie ih to be randomly replaced with tie iq. For a simple contagion ($\tau = 1/z$), the rewiring of the ih tie creates a shortcut across the ring that reduces the time required for a cascade to reach all the nodes. The deleted tie from h to i (indicated by the broken line) does not hinder the spread of a simple contagion around the ring since the critical width for $a = 1$ is $W_c = 1$, and

$W_{\max}=3$ provides sufficient redundancy to support local propagation even with the ih tie removed.

However, the need for bridges that are wider than a single tie implies a qualitative change in propagation dynamics as a increases above one. Figure C.2 shows how an increment in the threshold from $\tau=1/z$ to $\tau=2/z$ triples the critical width of the bridge required to create a short-cut, from one tie to three. Node j is the focal node of the seed neighborhood J in which j and all four of j's neighbors are activated (indicated by solid black and gray/black nodes). Node s is the focal node of an unacti-vated neighborhood S (shown in gray and gray/black). For a minimally complex contagion ($\tau = 2/z$), $W_c=3$, which means that three local ties must be rewired to create a bridge across the ring (indicated by the three bold lines). The two ties from i and k are sufficient to activate s, and the third tie from i to q is sufficient to activate q, given the tie from s to q.

Even for this minimally complex contagion on this very small ring (with only 16 nodes), the probability that three random ties will form a bridge is close to zero. We can expect to need many more random ties before the first bridge is formed across the ring, and that number in-creases exponentially as N increases. That is because the number of configurations in which all three random ties are between the same two neighborhoods is a very small fraction of the total number of possible configurations.[8] Further, as a increases, there is an exponential increase in the number of ties required to form a bridge, further reducing the prob-ability of bridge formation.

An obvious solution to the need for wider bridges is simply to re-wire more ties, thereby ensuring that shortcuts across the network will eventually form. However, the problem with extensive rewiring is the potential to erode the existing bridges that allow the contagion to spread locally. Figure C.2 shows how this happens. The deleted tie from h to i (indicated by the broken line) would not hinder the spread of a simple contagion. However, even for a minimally complex conta-gion, the three deleted ties (broken lines) reduce the width of the bridges on either side of i to less than $W_c=3$, preventing the contagion from spreading locally. The contagion can still spread out in both di-rections from s, but the JS bridge will not increase the rate of propaga-tion. Moreover, the probability that three random ties will form a bridge (like the one illustrated in figure C.2) is close to zero, while the probability that three deleted ties will break the ring and block the contagion is close to one.

Simply put, the effect of rewiring depends on whether random ties are more likely to form bridges across the ring than to break bridges

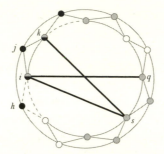

Figure C.2 Critical Bridge Width for a Complex Contagion

along the ring. This in turn depends on the magnitude of W_{max} relative to W_c. If $W_c = W_{max}$, there are no redundant ties in the bridge, and every tie that is removed creates a break along the ring. If $W_c < W_{max}$, some bridge ties may be redundant, and if they were to be rewired to form a new bridge, the rate of propagation would increase.

W_{max} increases exponentially with z while W_c increases exponentially with a. Holding a constant, an increase in z means a smaller fraction of neighbors need to be activated in order for a node to become active. It also means $W_c \ll W_{max}$, hence greater redundancy of bridge ties. As redundancy increases, the network becomes more efficient if some of the redundant ties are randomly rewired to create new bridges.

More generally, the redundancy, R, refers to the proportion of ties in a bridge that can be rewired without breaking the ring, or

$$R = (W_{max} - W_c) / W_{max} \tag{5}$$

$$R = 1 - [4a(a+1) / z(z+2)] \tag{6}$$

Equation 6 shows that if $a > z/2$ then $R < 0$, which means that the bridges will be too narrow for propagation. Thus, contagions cannot propagate on a ring lattice of any degree if $\tau > 0.5$ (Morris 2000). If $\tau = 0.5$, $R = 0$. This means that contagions can now pass, but there is no redundancy (as in figure C.2). The first tie that is randomized will break the ring.[9]

As R increases, more ties can be rewired without creating breaks along the ring, allowing complex contagions to benefit from randomization, just as simple contagions do. However, there is an important difference. For simple contagions, a connected network can never be too randomized. That is not true for complex contagions. Eventually, randomization will reach a critical upper limit (given by R) above which even minimally complex contagions can no longer propagate. For example, on a ring lattice with $z = 10$, $W_{max} = 15$ and $R = .75$. For a minimally complex contagion ($a = 2$ and $W_c = 3$), the high level of redundancy indicates that limited randomization could allow faster propagation than on the unperturbed ring. The unperturbed lattice consists of a chain of bridges that are linked to one another around the ring. As long as randomization does not create a break along this chain, rewiring redundant ties to create a shortcut will allow the contagion to jump across the network and fan out from multiple locations.

However, if randomization rewires more than R of the ties in an existing bridge, the chain will be cut. Although this rewiring may also create new bridges, the advantage of these shortcuts depends on the existence of other bridges to which the shortcut is linked. Bridges that are randomly created as the ring is perturbed are only useful to the extent that they are linked to other bridges. Otherwise the random rewiring creates a bridge to nowhere. As the links of the chain become increasingly disconnected, the probability increases that a random bridge will lead into a cul de sac.

The analysis of the ring lattice reveals two qualitative differences between simple and complex contagions:

1. While a single random tie is sufficient to promote the spread of simple contagions, complex contagions require more rewiring in order to benefit from randomization. The number of ties that need to be randomly rewired increases exponentially with the number required to form a bridge (W_c), and the number of ties needed to form a bridge in turn increases exponentially with the required number of activated neighbors (a).

2. As the ring becomes increasingly randomized, the width of the bridges that make up the lattice structure may be eroded below the critical width required for the contagion to spread. Simple contagions can propagate on a connected network even if every tie is random, and the rate of propagation increases monotonically with the proportion of random ties. In contrast, there is a critical upper limit of randomization above which complex contagions cannot propagate. As thresholds increase, this critical value decreases.

These conclusions for a one-dimensional lattice do not necessarily generalize to higher dimensional structures, which provide detours around local ties that have been deleted. Since higher dimensional

CLUSTERED   **REWIRED**

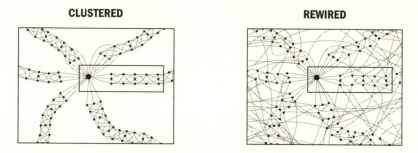

Figure C.3 Clustered and Rewired Scale-Free Networks (inset shown in detail in chapter 3)

structures lack the analytical simplicity of the ring lattice, computational models were used to confirm and extend the analysis of the ring lattice. The results on higher dimensional networks reveal three principal differences between simple and complex contagions in more complex geometries:

1. Complex contagions fail to benefit from low levels of randomization, as shown by an initial failure of propagation rates to improve as q increases above zero.
2. Increasing q has a non-monotonic effect on complex contagions, exhibiting a U-shaped effect, in which randomization starts to help, but ultimately impedes propagation.
3. As q exceeds a critical upper limit, complex contagions entirely fail to propagate.

In more complex networks with larger neighborhoods (i.e., greater redundancy) small levels of randomization can promote the spread of complex contagions so long as the randomization is not too great and the thresholds are not too large. This U-shaped effect of randomization is an important extension of the small world principle. Watts and Strogatz discovered that simple contagions could spread as fast on a highly clustered small world network as on a more randomized topology. This was important because social networks tend to be highly clustered and rarely (if ever) random. This "small world effect" becomes more pronounced for thresholds with low levels of complexity; that is, just above the level of simple contagions. In networks with greater density (i.e., more local redundancy), the potential for small amounts of rewiring to form wide bridges randomly, while local bridges remain intact, enables complex contagions with relatively low thresholds to spread *faster* on a highly clustered small world network than on either a network that is more random or one that is more clustered. However, as thresholds get higher, this small world effect disappears entirely.

Degree heterogeneity

Degree heterogeneity was tested using a scale-free degree distribution with $N=40,000$ and slope parameter $\gamma=2.3$, such that most nodes have a relatively low degree ($z<5$), and only a few have a very high degree ($z>100$). As noted above, the rewiring procedure reduces clustering through randomization without altering the degree of any node. Thus, it is possible to isolate the effects of randomization while preserving the scale-free degree distribution, as shown in figure C.3 (inset shown in detail in chapter 3).

For absolute thresholds, all nodes required the same number of activated neighbors (a), but since the degree varied, so too did the necessary proportion of activated neighbors. The very low degree in most nodes precluded the spread of contagions with $a>2$, even with $q=0$. However, for thresholds of $2/z$, the results were similar to those for the regular lattice, except that the drop off in cascade frequency is noticeably more gradual. This happens because the activation of large neighborhoods ($z>100$) occasionally allows cascades to spread through part of the network. However, even when an activated neighborhood is very large, the bridges between peripheral neighborhoods must remain intact in order for complex contagions to spread. The low degree in most neighborhoods means that there are very few, if any, redundant ties between neighborhoods, making bridges especially vulnerable to randomization. Thus, a scale-free network can be even more sensitive to perturbation than the regular lattices. For example, with $\tau=2/z$, minimally complex contagions were almost entirely inhibited above $q=.001$ (compared to $q\approx.1$ for a regular two-dimensional lattice).

When thresholds are fractional, degree heterogeneity can exacerbate the effects of randomization by increasing the exposure of hubs to large numbers of unactivated nodes. As degree becomes more skewed, the odds become much higher that a peripheral node will be randomly chosen as the seed. This might seem to make it more likely that a hub will become activated because of its greater access to the network. However, it is very difficult for a single peripheral node to activate a hub when all the other peripherals are exerting countervailing influence. Further, even if a hub is already activated, the hub still cannot activate peripherals who require social affirmation or reinforcement from others. Complex contagions can spread on hub-and-spoke structures only in the special case that hubs can compel activation of the peripheral nodes without reinforcement. Otherwise, the diffusion of complex contagions requires wide bridges, even on networks with skewed degree distributions.

The same reasoning also applies to rewiring procedures that increase network density.

Status

Status differences were created by assigning a few random nodes the ability to activate their neighbors without the need for social affirmation or reinforcement from additional sources. This enhanced influence might reflect higher social prestige, power, wealth, persuasiveness, etc. For convenience, we will refer to these as *high-status nodes*.

If there are sufficient numbers of high-status nodes to activate the remainder of the population in one step, the problem reduces to that of a simple contagion. The interesting case is one in which a few high-status nodes must trigger a cascade in order to activate the population. N/z of the nodes were randomly assigned to be high status (e.g., 5,000 high-status nodes in a population of 40,000). On average, this means that every neighborhood in the network can now be expected to have one high-status member. High-status nodes were given sufficient influence, t, to activate all of their neighbors (i.e., $t \geq a$ for $\tau = a/z$). In order not to conflate the effects of influence heterogeneity with an increase in mean influence (equivalent to a reduction in the average threshold), mean influence was held constant by reducing the status of all other nodes sufficiently to compensate for doubling the influence of a few "opinion leaders."

Results show that introducing a small fraction of high-status nodes does not mitigate the need for wide bridges. Under the assumption that the distribution of status is highly unequal, there is no improvement in the propagation of complex contagions as p increases.

To see why, suppose the high-status nodes are sufficiently influential to activate all their Moore neighbors on a network with $z = 48$. The problem is what happens next. Assuming $\tau = 2/z$ and influence homogeneity, an activated node would need only one other activated node to activate a common neighbor. However, with influence heterogeneity (and holding mean influence constant), two activated low-status nodes no longer have combined influence sufficient to activate a common neighbor with threshold $2/z$. Now three low-status nodes must be activated in order to extend the contagion beyond the reach of their high-status activated neighbor. This increases the width of the bridge needed to propagate the contagion.

Threshold heterogeneity

The effects of threshold heterogeneity were considered in a model that is otherwise identical to that the original complex contagions model, but with a Gaussian distribution of thresholds. The primary finding is that cascade times and frequencies behave much as they do for fixed thresholds. Initial perturbations to the network have no effect on cascade dynamics. As q increases, propagation times and cascade frequencies exhibit the same characteristic patterns that was observed for fixed thresholds.

The effects of heterogeneity were investigated within nodes as well as between nodes. Within-node heterogeneity relaxes the assumption that thresholds are stationary by allowing thresholds to change over time, which was implemented by randomly reassigning thresholds after each round of decision-making (that is, after all nodes had been given a chance to become activated). Thresholds were assigned using the same Gaussian distribution as with stationary threshold heterogeneity. The results are similar to what we observed with stationary thresholds.

Stochastic thresholds, in which nodes are activated with a probability that increases with the number of activated nodes in the neighborhood, were also tested. Using the cumulative logistic function, nodes have a 50% chance of activation when the proportion τ of the neighborhood is activated. Below τ, the probability approaches zero as a convex function of the number of active neighbors, and above τ the probability approaches one as a concave function. In infinite time, stochastic thresholds have a nonzero probability of activating the entire population. However, these results are for finite timescales comparable to those used for deterministic thresholds. The results for stochastic thresholds were similar to those for deterministic thresholds—random rewiring slowed complex contagions and ultimately prevented them from spreading. This result is due to the fact that as thresholds increase, the probability that an individual will stochastically "turn off" also increases, making the diffusion of complex contagions more difficult when random rewiring reduces pathways of local reinforcement.

Strength and weakness of ties

Regular unperturbed ties were given a weight of 1 and random ties were given a weight of .5. This 2:1 ratio is convenient in that it parallels the distinction between simple and minimally complex contagions. It means that a single close friend is now sufficient to activate a neighbor with a threshold of $1/z$, but it will take two acquaintances. As expected, the effects of randomization for simple contagions resembled what was previously observed for minimally complex contagions. In addition, when this procedure was repeated with heterogeneous thresholds and $z=48$, the inhibitory effects of long ties were found even for populations in which $\tau = 2/z$ (see below). More generally, the weaker the ties to acquaintances compared to friends, the wider must be the bridges connecting otherwise distant neighborhoods.

CHAPTER 6
Intervention seeding model

For every agent, the threshold t is represented as a fixed fraction of the neighborhood. This means that some agents require only one neighbor to become activated; however, most require reinforcement from several neighbors. In Networks A and B, the threshold $t=0.4$. Network A has a population size of 1,082, an average degree of 6, and an average clustering of 0.171 and consists of one component. Network B has a population size of 1,525, an average degree of 5.13, and an average clustering of 0.143 and consists of one component. In Network C, $t=0.6$. Network C has a population size of 2,033, an average degree of 5.03, and an average local clustering of 0.69 and consists of one component. Thresholds for adoption are deterministic.

In the random seeding simulations, the population is seeded by selecting a fixed percentage of the population (10% in Networks A and B, and 15% in Network C) at random and exogenously activating them as seed nodes. In the clustered seeding simulations, the population is seeded by randomly selecting individual nodes to become focal nodes of seed neighborhoods. The randomly selected individual and all of their neighbors are exogenously activated. This procedure is repeated until the same fixed percentage of the population is activated as in the corresponding random seeding simulations, producing a seed population equivalent to the one used in the corresponding random seeding procedure.

In each round, the model iterates through all agents in the population in random order. Each agent evaluates whether or not to become activated based on whether enough of their contacts are activated. In every case, the model iterates for five rounds, and then the seeds become susceptible

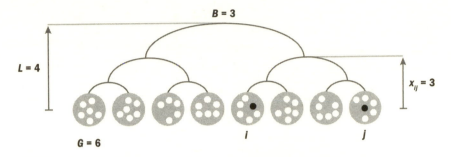

Figure C.4 Formal Structure of Social Identities in Network Formation Model

to social influence. Starting at round six, seeds require their threshold *t* to be triggered in order to stay activated. The choice of five rounds is arbitrary. If the model iterates for fewer rounds before seeds become vulnerable to social influence, diffusion with clustered seeding is not affected; however, diffusion with random seeding does not spread as far. Once seeds are vulnerable to social influence, if there are insufficient active neighbors to activate a seed, the seed becomes unactivated. Similarly, for all agents in the model, if there are insufficient activated neighbors to keep triggering an activated agent, the agent becomes unactivated. The model iterates until there are no further changes in activation.

Innovation diffusion model

This discussion is based on the models developed by Glenn Ellison and H. Peyton Young.[10] Agents play a pairwise coordination game with their neighbors. They base their decision whether to choose A or B on the expected payoff for both options. Agents have a fixed memory size, *m*, and they select the option with highest expected payoff given their history of past interactions.

CHAPTER 7*

Identity-based network formation model

The model of social network formation is based on the premise that people in social networks not only have social ties, but they also have social identities, which define their proximity or distance from others

* From Centola, "Social Origins of Networks"

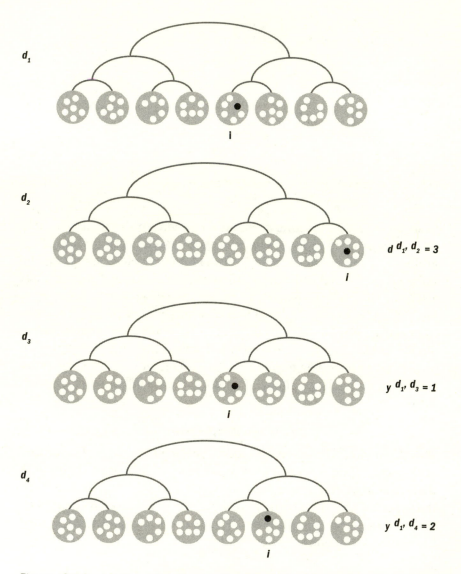

Figure C.5 Social Consolidation as Correlated Position across Several Dimensions of Social Life

within a dimension of social life. The approach used here follows from five contentions about social networks:

1. Individuals' social identities are defined by their association with, and participation in, social groups.

2. Each dimension of social life can be partitioned into groups using a hierarchical representation, as shown in figure C.4. This representation of a social dimension is not the actual network but rather a cognitive construct for measuring social distance between individuals.[11] As in figure C.4, this partitioning ends with specialized subgroups that are relatively small and socially proximate. The parameter G refers to the number of people in each subgroup. The social distance between individuals i and j, x_{ij}, within a dimension of social life is defined as their closest partition level. $x_{ij} = 1$ if i and j belong to the same group, $x_{ij} = 2$ if i and j are both under the next highest partition, etc. As shown in figure C.4, a hierarchy is fully defined by the number of levels of partitioning L and the branching ratio B. The number of groups, or social positions, in a dimension is given by B^{L-1}.

3. The actual social network is created based on the principle that group memberships are the primary basis for social interaction and therefore the formation of social ties. The probability that a social tie will form between individuals i and j increases with their social proximity. This is modeled by choosing an individual i at random, and a distance x with probability $p(x) = ce^{-\alpha x}$, where α is a tunable parameter that controls homophily, and c is a normalizing constant. A node j is then chosen randomly from among all nodes at distance x from i. This process is repeated until a network is constructed in which all individuals have an average number of friends, Z. When homophily is high, $e^{-\alpha} \ll 1$, individuals will be connected only to people within their immediate subgroup ($x_{ij} = 1$, for all i and j who have network ties to one another). By contrast, when there is no homophily, $e^{-\alpha} = B$, ties are equally likely to form at all distances.

4. There are multiple dimensions of social life. The parameter $D \geq 1$ determines the number of dimensions. As shown in figure C.5, each dimension is represented as its own independent hierarchy. Each individual is randomly assigned to a position in dimension h_1. The correlation between an individual's social positions across dimensions (i.e., social consolidation) is modeled by assigning an individual's social positions in h_2–h_H at distance y from her position in h_1 with the probability $p(y) = ce^{-\beta y}$, where β is a tunable social consolidation parameter and c is a

normalizing constant. When social consolidation is very high, $e^{-\beta} \ll 1$, individuals will be located in the same subgroup, or social position, across all dimensions (i.e., $y^{h_1 h_2} = y^{h_1 h_3} = y^{h_1 h_4} = 1$). By contrast, when there is no consolidation, $e^{-\beta} = B$, people are equally likely to be located in any social position, making social positions uncorrelated across dimensions.

5. Social distance, unlike Euclidean space, is not transitive. Two people i and j may have high social similarity in dimension h_1, while i may be close to k in dimension h_2. But, this does not imply that j and k are close to each other in any dimension. The ultrametric distance used here to measure the social distance between people preserves this intransitivity of social relations.

Acknowledgments

This is a book about networks, so it is only fitting that it would never have come into being without the vast network of scholars who comprise the intersecting fields of sociology, complex systems, health research, data science, and network science. Among the many people that I am eager to thank, I first want to acknowledge my indebtedness to my PhD adviser, Michael Macy, who encouraged me to keep following the thread of these ideas as I began working on them, and gave me invaluable guidance as we worked together to publish the initial papers on this project. I am grateful for his intellectual support and rigorous engagement throughout my many years thinking through these topics. I also want to acknowledge Mark Granovetter and Duncan Watts, who have both spent considerable time giving me advice and suggestions on many parts of this project over a decade of conversations. If the contributions herein provide any useful advance for the study of diffusion, it is only because of the remarkable clarity of their insights, upon which this work attempts to build.

Of the many institutions that have generously supported this work, the closest to my heart is the Annenberg School for Communication at the University of Pennsylvania. It has provided me with not only the time and support to undertake the writing of this book but also a superb research community that has offered me the unexpected pleasure of being immersed in a culture of book writing. My colleagues at Annenberg have kept me excited and optimistic about this book throughout the journey of writing it. I want to make particular note of the valuable conversations I have had with Kathleen Hall Jamieson, Joe Cappella, Joe Turrow, Diana Mutz, Guobin Yang, Marwan Kraidy, John Jackson, John Jemmott, Vincent Pickard, Sharrona Pearl, and Barbie Zelizer about this project. Additionally, I would be remiss if I did not make special mention of my colleague, and dean, Michael Delli Carpini, whose uncompromising leadership, and striking perspicacity in managing the well-being of the faculty, has given us all an environment in which we can easily balance the demands of scholarship with our investments in teaching and our active participation in Annenberg's strong culture of civic engagement and public policy.

I am also deeply grateful for the guidance I received from the members of my PhD committee, including Peter Bearman and Doug Heckathorn, both of whom encouraged me to find connections between this emerging theory of diffusion and the practice of health policy, and Steve Strogatz, who encouraged me to adopt an approach to my research that would make it accessible to a much broader audience than I had initially intended.

I owe a tremendous debt of gratitude to Harvard University and the Robert Wood Johnson Foundation for their unwavering support of this project. It is fair to say that the majority of work reported in this book would have never been started without the Scholars in Health Policy Research program and the early mentorship that I received from Nicholas Christakis, who dedicated many hours to discussing these ideas with me, and who encouraged me to find the new approaches to empirical research that would ultimately be decisive for putting me onto my current path. Invaluable guidance also came from Gary King, Joseph Newhouse, and Kathy Swartz, as well as the members of the National Program Committee, Lori Melichar and Alan Cohen, all of whom have been faithful supporters of this work. Particular thanks must also to go Graham Colditz for guiding my initial leap into the world of health policy practice.

I am also indebted to MIT for generously providing me with additional award funding for this research, as well as giving me many years of support to pursue the experimental studies presented here. My colleagues there—Ray Reagans, Ezra Zuckerman, John Sterman, Nelson Repenning, and Roberto Fernandez—dedicated untold hours to discussing these studies with me and offering insightful suggestions that helped to improve the ideas in this book. I must also gratefully acknowledge Paul DiMaggio and Karen Cook, who hosted me during my first sabbatical year, respectively, at Princeton University's Center for the Study of Social Organization during the autumn term, and at Stanford University's Institute for Research in the Social Sciences in the winter/spring term, the latter allowing me to escape the East Coast winter and continue these experimental studies while enjoying the rolling hills above the Stanford campus. These experiments also would not have been possible without the generous support of a Complex Systems Grant from the James S. McDonnell Foundation. I have deep admiration for the McDonnell Foundation and its vision of funding quite unorthodox basic research in the complexity sciences—without which funding most of the work in this book would never have left my head.

This book has also benefitted far more than it is possible to acknowledge here from my year at the Center for Advanced Study in the Behavioral Sciences at Stanford University. The intimidating library of CASBS classics that greets arriving fellows stands as a constant reminder of the great books that have been written there over the years, to which we can aspire, if not achieve. Amid all of the important discussions that I had during that year, a few conversations were particularly impactful on this book. Specifically, I want to acknowledge discussions with my colleagues Margaret Levi, Robert Gibbons, Jennan Ismael, Richard Leo, Massimo Tavoni, Michael Chwe, Valentina Bosetti, Mary Dudziak, David Yeager, and most of all, Paul Starr, whose influence on my thinking continues to inform my theoretical ideas and empirical aspirations to this day.

Additionally, my sincere gratitude goes to all of the generous colleagues who spent time reading and commenting on various sections of this book. I am particularly grateful for the efforts of my friend and colleague Arnout van de Rijt, who has been productively discussing these ideas with me for years and has thoughtfully engaged with many parts of this book that required several stages of revision (as well as engaging with the chapters that he ultimately, and very helpfully, convinced me to exclude). I am also deeply grateful for the innumerable suggestions on various parts of this manuscript that came from H. Peyton Young, Urmimala Sarkar, Arline Geronimus, Robert Gross, Sarah Wood, Paul DiMaggio, Neil Fligstein, Brooke West, Emily Erikson, and Mario Small, without whose scholarly insights the rudimentary ideas that I started out with would never have been sufficiently developed to meet the light of day.

Other insights have come in the form of contributions from my former student, Devon Brackbill, who offered excellent editorial suggestions and revisions to this book, and from the talented artist Brittany Bennett, who painstakingly worked with me to design every image in the main text of this book. Soojong Kim provided valuable help with the simulations and figures for chapter 6, and several members of the Network Dynamics Group, including Jingwen Zhang, Joshua Becker, Natalie Herbert, Sijia Yang, and Douglas Guilbeault, participated in the research discussed in chapters 5 and 9. I must also gratefully acknowledge the support of the National Institutes of Health, for award number P20CA095856, and the National Science Foundation, for award number SES-0432917.

For this kind of book, it is impossible to overstate the importance of a good editor. Elizabeth Knoll and Eric Swartz both made important contributions during the early stages of my thinking on this project. However, this book came into its present form in the remarkably talented hands of Meagan Levinson. I will always be enormously grateful for the thoughtfulness and attention she has brought to this project, which has undoubtedly made this a much better book. I must also thank PUP's extraordinary editorial staff, in particular Gail Schmitt and Debbie Tegarden, for their peerless and tireless efforts on this project.

Finally, my family and friends deserve the lion's share of my gratitude for enduring my many years' obsession with these topics and for their continual inquiries into how these ideas might be applied to the real world, as opposed to the abstract world that I often find myself contemplating. Over the course of completing the studies presented in this book, I endured two long and difficult hospitalizations in 2010–11 and 2011–12, both of which required many months of recovery. This book would never have been completed without the people who got me back on my feet. Thank you to my family and friends for your unceasing support, and consummate good cheer.

On this point, the position of honor is reserved for my wife, Susana. The writing of this manuscript has only been possible because of your kindness, generosity, and loving encouragement.

Notes

PREFACE

1. Damon Centola and Michael Macy, "Complex Contagions and the Weakness of Long Ties," *American Journal of Sociology* 113, no. 3 (2007): 702–734.

2. Damon Centola, "The Spread of Behavior in an Online Social Network Experiment," *Science* 329, no. 5996 (2010): 1194–1197.

CHAPTER 1. INTRODUCTION

1. Carl Haub, "Did South Korea's Population Policy Work Too Well?," Population Reference Bureau, 2010.

2. Icek Ajzen, "The Theory of Planned Behavior," *Organizational Behavior and Human Decision Processes* 50, no. 2 (1991): 179–211; Icek Ajzen and Martin Fishbein, *Understanding Attitudes and Predicting Social Behaviour* (Englewood Cliffs, NJ: Prentice-Hall, 1980); John T. Cacioppo et al., "Central and Peripheral Routes to Persuasion: An Individual Difference Perspective," *Journal of Personality and Social Psychology* 51, no. 5 (1986): 1032–1043; A. Bankole, G. Rodríguez, and C. F. Westoff, "Mass Media Messages and Reproductive Behaviour in Nigeria," *Journal of Biosocial Science* 28, no. 2 (1996): 227–239; Sarah N. Keller and Jane D. Brown, "Media Interventions to Promote Responsible Sexual Behavior," *Journal of Sex Research* 39, no. 1 (2002): 67–72; Everett M. Rogers and D. Lawrence Kincaid, *Communication Networks: Toward a New Paradigm for Research.* (New York: Free Press, 1981); Robert Hornik, "Channeling Effectiveness in Development Communication Programs," in *Public Communication Campaigns*, ed. R. Rice and C. Atkins (Newbury Park, CA: Sage, 1989), 309–330; Thomas W. Valente, "Mass-Media-Generated Interpersonal Communication as Sources of Information about Family Planning," *Journal of Health Communication* 1, no. 3 (1996): 247–266; Thomas W. Valente, *Social Networks and Health: Models, Methods, and Applications* (Oxford University Press, 2010); Thomas W. Valente et al., "Social Network Associations with Contraceptive Use among Cameroonian Women in Voluntary Associations," *Social Science & Medicine* 45, no. 5 (1997): 677–687.

3. Rogers and Kincaid, *Communication Networks.*

4. Everett M. Rogers, *Diffusion of Innovations*, 5th ed. (New York: Free Press, 2003), 333–335; Rogers and Kincaid, *Communication Networks*; Hans-Peter Kohler, "Learning in Social Networks and Contraceptive Choice," *Demography* 34, no. 3 (1997): 369–383; Barbara Entwisle, John B. Casterline, and Hussein A. A. Sayed, "Villages as Contexts for Contraceptive Behavior in Rural Egypt," *American Sociological Review* 54, no. 6 (1989): 1019–1034; Barbara Entwisle et al., "Community and Contraceptive Choice in Rural Thailand: A Case Study of Nang Rong," *Demography* 33, no. 1 (1996): 1–11; Mark R. Montgomery and John B. Casterline, "The Diffusion of Fertility Control in Taiwan: Evidence from Pooled Cross-Section Time-Series Models," *Population Studies* 47, no. 3 (1993):

457–479; Thomas W. Valente, *Network Models of the Diffusion of Innovations* (Cresskill, NJ: Hampton Press, 1995).

5. Malcolm Gladwell, *The Tipping Point: How Little Things Can Make a Big Difference* (Little, Brown, 2000); Malcolm Gladwell, "Q and A with Malcolm," accessed January 5, 2017, http://gladwell.com/the-tipping-point/the-tipping-point-q-and-a/. This research tradition dates back to the pioneering work of Bryce Ryan and Neil Gross, "The Diffusion of Hybrid Seed Corn in Two Iowa Communities," *Rural Sociology* 8, no. 1 (1943); and to Gabriel Tarde, *The Laws of Imitation*, trans. E. C. Parsons (New York: Holt: 1903).

6. Richard H. Thaler and Cass R. Sunstein, *Nudge: Improving Decisions About Health, Wealth, and Happiness.* (New Haven, CT: Yale University Press, 2008).

7. Mark Granovetter, "The Strength of Weak Ties," *American Journal of Sociology* 78, no. 6 (1973), 1366.

8. Duncan J. Watts and Steven H. Strogatz, "Collective Dynamics of 'Small-World' Networks," *Nature* 393, no. 6684 (1998): 440–442.

9. Robert M. Axelrod, *The Evolution of Cooperation*, rev. ed. (New York: Basic Books, 1984); Cristina Bicchieri, *The Grammar of Society: The Nature and Dynamics of Social Norms* (Cambridge: Cambridge University Press, 2006); H. Peyton Young, "The Evolution of Conventions," *Econometrica* 61, no. 1 (1993): 57–84; Peter M. Blau, Terry C. Blum, and Joseph E. Schwartz, "Heterogeneity and Intermarriage," *American Sociological Review* 47, no. 1 (1982): 45–62; Nicholas A. Christakis and James H. Fowler, "The Spread of Obesity in a Large Social Network over 32 Years," *New England Journal of Medicine* 357, no. 4 (2007): 370–379; Robert M. Bond et al., "A 61-Million-Person Experiment in Social Influence and Political Mobilization," *Nature* 489, no. 7415 (2012): 295–298; Rogers, *Diffusion of Innovations*; Serguei Saavedra, Kathleen Hagerty, and Brian Uzzi, "Synchronicity, Instant Messaging, and Performance among Financial Traders," *Proceedings of the National Academy of Sciences* 108, no. 13 (2011): 5296–5301. While several popular books on diffusion have reinforced the broad appeal of Granovetter's theory, such as Albert-László Barabási's *Linked: How Everything Is Connected to Everything Else and What It Means for Business, Science, and Everyday Life* (New York: Perseus Books, 2002), Gladwell's *Tipping Point*, and Jonah Berger's *Contagious: Why Things Catch On* (New York: Simon and Schuster, 2013), other earlier studies have anticipated the idea that different kinds of social contagions may spread differently in various network contexts, including Susan Watkins and I. Warriner, "How Do We Know We Need to Control for Selectivity?," *Demographic Research*, Special Collection 1 (2003):109–142; Paul DiMaggio et al., "Digital Inequality: From Unequal Access to Differentiated Use," in *Social Inequality*, ed. K Neckerman, (New York: Russell Sage Foundation, 2004), 355–400; and D. McFarland and H. Pals, "Motives and Contexts of Identity Change: A Case for Network Effects," *Social Psychology Quarterly* 68, no. 4 (2005): 289–315. See Paul DiMaggio and Filiz Garip, "Network Effects and Social Inequality," *Annual Review of Sociology* 38 (2012): 93–118.

CHAPTER 2. UNDERSTANDING DIFFUSION

1. Roger V. Gould, "Collective Action and Network Structure," *American Sociological Review* 58, no. 2 (1993): 182–196; Gerald Marwell and Pamela Oliver, *The Critical Mass in Collective Action: A Micro-Social Theory* (Cambridge: Cambridge University Press, 1993); Pamela Oliver, Gerald Marwell, and Ruy Teixeira, "A Theory of the Critical Mass. I. Interdependence, Group

Heterogeneity, and the Production of Collective Action," *American Journal of Sociology* 91, no. 3 (1985): 522–556. See also Thomas J. Coates, Linda Richter, and Carlos Caceres, "Behavioural Strategies to Reduce HIV Transmission: How to Make Them Work Better," *Lancet* 372, no. 9639 (2008): 669–684; Jeanne M. Marrazzo et al., "Tenofovir-Based Preexposure Prophylaxis for HIV Infection among African Women," *New England Journal of Medicine* 372, no. 6 (2015): 509–518.

2. WHO, "HIV/AIDS," accessed January 5, 2017, http://www.who.int/gho/hiv/en/; Sunetra Gupta, Roy M. Anderson, and Robert M. May, "Networks of Sexual Contacts: Implications for the Pattern of Spread of HIV," *AIDS* 3, no. 12 (1989): 807–818; Coates, Richter, and Caceres, "Behavioural Strategies."

3. Male circumcision was found to provide "a degree of protection against acquiring HIV infection, equivalent to what a vaccine of high efficacy would have achieved." Bertran Auvert et al., "Randomized, Controlled Intervention Trial of Male Circumcision for Reduction of HIV Infection Risk: The ANRS 1265 Trial," *PLOS Medicine* 2, no. 11 (2005): e298; Robert C. Bailey et al., "Male Circumcision for HIV Prevention in Young Men in Kisumu, Kenya: A Randomised Controlled Trial," *Lancet* 369, no. 9562 (2007): 643–656; Ronald H. Gray et al., "Male Circumcision for HIV Prevention in Men in Rakai, Uganda: A Randomised Trial," *Lancet* 369, no. 9562 (2007): 657–666; Helen A. Weiss, Maria A. Quigley, and Richard J. Hayes, "Male Circumcision and Risk of HIV Infection in Sub-Saharan Africa: A Systematic Review and Meta-analysis," *AIDS* 14, no. 15 (2000): 2361–2370. Recent studies have shown that circumcision reduces the chances of heterosexual transmission by 53–60%. UNAIDS and WHO, *Joint Strategic Action Framework to Accelerate the Scale-Up of Voluntary Medical Male Circumcision for HIV Prevention in Eastern and Southern Africa (2012–2016)* (Geneva: UNAIDS, 2011).

4. For instance, in Malawi, "members of the Tumbuka ethnic group, who are primarily Christian and do not traditionally practice circumcision, [consider] male circumcision a Muslim and Yao tradition . . . referring to it as a 'bad cultural practice.'" Justin O. Parkhurst, David Chilongozi, and Eleanor Hutchinson, "Doubt, Defiance, and Identity: Understanding Resistance to Male Circumcision for HIV Prevention in Malawi," *Social Science & Medicine* 135 (2015): 15–22. See also Aaron A. R. Tobian, Seema Kacker, and Thomas C. Quinn, "Male Circumcision: A Globally Relevant but Under-Utilized Method for the Prevention of HIV and Other Sexually Transmitted Infections," *Annual Review of Medicine* 65 (2014): 293–306; National AIDS Control Council, *Kenya Aids Strategic Framework 2014/2015—2018/2019* (Nairobi: Kenya Ministry of Health, 2015); Verah Okeyo, "Lessons from Voluntary Medical Male Circumcision," *Daily Nation*, June 14, 2016.

5. Marrazzo et al., "Tenofovir-Based Preexposure Prophylaxis."

6. Elizabeth T. Montgomery et al., "Misreporting of Product Adherence in the MTN-003/VOICE Trial for HIV Prevention in Africa: Participants' Explanations for Dishonesty," *AIDS and Behavior* 21, no. 2 (2017): 481–491; Ariane van der Straten et al., "Perspectives on Use of Oral and Vaginal Antiretrovirals for HIV Prevention: The VOICE-C Qualitative Study in Johannesburg, South Africa," *Journal of the International AIDS Society* 17, no. 3 (2014): 19146, doi: 10.7448/IAS.17.3.19146; Marrazzo et al., "Tenofovir-Based Preexposure Prophylaxis." Thanks to Sarah Wood for this discussion on PrEP.

7. Even a relatively easy behavior like condom use can run into similar problems. In some countries, the adoption of condoms has been limited by social norms that encouraged young men to engage in risk-seeking behaviors such as condomless sex. See Catherine MacPhail and Catherine Campbell,

"'I Think Condoms Are Good But, Aai, I Hate Those Things': Condom Use among Adolescents and Young People in a Southern African Township," *Social Science and Medicine* 52, no. 11 (2001): 1613–1627; Seth M. Noar and Patricia J. Morokoff, "The Relationship between Masculinity Ideology, Condom Attitudes, and Condom Use: Stage of Change; A Structural Equation Modeling Approach," *International Journal of Men's Health* 1, no. 1 (2002): 43–58; Jason Chan and Anindya Ghose, "Internet's Dirty Secret: Assessing the Impact of Online Intermediaries on HIV Transmission," *MIS Quarterly* 38, no. 4 (2013): 955–976. In other communities, resistance has turned into active opposition. Among some of the most affected populations in the United States, an unexpected response to the extensive diffusion of public health information about condom use has been the emergence of a new subculture in which the explicit choice for condomless sex has become a vehicle for establishing partner intimacy and social identity within the community. See Tim Dean, *Unlimited Intimacy: Reflections on the Subculture of Barebacking* (Chicago: University of Chicago Press, 2009).

8. Claude Compagnone and Peter Hamilton, "Burgundy Winemakers and Respect of the Environment," *Revue Française de Sociologie* 55, no. 2 (2014): 319–358; Sigmund Freud, *Beyond the Pleasure Principle*, trans. C.J.M. Hubback (London: International Psycho-Analytical, 1922); Rogers, *Diffusion of Innovations*.

9. Berger, *Contagious*; Cristina Bicchieri, *Norms in the Wild: How to Diagnose, Measure and Change Social Norms* (Oxford: Oxford University Press, 2016).

10. Michael Dietler and Ingrid Herbich, "Habitus, Techniques, Style: An Integrated Approach to the Social Understanding of Material Culture and Boundaries," in *The Archaeology of Social Boundaries*, ed. Miriam T. Stark (Washington, DC: Smithsonian Institution Press, 1998), 232–263.

11. Freud, *Beyond the Pleasure Principle*; Bicchieri, Norms in the Wild; Dietler and Herbich, "Habitus, Techniques, Style."

12. Daniel DellaPosta, Victor Nee, and Sonja Opper, "Endogenous Dynamics of Institutional Change," *Rationality and Society* (2016): 1–44; Philip Ross, "Marin County and California's Measles Outbreak: A Look into the Epicenter of The Anti-vaccination Trend," *International Business Times*, February 6, 2015, http://www.ibtimes.com/marin-county-californias-measles-outbreak-look -epicenter-anti-vaccination-trend-1808182.

13. Carl Knappett and Sander Van Der Leeuw, "A Developmental Approach to Ancient Innovation: The Potter's Wheel in the Bronze Age East Mediterranean," *Pragmatics & Cognition* 22, no. 1 (2014): 64–92; Aharon Levy et al., "Ingroups, Outgroups, and the Gateway Groups Between: The Potential of Dual Identities to Improve Intergroup Relations," *Journal of Experimental Social Psychology* 70 (2016): 260–271.

14. This brief caricature of the long and storied field of social networks research is intended only to provide a conceptual orientation for the reader who is new to social networks. It is inadequate for any other purpose. Readers interested in a summary of the field, including either its history, or the contemporary scale of social networks research, should consult the excellent, and very accessible, overviews of the field found in David Easley and Jon Kleinberg, *Networks, Crowds, and Markets: Reasoning about a Highly Connected World* (New York: Cambridge University Press, 2010); Peter J. Carrington, John Scott, and Stanley Wasserman, eds., *Models and Methods in Social Network Analysis* (New York: Cambridge University Press, 2005), Matthew O. Jackson, *Social and Economic Networks* (Princeton, NJ: Princeton University Press, 2008); Mark Newman, Albert-László Barabási, and Duncan J. Watts, *The Structure and Dynamics of Networks* (Princeton, NJ: Princeton University Press, 2008).

15. Peter V. Marsden, "Network Data and Measurement," *Annual Review of Sociology* (1990): 435–463; Jacob Levy Moreno, *Sociometry, Experimental Method and the Science of Society* (New York: Beacon House, 1951).

16. Scott L. Feld, "The Focused Organization of Social Ties," *American Journal of Sociology* 86, no. 5 (1981): 1015–1035; Ronald L. Breiger, "The Duality of Persons and Groups," *Social Forces* 53, no. 2 (1974): 181–190; Granovetter, "Strength of Weak Ties"; Peter V. Marsden, "Homogeneity in Confiding Relations," *Social Networks* 10, no. 1 (1988): 57–76; Peter V. Marsden, *Social Trends in American Life: Findings from the General Social Survey since 1972* (Princeton, NJ: Princeton University Press, 2012); Christakis and Fowler, "Spread of Obesity"; Nicholas A. Christakis and James H. Fowler, "The Collective Dynamics of Smoking in a Large Social Network," *New England Journal of Medicine* 358, no. 21 (2008): 2249–2258; Cosma Rohilla Shalizi and Andrew C. Thomas, "Homophily and Contagion Are Generically Confounded in Observational Social Network Studies," *Sociological Methods & Research* 40, no. 2 (2011): 211–239.

17. Granovetter, "Strength of Weak Ties"; Georg Simmel, *The Sociology of Georg Simmel*, trans. Kurt H. Wolff (New York: Free Press, 1950).

18. Mark Granovetter, "The Strength of Weak Ties: A Network Theory Revisited," *Sociological Theory* 1, no. 1 (1983): 201–233; Scott L. Feld and William C. Carter, "When Desegregation Reduces Interracial Contact: A Class Size Paradox for Weak Ties," *American Journal of Sociology* 103, no. 5 (1998): 1165–1186; John A. Schneider et al., "Network Mixing and Network Influences Most Linked to HIV Infection and Risk Behavior in the HIV Epidemic among Black Men Who Have Sex with Men," *American Journal of Public Health* 103, no. 1 (2012): e28–e36.

19. Watts and Strogatz, "Collective Dynamics"; Albert-László Barabási and Réka Albert, "Emergence of Scaling in Random Networks," *Science* 286, no. 5439 (1999): 509–512.

20. Simmel, *Sociology of Georg Simmel*; Georg Simmel, *Conflict and the Web of Group Affiliations* (New York: Free Press, 1955); see also, Emile Durkheim, *Suicide: A Study in Sociology*, trans. J. A. Spaulding and G. Simpson (New York: Free Press, 1951).

21. Dawn K. Smith et al., "Condom Effectiveness for HIV Prevention by Consistency of Use among Men Who Have Sex with Men in the United States," *JAIDS Journal of Acquired Immune Deficiency Syndromes* 68, no. 3 (2015): 337–344.

22. Granovetter, "Strength of Weak Ties"; Rogers, *Diffusion of Innovations*, 340.

23. Granovetter, "Strength of Weak Ties"; Gueorgi Kossinets and Duncan J. Watts, "Empirical Analysis of an Evolving Social Network," *Science* 311, no. 5757 (2006): 88–90.

24. Centola and Macy, "Complex Contagions"; Robert D. Putnam, *Bowling Alone: The Collapse and Revival of American Community* (Simon and Schuster, 2001); Joel M. Podolny, "Networks as the Pipes and Prisms of the Market," *American Journal of Sociology* 107, no. 1 (2001): 33–60.

25. While there are several possible implementations of this model—Watts and Strogatz, "Collective Dynamics"; Duncan J. Watts, *Small Worlds: The Dynamics of Networks between Order and Randomness* (Princeton, NJ: Princeton University Press, 1999); Mark E. J. Newman and Duncan J. Watts, "Scaling and Percolation in the Small-World Network Model," *Physical Review E* 60, no. 6 (1999): 7332; Duncan J. Watts, "Networks, Dynamics, and the Small-World Phenomenon," *American Journal of Sociology* 105, no. 2 (1999): 493–527; Sergei Maslov and Kim Sneppen, "Specificity and Stability in Topology of Protein Networks,"

Science 296, no. 5569 (2002): 910–913—the original (1998) model serves to illustrate the basic idea.

26. John Guare, *Six Degrees of Separation: A Play* (New York: Random House: 1990). Decades of research on both the degrees of separation in social networks, and the "small world problem" stand behind Guare's 1990 play, including Michael Gurevich, *The Social Structure of Acquaintanceship Networks* (Cambridge, MA: MIT Press, 1961); Stanley Milgram, "The Small World Problem," *Psychology Today* 2 (1967): 60–67; Jeffrey Travers and Stanley Milgram, "An Experimental Study of the Small World Problem," *Sociometry* 32 (December 4, 1969): 425–443; and Ithiel de Sola Pool and Manfred Kochen, "Contacts and Influence," *Social Networks* 1, no. 1 (1978–79): 5–51.

27. Mark E. J. Newman, "Models of the Small World," *Journal of Statistical Physics* 101, no. 3–4 (2000): 819–841; Watts, "Networks, Dynamics"; Centola and Macy, "Complex Contagions." One technical point worth noting is that if long-distance links are randomly "added" to the population instead of "rewired" from the original network (Newman and Watts, "Scaling and Percolation"), this will change the topology, but it will also increase the overall density of the social network. Rewiring methods permit us to identify the effects of changing network structure without the confounding effects of changing density. Nevertheless, the discussion in chapter 3 explores the effects of this alternative approach, changing both topology and density, on the dynamics of diffusion.

28. Jeffrey Travers and Stanley Milgram, "An Experimental Study of the Small World Problem," *Sociometry* 32, no. 4 (1969): 425–443; Peter Sheridan Dodds, Roby Muhamad, and Duncan J. Watts, "An Experimental Study of Search in Global Social Networks," *Science* 301, no. 5634 (2003): 827–829; Duncan J. Watts, *Small Worlds: The Dynamics of Networks between Order and Randomness* (Princeton, NJ: Princeton University Press, 1999); Harrison C. White, "Search Parameters for the Small World Problem," *Social Forces* 49, no. 2 (1970): 259–264.

29. Granovetter, "Strength of Weak Ties."

30. Mark Granovetter, *Getting a Job: A Study of Contacts and Careers* (Chicago: University Of Chicago Press, 1974).

31. Blau, Blum, and Schwartz, "Heterogeneity and Intermarriage"; Diana C. Mutz, "The Consequences of Cross-Cutting Networks for Political Participation," *American Journal of Political Science* 46, no. 4 (2002): 838–855.

32. Granovetter, "Strength of Weak Ties," 1366.

33. Watts and Strogatz, "Collective Dynamics"; Lisa Sattenspiel and Carl P. Simon, "The Spread and Persistence of Infectious Diseases in Structured Populations," *Mathematical Biosciences* 90, no. 1–2 (1988): 341–366; Ira M. Longini Jr., "A Mathematical Model for Predicting the Geographic Spread of New Infectious Agents," *Mathematical Biosciences* 90, no. 1–2 (1988): 367–383; George Hess, "Disease in Metapopulation Models: Implications for Conservation," *Ecology* 77, no. 5 (1996): 1617–1632; Marwell and Oliver, *Critical Mass*; Oliver, Marwell, and Teixeira, "Theory of Critical Mass"; Mark Granovetter, "Threshold Models of Collective Behavior," *American Journal of Sociology* 83, no. 6 (1978): 1420–1443.

34. Putnam, *Bowling Alone*, 152–153.

35. Granovetter, "Strength of Weak Ties."

36. Michael Biggs, "Strikes as Forest Fires: Chicago and Paris in the Late Nineteenth Century," *American Journal of Sociology* 110, no. 6 (2005):

1684–1714; Francesca Polletta, " 'It Was Like A Fever . . .': Narrative and Identity in Social Protest," *Social Problems* 45, no. 2 (1998): 137–159; David Strang and John W. Meyer, "Institutional Conditions for Diffusion," *Theory and Society* 22, no. 4 (1993): 487–511; Sarah A. Soule, "The Student Divestment Movement in the United States and Tactical Diffusion: The Shantytown Protest," *Social Forces* 75, no. 3 (1997): 855–882; Malcolm Gladwell, "Small Change: Why the Revolution Will Not Be Tweeted," *New Yorker*, October 4, 2010, http://www.newyorker.com/magazine/2010/10/04/small-change-malcolm -gladwell.

37. Roger V. Gould, "Multiple Networks and Mobilization in the Paris Commune, 1871," *American Sociological Review* 56, no. 6 (1991): 716–729.

38. Adolph Fick, "On Liquid Diffusion," *Poggendorffs Annalen* 94, no. 59 (1855), reprinted in *Journal of Membrane Science* 100 (1995): 33–38; Howard C. Berg, *Random Walks in Biology* (Princeton, NJ: Princeton University Press, 1993).

39. Granovetter, "Strength of Weak Ties," 1367.

40. Peter Hedström, "Contagious Collectivities: On the Spatial Diffusion of Swedish Trade Unions, 1890–1940," *American Journal of Sociology* 99, no. 5 (1994): 1176.

41. Doug McAdam and Ronnelle Paulsen, "Specifying the Relationship between Social Ties and Activism," *American Journal of Sociology* 99, no. 3 (1993): 640–667.

42. Rogers, *Diffusion of Innovations*; H. Peyton Young and Gabriel E. Kreindler, "Rapid Innovation Diffusion in Social Networks," *Proceedings of the National Academy of Sciences* 111, suppl. 3 (2014): 10881–10888; H. Peyton Young, "The Dynamics of Social Innovation," *Proceedings of the National Academy of Sciences* 108, no. 4 (2011): 21285–21291; Lisa F. Berkman, Ichiro Kawachi, and M. Maria Glymour, *Social Epidemiology* (Oxford: Oxford University Press, 2014); Ichiro Kawachi and Lisa Berkman. "Social Cohesion, Social Capital, and Health," in *Social Epidemiology*, ed. Lisa Berkman and Ichiro Kawachi, 174–190 (New York: Oxford University Press, 2000); Ka-Yuet Liu, Marissa King, and Peter S. Bearman, "Social Influence and the Autism Epidemic," *American Journal of Sociology* 115, no. 5 (2010): 1387–1434; Dingxin Zhao, "Ecologies of Social Movements: Student Mobilization during the 1989 Prodemocracy Movement in Beijing," *American Journal of Sociology* 103, no. 6 (1998): 1493–1529; Michael Biggs, "Positive Feedback in Collective Mobilization: The American Strike Wave of 1886," *Theory and Society* 32, no. 2 (2003): 217–254; Soule, "Student Divestment Movement"; William H. Whyte Jr., "The Web of Word of Mouth," *Fortune* 50, no. 5 (1954): 140–143; Rogers and Kincaid, *Communication Networks*; Lisa F. Berkman and Ichiro Kawachi, eds., *Social Epidemiology* (Oxford: Oxford University Press, 2000); Jeffrey D. Morenoff and Robert J. Sampson, "Violent Crime and the Spatial Dynamics of Neighborhood Transition: Chicago, 1970–1990," *Social Forces* 76, no. 1 (1997): 31–64; DellaPosta, Nee, and Opper, "Endogenous Dynamics"; Knappett and Van Der Leeuw, "Developmental Approach"; Torsten Hagerstrand, *Innovation Diffusion as a Spatial Process* (Chicago: University of Chicago Press, 1968); Simone Gabbriellini et al., "Complex Contagions in Ethnically Diverse Non-Western Societies: Explaining Diffusion Dynamics among Indian and Kenyan Potters" (paper, DIFFCERAM Workshop, Paris, France, June 16, 2016); Kawachi and Berkman, "Social Cohesion."

Spatial concentration in the entrepreneurial counties thus provided conditions that favored the unfettered growth of private manufacturing" (DellaPosta, Nee, and Opper, "Endogenous Dynamics," 19–20).

18. Hedström, "Contagious Collectivities," 1163.

19. Mark E. J. Newman, "Models of the Small World," *Journal of Statistical Physics* 101, no. 3–4 (2000): 819–841; Mark E. J. Newman, Albert-László Barabási, and Duncan J. Watts, *The Structure and Dynamics of Networks* (Princeton, NJ: Princeton University Press, 2006).

20. Barabási and Albert, "Emergence of Scaling"; Albert-László Barabási, Réka Albert, and Hawoong Jeong, "Scale-Free Characteristics of Random Networks: The Topology of the World-Wide Web," *Physica A: Statistical Mechanics and Its Applications* 281, no. 1 (2000): 69–77; Réka Albert, Hawoong Jeong, and Albert-László Barabási, "Error and Attack Tolerance of Complex Networks," *Nature* 406, no. 6794 (2000): 378–382.

21. Fredrik Liljeros et al., "The Web of Human Sexual Contacts," *Nature* 411, no. 6840 (2001): 907–908; Fredrik Liljeros et al., "Social Networks (Communication Arising): Sexual Contacts and Epidemic Thresholds," *Nature* 423, no. 6940 (2003): 606–606; Gladwell, *Tipping Point*.

22. Konstantin Klemm and Víctor M. Eguíluz, "Highly Clustered Scale-Free Networks," *Physical Review E* 65, no. 3 (2002): 36123; Maslov and Sneppen, "Specificity and Stability"; Damon Centola, "Failure in Complex Social Networks," *Journal of Mathematical Sociology* 33, no. 1 (2008): 64–68.

23. Centola and Macy, "Complex Contagions."

24. McAdam and Paulsen, "Specifying the Relationship." Chapter 5 presents several empirical examples of diffusion on Facebook and Twitter that show how fractional thresholds make hubs difficult to activate.

25. The implications of countervailing influences for social inertia among highly connected individuals suggest that leaders of Fortune 500 firms may be selected based on "risk-seeking" personalities to offset the forces of social inertia that accompany high levels of connectedness.

26. James G. March, "Exploration and Exploitation in Organizational Learning," *Organization Science* 2, no. 1 (1991): 71–87; Damon J. Phillips and Ezra W. Zuckerman, "Middle-Status Conformity: Theoretical Restatement and Empirical Demonstration in Two Markets," *American Journal of Sociology* 107, no. 2 (2001): 379–429.

27. See, for instance, the discussion of social movements on Twitter in chapter 5.

28. E. E. Evans-Pritchard, *The Nuer: A Description of the Modes of Livelihood and Political Institutions of a Nilotic People* (Oxford: Clarendon Press, 1940); R.I.M. Dunbar, "Neocortex Size as a Constraint on Group Size in Primates," *Journal of Human Evolution* 22, no. 6 (1992): 469–493. The idea of determining which subset of contacts is relevant for social influence is explored in more detail in part 3 of this book.

29. Gould, "Collective Action"; Roger V. Gould, "The Origins of Status Hierarchies: A Formal Theory and Empirical Test," *American Journal of Sociology* 107, no. 5 (2002): 1143–1178; Hyojoung Kim and Peter S. Bearman, "The Structure and Dynamics of Movement Participation," *American Sociological Review* 62, no. 1 (1997): 70–93.

30. Elihu Katz and Paul Lazarsfeld, *Personal Influence* (New York: Free Press, 1955); Centola and Macy, "Complex Contagions."

31. Valente, *Network Models*; Rogers, *Diffusion of Innovations*.

32. See appendix C for more details. Excessive numbers of low-threshold individuals can trigger a "critical mass" phenomenon, as detailed in Centola, "Social Media," and in Vladimir Barash, Christopher Cameron, Michael Macy, "Critical Phenomena in Complex Contagions," *Social Networks* 34 (2012): 451– 461. See chapters 6 and 7 for practical applications.

33. The well-known Bass model of diffusion does not account for the possibility that actors "turn off," which limits its applicability to "durable" consumer items. Frank M. Bass, "A New Product Growth for Model Consumer Durables," *Management Science* 15, no. 5 (1969): 215–227.

34. See appendix C for more details about this model.

35. In some circumstances, weak ties may be even more likely to transmit diseases than strong ties because there is a greater likelihood of using condoms with longer-term partners (with greater emotional attachment) than with casual sexual contacts or prostitutes. See R. Damani et al., "Emotional Intimacy Predicts Condom Use: Findings in a Group at High Sexually Transmitted Disease Risk," *International Journal of STD & AIDS* 20, no. 11 (2009): 761–764.

36. Granovetter, "Strength of Weak Ties," 202, 201.

CHAPTER 4. A SOCIAL EXPERIMENT ON THE INTERNET

1. Granovetter, "Threshold Models"; Mark Huisman, "Imputation of Missing Network Data: Some Simple Procedures," *Journal of Social Structure* 10, no. 1 (2009): 1–29; Matthew Burgess, Eytan Adar, and Michael Cafarella, "Link-Prediction Enhanced Consensus Clustering for Complex Networks," *PLOS ONE* 11, no. 5 (2016): e0153384.

2. Shalizi and Thomas, "Homophily and Contagion"; See also Tom A. B. Snijders, "The Statistical Evaluation of Social Network Dynamics," *Sociological Methodology* 31, no. 1 (2001): 361–395; Tom A. B. Snijders, "Stochastic Actor-Oriented Models for Network Change," *Journal of Mathematical Sociology* 21, no. 1–2 (1996): 149–172; Tom A. B. Snijders, Gerhard G. Van de Bunt, and Christian E. G. Steglich, "Introduction to Stochastic Actor-Based Models for Network Dynamics," *Social Networks* 32, no. 1 (2010): 44–60; Ethan Cohen-Cole and Jason M. Fletcher, "Is Obesity Contagious? Social Networks vs. Environmental Factors in the Obesity Epidemic," *Journal of Health Economics* 27, no. 5 (2008): 1382–1387. Some interesting progress has been made on the problem of distinguishing homophily from diffusion, but so far these approaches do not tell much about causal factors that affect the success of diffusion.

3. Philip W. Anderson, "More Is Different," *Science* 177, no. 4047 (1972): 393–396; Watts, "Networks, Dynamics"; Centola and Macy, "Complex Contagions"; Damon Centola et al., "Homophily, Cultural Drift, and the Co-evolution of Cultural Groups," *Journal of Conflict Resolution* 51, no. 6 (2007): 905–929.

4. For technical detail, see Centola et al., "Homophily, Cultural Drift"; Centola and Macy, "Complex Contagions."

5. It is also important that the social network structure is static over the course of studying a diffusion process. If the network can change, then diffusion may be the cause of the topology (e.g., because people who adopt a behavior choose to form ties to each other), instead of the topology causing diffusion.

6. Solomon E. Asch, "Effects of Group Pressure upon the Modification and Distortion of Judgments," in *Groups, Leadership, and Men: Research in Human Relations*, ed. Harold S. Guetzkow (Pittsburgh: Carnegie Press, 1951), 222–236;

Muzafer Sherif, *Experimental Study of Positive and Negative Intergroup Attitudes between Experimentally Produced Groups: Robbers Cave Study* (Norman, OK: University of Oklahoma, 1954); James A. Kitts, "Egocentric Bias or Information Management? Selective Disclosure and the Social Roots of Norm Misperception," *Social Psychology Quarterly* 66, no. 3 (2003): 222–237; Craig T. Nagoshi et al., "College Drinking Game Participation within the Context of Other Predictors of Alcohol Use and Problems," *Psychology of Addictive Behaviors* 8, no. 4 (1994): 203–213; H. Wesley Perkins and Henry Wechsler, "Variation in Perceived College Drinking Norms and Its Impact on Alcohol Abuse: A Nationwide Study," *Journal of Drug Issues* 26, no. 4 (1996): 961–974; John S. Baer, "Effects of College Residence on Perceived Norms for Alcohol Consumption: An Examination of the First Year in College," *Psychology of Addictive Behaviors* 8, no. 1 (1994): 43; Brian Borsari and Kate B. Carey, "Peer Influences on College Drinking: A Review of the Research," *Journal of Substance Abuse* 13, no. 4 (2001): 391–424; Granovetter, "Threshold Models"; Rachel Manning, Mark Levine, and Alan Collins, "The Kitty Genovese Murder and the Social Psychology of Helping: The Parable of the 38 Witnesses," *American Psychologist* 62, no. 6 (2007): 555–562.

7. Jeana Frost and Michael Massagli, "Social Uses of Personal Health Information within PatientsLikeMe, an Online Patient Community: What Can Happen When Patients Have Access to One Another's Data," *Journal of Medical Internet Research* 10, no. 3 (2008): e15; Janna Anderson and Lee Rainie, "Millennials Will Make Online Sharing in Networks a Lifelong Habit," Pew Research Center: Internet, Science & Tech, July 9, 2010; "ACOR.org—Association of Cancer Online Resources," accessed February 5, 2017, http://www.acor.org/.

8. Christakis and Fowler, *Connected*; Berkman, Kawachi, and Glymour, *Social Epidemiology*.

9. Watts, "Networks, Dynamics"; Watts and Strogatz, "Collective Dynamics"; Maslov and Sneppen, "Specificity and Stability"; Granovetter, "Strength of Weak Ties."

10. See the introduction to part 2 for a discussion of this point.

11. It is useful to consider an alternative experimental design that could have been used, in which, instead of constructing the health forum, the study measured the diffusion of an existing health service or product—such as signing up for a Weight Watchers account. Let's imagine that we ran this hypothetical Weight Watchers study and that adoption of Weight Watchers did indeed spread through the networks such that there were significantly different levels of adoption across experimental conditions. What would we learn?

Because of the controlled experimental design of the study, that outcome could indeed demonstrate the existence of a causal effect of network structure on behavior change. However, the problem with the Weight Watchers study is that we might not learn much about the process of how behaviors spread through social networks. This is because in the Weight Watchers study, subjects might discover the Weight Watchers program from friends who are not in the study or from exogenous media sources, or they might already be existing users of the product. These exogenous influences could create situations in which actors spontaneously adopted without having received any health-buddy messages. This would not compromise the internal validity of the experimental design, but it would make it very difficult to determine how the network structure mediated the flow of social influence through the population. Further, it would make it nearly impossible to identify how network structure affected the speed of diffusion from an initial seed to the rest of population, since spontaneous adopters would be able to introduce the contagion at any point in the network without it having to follow the topology in order to get there. The Weight Watchers study is not a bad design, but it would limit the ability to identify the flow of adoption in the network, and it would make it impossible to control the social and nonsocial influences on adoption outside of the experimental design.

To address these concerns, the health forum website was constructed exclusively for the Healthy Lifestyle Network and was used as the only dependent variable for this study. As a result, each experimental trial produced a clear time series of adoption decisions that show the cascade of behavior change through each of the social networks.

12. Differences in both the success of diffusion and the rate of diffusion between experimental conditions were statistically significant ($p < 0.01$, using the Wilcoxon rank sum test / Mann-Whitney U test); Centola, "Spread of Behavior."

I measured the success of diffusion in terms of the fraction of the population that ultimately adopted the behavior. The fraction of adopters, S_j, in network j, is defined as

$$S_j = \frac{\sum_{i=1}^{(N_j-1)} a_i}{(N_j-1)}, \tag{1}$$

where N_j is the number of nodes in network j (1 is subtracted to account for the seed node), and $a_i = 1$ iff node i adopted, otherwise $a_i = 0$. Within each trial, both networks in both conditions had the same size and degree distribution. However, across trials some networks had different sizes and degree distributions. This was done to ensure that the results from this study were not an artifact of a specific choice of neighborhood size or network size. To make comparisons across trials possible, success is measured in terms of the *fraction* of the population that adopted, not the absolute number.

I used the Wilcoxon rank sum test (also known as the Mann-Whitney U test) to evaluate the statistical significance of differences in success across the six trials. The Wilcoxon is a nonparametric test of the likelihood that observations drawn from one population will be greater than those drawn from another population. In essence, it tests whether there is a statistical significance in the difference of the medians of two populations. Thus, it is very similar to the two-sample t-test; however, it provides a more conservative estimate of significance since it does not rely on the assumption of normality in the distribution. The Wilcoxon test shows that the null hypothesis that there is no difference in the success of diffusion between the two conditions can be accepted with a probability of $p < 0.01$.

To measure the rate of diffusion, I compared the time it took for the diffusion process to reach the farthest node that was reached by both conditions in a given trial. For example, in trial 1, diffusion in the random network condition reached 38.14% of the network (37 nodes), while diffusion in the clustered lattice network condition reached 51.54% of the network (50 nodes). Thus, the rates of diffusion for trial 1 are compared by evaluating the time it took each network to reach 37 nodes. More generally, the rate of diffusion in network j in trial T, R_{Tj}, is defined as

$$R_{T_j} = \frac{\min(S_{T_0}, S_{T_1})}{time_{T_j}[\min(S_{T_0}, S_{T_1})]},\tag{2}$$

where S_{T_0} and S_{T_1} are the fraction of adopters in conditions 0 (random network) and 1 (clustered lattice network) of trial T, respectively. $time_{T_j}[\min(S_{T_0}, S_{T_1})]$ reports the time it took in network j of trial T for the behavior to reach the largest fraction of nodes reached by both networks in trial T. This analysis identifies the distances, times, and rates corresponding to each condition in each trial, and the mean and standard deviation of the rates of diffusion across all trials.

An alternative approach to measuring diffusion rates is to pick a specific prevalence (say 50% adoption) and compare all networks at this same prevalence point. However, since many of the random networks did not reach 50%, this comparison would omit some of the data. To include all of the data in such a comparison, the prevalence point would have to be below 27% adoption. Yet, since many of the networks (both clustered lattice networks and random networks) spread well past 27%, this measure does not provide a good representation of the overall diffusion processes recorded in these trials.

The approach that I adopted of comparing the network conditions on a trial-by-trial basis ensures that all networks are included in the comparison. Further, this approach also ensures that the greatest possible number of data points is included to give the most accurate picture of the rate at which the behavior spread through each of the networks. Finally, because the network conditions are already paired into trials, comparing the time it takes to reach an equivalent distance within each trial is a natural way to evaluate the rate of diffusion across conditions. Because these rate measurements have commensurate units across trials (i.e., nodes/sec), they can be aggregated to provide a summary statistic.

To evaluate the significance of the differences in rates across the six trials, I used the same Wilcoxon rank sum test described above. The logic for using this test to compare rates is the same as it was for the evaluating the differences in success: I am trying to determine the likelihood that one condition will consistently produce observations that are greater than those for the other condition. The Wilcoxon test shows that the null hypothesis that there is no difference in the rates of diffusion between the two conditions can be accepted with a probability of $p < 0.01$.

To test for the possible effects of population size (N) and degree (Z)—that is, the number of health buddies each person had—on the diffusion dynamics, I used three different versions of the experiment, which are shown in figure 4.2: panel A: $N = 98$, $Z = 6$; panels B–D: $N = 128$, $Z = 6$; and panels E and F: $N = 144$, $Z = 8$. The modest range of population sizes tested and the correspondingly narrow range of degrees were due to the challenges of recruiting large numbers of people simultaneously. Among the networks I used, there were no effects of population size. The experimental findings were qualitatively the same across different network and neighborhood sizes. However, networks with a greater degree ($Z = 8$) performed better than those with a lower degree ($Z = 6$). This finding is consistent with the hypothesis that more-redundant ties between neighborhoods can improve the global spread of behavior.

13. Hagerstrand, *Innovation Diffusion*; Hedström, "Contagious Collectivities"; David Strang and Sarah A. Soule, "Diffusion in Organizations and Social Movements: From Hybrid Corn to Poison Pills," *Annual Review of Sociology* 24 (January 1, 1998): 265–290;

14. Gould, "Multiple Networks," 727–728.

15. The effect of social reinforcement on the individual likelihood of adoption was calculated using the Cox proportional hazards model. The Cox model is a semi-parametric test of hazard rates, which does not assume an underlying functional form for the hazard of adoption. The baseline hazard for adoption is based on the individuals who adopted after one signal. This hazard function was then used to evaluate the conditional hazard of adoption for individuals receiving additional signals. This test thus measures the increase in likelihood that an individual will adopt the behavior from receiving multiple social signals, conditioned on the likelihood of adoption from receiving a single social signal.

The results of the Cox model showed that receiving a second social signal increased the probability of adoption by 1.67 times, with 95% confidence intervals ranging from 1.35 to 2.05. The null hypothesis—that there was no effect of receiving a second signal on the likelihood of adoption—can be accepted with a probability of $p < 0.001$. Receiving a third signal increased the likelihood of adoption by an additional 1.32 times, with 95% confidence intervals ranging from 1.01 to 1.73. The null hypothesis can be accepted with a probability of $p < 0.05$. There was no significant effect of additional social signals on the likelihood of adoption. See Centola, "Spread of Behavior."

16. Barry Wellman and Scot Wortley, "Different Strokes from Different Folks: Community Ties and Social Support," *American Journal of Sociology* 96, no. 3 (November 1990): 558–588.

17. Centola, "Spread of Behavior"; Damon Centola, "Social Media and the Science of Health Behavior," *Circulation* 127, no. 21 (2013): 2135–2144; Bess H. Marcus et al., "Physical Activity Behavior Change: Issues in Adoption and Maintenance," *Health Psychology* 19, no. 1, suppl. (2000): 32–41.

18. To investigate the effects of social reinforcement on individuals' level of commitment to their memberships in the health forum, pairwise statistical comparisons were made between group 1 and groups 2–5 using the Kolmogorov-Smirnov test. The results show that the null hypothesis can be rejected that group 1 was drawn from the same distribution as groups 2–5 for all four comparisons. See Centola "Spread of Behavior."

19. Cornelia Pechmann et al., "Randomised Controlled Trial Evaluation of Tweet2Quit: A Social Network Quit-Smoking Intervention," *Tobacco Control* 26, no. 2 (2017): 188–194; Cynthia M. Lakon et al., "Mapping Engagement in Twitter-Based Support Networks for Adult Smoking Cessation," *American Journal of Public Health* 106, no. 8 (2016): 1374–1380.

20. Rogers, *Diffusion of Innovations*; McAdam and Paulsen, "Specifying the Relationship"; Kossinets and Watts, "Empirical Analysis"; Gueorgi Kossinets and Duncan J. Watts, "Origins of Homophily in an Evolving Social Network," *American Journal of Sociology* 115, no. 2 (2009): 405–450.

21. Centola, "Spread of Behavior."

INTRODUCTION TO PART II

1. Michael T. Madigan et al., *Brock Biology of Microorganisms*, 14th ed. (Boston: Pearson, 2014); John G. Holt, *Bergey's Manual of Determinative Bacteriology*, 9th ed. (Philadelphia: Lippincott Williams & Wilkins, 1994); Laurent Hébert-Dufresne and Benjamin M. Althouse, "Complex Dynamics of Synergistic Coinfections on Realistically Clustered Networks," *Proceedings of the National Academy of Sciences* 112, no. 33 (2015): 10551–10556. See chapter 5.

2. A surprising variety of "social" contagions in the nonhuman world exhibit the spreading dynamics of complex contagions. For instance, quorum sensing is a phenomenon in which bacteria will only activate certain behaviors when they are triggered by a sufficient number of other bacteria. One of the most famous examples of this is the bioluminescent bacterium *Aliivibrio fischeri*, which lives symbiotically inside the Hawaiian bobtail squid (*Euprymna scolopes*). The bacteria are surprisingly social. They will not release bioluminescent enzymes if there are too few other bacteria to create a visible display. But when they sense a sufficient density of peers, a cascade of activation is triggered throughout the colony, resulting in large spatial swaths of connected bioluminescent patches that make the squid visible at night.

While the display of *A. fischeri* can be quite beautiful to observe, these same social dynamics of bacteria can also be quite dangerous. A number of harmful pathogens such as *Escherichia coli* (*E. coli*), *Salmonella enterica*, and *Pseudomonas aeruginosa* also use the dynamics of complexity for managing their collective behaviors, sometimes to quite lethal effect. In the case of *P. aeruginosa*, the pathogen will grow harmlessly in a host until there is a sufficient concentration of the bacteria to overwhelm the host's immune system. In small groups, the bacteria are inert; however, once there is safety in numbers, a biological change is triggered in the previously harmless bacteria, leading to a cascade of pathogenic function throughout the colony. This change results in a concerted attack on the host organism and the rapid formation of a protective biofilm that insulates the colony against retaliation.

Recent research on these aggressive bacteria has found that while *P. aeruginosa* can be resistant to antibiotic treatments, an alternative approach is to target the collective dynamics of social signaling rather than the bacteria themselves. These new treatments are effective because of their ability to block the signaling process that triggers the onset of pathogenic behaviors. This therapeutic strategy of "quorum sensing inhibition" prevents concentrations of bacteria like *P. aeruginosa* from triggering aggressive behavior. If the bacteria can be prevented from sending reinforcing signals to each other, the colony will never be activated. The colony may therefore remain inert even though the number of bacteria may be quite large. Interestingly, this means that the structure of the sensing network among bacteria can determine whether a harmful change in behavior is triggered—in some cases, the spatial distribution of cells can be more important for triggering quorum sensing than the overall size of the colony.

These same dynamics of complexity have been found among social insects, whose collective behaviors can also be organized by a process of quorum sensing. For instance, in colonies of the ant species *Temnothorax albipenni*, when a nest is destroyed the workers scatter looking for a suitable replacement. Each individual leaves a distinct pheromone trail for its peers to follow. When enough ants choose one site, they collectively release a large enough pheromone signal that it triggers a threshold in the other ants, who abandon the other sites, and all converge on the popular option. Together, the reinforcing signals from these workers trigger a rapid cascade of self-organization throughout the colony. With remarkable efficiency the entire population coordinates to initiate the move.

The efficiency of these threshold dynamics for producing coordinated behavior in insects has also led them to be applied to the design of semiautonomous robots. Recent studies have found that distributed groups of robots that use local threshold rules and sensing networks, very similar to those found in ant and termite colonies, can be used collectively to solve complex engineering tasks.

These same strategic dynamics are also found in the collective behavior of honeybee colonies (*Apis mellifera*), which use social thresholds to decide how to locate new sites for nests. A colony's move is triggered when social reinforcement from several drones—which is exhibited through coordinated "dancing" behavior—signals that a sufficiently popular option has been found. At this point, social recruitment spreads through the colony through a series of intensifying vibrational signals, ultimately leading to a synchronized move of the entire hive. Perhaps most surprisingly, experimental tests of these collective dynamics have shown that this system of social reinforcement leads to near-optimal levels of collective intelligence in a colony's selection of desirable sites.

CHAPTER 5. COMPLEX CONTAGIONS IN OTHER CONTEXTS

1. Lori Beaman et al., "Can Network Theory-Based Targeting Increase Technology Adoption?" (working paper, Northwestern University, Evanston, IL, June); Vincent Traag, "Complex Contagion of Campaign Donations," *PLOS ONE* 11 no. 4 (2016): e0153539. A complete review of the theoretical and empirical applications and extensions of research on complex contagions during the decade from 2007 to 2017 can be found in Douglas Guilbeault, Joshua Becker, and Damon Centola, "Complex Contagions: A Decade in Review," in *Spreading Dynamics in Social Systems*, ed. Yong Yeol Ahn and Sune Lehmann (New York: Springer Nature, forthcoming).

2. Daniel M. Romero, Brendan Meeder, and Jon Kleinberg, "Differences in the Mechanics of Information Diffusion across Topics: Idioms, Political Hashtags, and Complex Contagion on Twitter," in *Proceedings of the 20th International Conference on World Wide Web*, 695–704 (New York: ACM, 2011).

3. Nicholas Harrigan, Palakorn Achananuparp, and Ee-Peng Lim, "Influentials, Novelty, and Social Contagion: The Viral Power of Average Friends, Close Communities, and Old News, *Social Networks* 34, no. 4 (2012): 470–480; Sanjay Sharma, "Black Twitter?: Racial Hashtags, Networks and Contagion," *New Formations* 78, no. 1 (2013): 46–64; Zachary C. Steinert-Threlkeld, "Spontaneous Collective Action: Peripheral Mobilization during the Arab Spring," *American Political Science Review* 111, no. 2 (May 2017): 379–403. These observations from Twitter resonate with the theoretical findings on diffusion in networks with hubs from chapter 3.

4. Doug McAdam, "Recruitment to High-Risk Activism: The Case of Freedom Summer," *American Journal of Sociology* 92, no. 1 (1986): 64–90.

5. McAdam (ibid.) distinguishes between high-risk/high-cost and low-risk/low-cost collective action. All possible permutations may exist (e.g., low-risk/high-cost collective action, such as writing daily petitions to government officials in a democratic society). The discussion here focuses on high-risk collective action; however, it generalizes to high-cost collective action, *mutatis mutandis*; see also Gladwell, "Small Change."

6. McAdam, "Recruitment," 68–69.

7. Quoted in James S. Coleman, "Social Capital in the Creation of Human Capital," *American Journal of Sociology* 94 (1988): S99.

8. Centola, "Social Media."

9. Hannah Arendt, *The Origins of Totalitarianism* (New York: Schocken Books, 1951). As discussed in Damon Centola, Robb Willer, and Michael Macy,

"The Emperor's Dilemma: A Computational Model of Self-Enforcing Norms" (*American Journal of Sociology* 110, no. 4 [2005]: 19–31), clustered networks can be effective channels for mobilizing an oppressive system of self-enforcing unpopular norms, known as an Emperor's Dilemma. Clustered networks can also be used by regimes for maintaining local enforcement through collective sanctions. However, once a totalitarian regime is in power, clustered networks of strong ties also pose a risk of counter-mobilization.

10. McAdam, "Recruitment," 89; Summer Harlow, "Social Media and Social Movements: Facebook and an Online Guatemalan Justice Movement That Moved Offline," *New Media & Society* 14, no. 2 (2012): 225–243; Nahed Eltantawy and Julie B. Wiest, "Social Media in the Egyptian Revolution: Reconsidering Resource Mobilization Theory," *International Journal of Communication* 5 (2011): 18; Gladwell, "Small Change"; Bond et al., "61-Million-Person Experiment"; John D. McCarthy and Mayer N. Zald, "Resource Mobilization and Social Movements: A Partial Theory," *American Journal of Sociology* 82, no. 6 (1977): 1212–1241; Steinert-Threlkeld, "Spontaneous Collective Action"; Gerald F. Davis and Mayer Zald, "Social Change, Social Theory, and the Convergence of Movements and Organizations," in *Social Movements and Organization Theory*, ed. Gerald F. Davis et al. (New York: Cambridge University Press, 2005), 335–350; Jameson L. Toole, Meeyoung Cha, and Marta C. González, "Modeling the Adoption of Innovations in the Presence of Geographic and Media Influences," *PLoS ONE* 7, no. 1 (2012): e29528; Farshad Kooti et al., "Predicting Emerging Social Conventions in Online Social Networks," in *CIKM '12, Proceedings of the 21st ACM International Conference on Information and Knowledge Management*, 445–454 (New York: Association of Computing Machinery, 2012); Johan Ugander et al., "Structural Diversity in Social Contagion," *Proceedings of the National Academy of Sciences*, 109, no. 16 (2012): 5962–5966; Márton Karsai et al., "Local Cascades Induced Global Contagion: How Heterogeneous Thresholds, Exogenous Effects, and Unconcerned Behaviour Govern Online Adoption Spreading," *Scientific Reports* (2016): 27178, doi.org/10.1038/srep27178.

11. Toole, Cha, and Gonzalez, "Modeling the Adoption"; Kooti et al., "Predicting Emerging Social Conventions"; Ugander et al., "Structural Diversity"; Karsai et al., "Local Cascades."

12. Etan Bakshy, B. Karrer and L. Adamic, "Social Influence and the Diffusion of User-Created Content," in *Proceedings of the 10th ACM conference on Electronic Commerce*, 325–334 (New York: Association of Computing Machinery, 2009); Nathan O. Hodas and Kristina Lerman, "How Visibility and Divided Attention Constrain Social Contagion," in *Proceedings, 2012 ASE/IEEE International Conference on Privacy, Security, Risk and Trust and 2012 ASE/IEEE International Conference on Social Computing*, 249–257 (Piscataway, NJ: Institute of Electrical and Electronic Engineers, 2012).

13. Another design issue that affects diffusion in social media is the visual display of user content. In some cases, screen position can become a stronger factor than social influence for determining diffusion. For instance, social media sites such as Reddit promote "upvoted" material to the top of the user feed, which can push other user-nominated content off of the front page of the website. This media selection process creates a discontinuity in users' exposure to media content, giving disproportionately greater influence to signals that stay on the front page but that may have only marginally more social support. As a result, these digital interfaces can create an incongruity in the social influence dynamics, whereby diffusion is driven more by screen position effects than by social influences.

14. Bogdan State and Lada Adamic, "The Diffusion of Support in an Online Social Movement: Evidence from the Adoption of Equal-Sign Profile Pictures," in *CSCW '15, Proceedings of the 18th ACM Conference on Computer Supported Cooperative Work & Social Computing*, 1741–1750 (New York: Association of Computing Machinery, 2015).

15. Ibid., 1742.

16. Ibid.; Yong Ming Kow et al., "Mediating the Undercurrents: Using Social Media to Sustain a Social Movement," in *Proceedings of the 2016 CHI Conference on Human Factors in Computing Systems*, 3883–3894 (New York: Association of Computing Machinery, 2016); J. Nathan Matias, "Going Dark: Social Factors in Collective Action Against Platform Operators in the Reddit Blackout," in *Proceedings of the 2016 CHI Conference on Human Factors in Computing Systems*, 1138–1151 (New York: Association of Computing Machinery, 2016).

17. Sinan Aral and Christos Nicolaides, "Exercise Contagion in a Global Social Network," *Nature Communications* 8: 14753 (2017), doi:10.1038/ncomms14753. As discussed in chapter 7, these findings resonate with the structural implications of wide bridges for the design of organizational networks. When individuals have overlapping memberships to multiple groups, social reinforcement can flow through wide bridges that connect diverse segments of a population.

18. Christakis and Fowler, "Collective Dynamics."

19. Chris Kuhlman et al., "Effects of Opposition on the Diffusion of Complex Contagions in Social Networks: An Empirical Study," in *Social Computing, Behavioral-Cultural Modeling and Prediction, SBP 2011*, ed. J. Salerno et al., 188–196, vol. 6589 of Lecture Notes in Computer Science (Heidelberg: Springer, 2011); Chris Kuhlman et al., "A Bi-Threshold Model of Complex Contagion and its Application to the Spread of Smoking Behavior" (paper, Fifth SIGKDD Workshop on Social Network Mining and Analysis [SNA-KDD], San Diego, CA, 2011); Sahiti Myneni et al., "Content-Driven Analysis of an Online Community for Smoking Cessation: Integration of Qualitative Techniques, Automated Text Analysis, and Affiliation Networks," *American Journal of Public Health* 105, no. 6 (2015): 1206–1212, doi: 0.2105/AJPH.2014.302464.

20. Marcel Salathé and Sebastian Bonhoeffer, "The Effect of Opinion Clustering on Disease Outbreaks," *Journal of the Royal Society: Interface* 5, no. 29 (2008): 1505–1508; Ellsworth Campbell and Marcel Salathé, "Complex Social Contagion Makes Networks More Vulnerable to Disease Outbreaks," *Scientific Reports* 3 (2013): 1–6; See Centola, Willer, and Macy, "Emperor's Dilemma," for connections to the Emperor's Dilemma. An example of this emerged recently in Northern California, as reported by Philip Ross:

Marin County, California, an enclave of expensive homes, private schools and yoga studios nestled along the Pacific coast just north of San Francisco, has been considered by many to be the epitome of active, healthy living. But in recent years the birthplace of modern mountain biking and competitive trail running has become the epicenter of the country's anti-vaccination movement, a trend that goes back at least a decade and has been largely to blame for California's ongoing measles outbreak that has put health officials and parents on edge.

Despite its reputation for being physically fit and contaminant-free, Marin County has a serious public health problem. Too few parents have chosen to vaccinate their children against such contagious diseases as measles and pertussis, commonly known as whooping cough. So-called anti-vaxxers have often eschewed modern medicine for more traditional health regimens, turning to the Internet's flood of health and wellness blogs for direction.

Many anti-vaxxers said they believed vaccines were toxic and latched on to wild health claims such as the link between vaccines and autism, an idea that began circulating in the late 1990s and has since been debunked. Other anti-vaxxers said they thought that administering too many at once could somehow overload the child's immune system.

Marin children were nearly twice as likely in recent years not to have received the measles, mumps and rubella, or MMR, vaccine, compared with the average California kindergartner, according to county officials. Full vaccine opt-out rates peaked in Marin in 2012 at 7.8 percent—more than twice the state's average. Underimmunization rates, in which children received some but not all federally recommended vaccines, were as high as 17.9 percent. Nonvaccination tends to be higher at Marin County's private schools compared with its public schools. Some classrooms had nonvaccination rates as high as 74 percent, according to officials. With the state's measles outbreak on most every California parent's mind, health officials in Marin have feared that just a few cases could spark an outbreak.

("Marin County and California's Measles Outbreak: A Look into the Epicenter of the Anti-vaccination Trend," *International Business Times*, February 6, 2015, http://www.ibtimes.com/marin-county-californias-measles-outbreak -look-epicenter-anti-vaccination-trend-1808182).

21. The interplay of behavior and disease becomes even more nuanced when we appreciate that there may also be situations in which biological pathogens are complex, such as cases when patients suffer multiple, simultaneous "co-infections" from several diseases. In these situations, each disease increases a patient's susceptibility to the other one, making it more likely that both infections will take in hold. For instance, infection with the influenza virus can increase the likelihood of coinfection with other respiratory diseases, such as the *Streptoccocus pneumoniae* bacterium (a leading cause of pneumonia). Co-infections cannot spread across long ties because they require multiple reinforcing sources of transmission. However, clustered social networks can significantly increase the likelihood that individuals who are exposed to complementary infections, such as pneumonia and flu, or syphilis and HIV, will spread reinforcing co-infections to others, leading to epidemic outbreaks of simultaneous infections; see Hébert-Dufresne and Althouse, "Complex Dynamics."

CHAPTER 6. DIFFUSING INNOVATIONS THAT FACE OPPOSITION

1. University of North Carolina at Chapel Hill, Add Health: The National Longitudinal Study of Adolescent to Adult Health, accessed January 18, 2017, http://www.cpc.unc.edu/projects/addhealth; Framingham Heart Study, Framingham Heart Study: A Project of the National Heart, Lung, and Blood Institute and Boston University, accessed January 18, 2017, https://www.framing hamheartstudy.org/. Use of these data comes from NCBI dbGaP research approval #63796-2 for project #16556 "Social Network Analysis for Developing Behavioral Interventions."

2. The AddHealth data are drawn from the National Longitudinal Study of Adolescent Health, a nationally representative study of students enrolled in

grades 7–12 in 1994–95. Networks A and B were selected at random from the Add Health archive. The data for networks A and B were downloaded from the public AddHealth website at http://www.cpc.unc.edu/projects/addhealth/documentation/publicdata. Students were asked to nominate friends in their community. For each friend named, the student was asked to check off whether he or she participated in any of five activities with the friend.

These activities were the following: 1. You went to (his/her) house in the last seven days; 2. You met (him/her) after school to hang out or go somewhere in the last seven days; 3. You spent time with (him/her) last weekend; 4. You talked with (him/her) about a problem in the last seven days; 5. You talked with (him/her) on the telephone in the last seven days. These activities were summed to create a valued network. Ties range in value from 1, meaning the student nominated the friend but reported no activities, to 6, meaning the student nominated the friend and reported participating in all five activities with the friend. For the simulations, all edges with value of 1 were deleted. All values 2–6 were assigned a uniform value tie. We then extracted the largest connected component from the community. Network A has a population size of 1,082, an average degree of 6, average clustering of 0.171, and consists of 1 component. Network B has a population size of 1,525, an average degree of 5.13, average clustering of 0.143, and consists of 1 component.

3. The Framingham data are drawn from the Framingham Heart Study (1971–2003), a thirty-two-year longitudinal study of health in Framingham, Massachusetts, under the direction of the National Heart, Lung, and Blood Institute; see https://www.framinghamheartstudy.org/about-fhs/index.php. Network C is based on data collection and network construction conducted by Nicholas Christakis and James Fowler, and made available by the Framingham SHARe Social Network in the NCBI dbGaP data portal, as reported in Christakis and Fowler, "Spread of Obesity," and Nicholas Christakis and James Fowler, "Social Contagion Theory: Examining Dynamic Social Networks and Human Behavior," *Statistics in Medicine* 61, no.4 (2013): 556–577. Network C has a population size of 2,033, average degree of 5.03, average local clustering of 0.69, and consists of 1 component. Use of these data comes from NCBI dbGaP research approval #63796-2 for project #16556 "Social Network Analysis for Developing Behavioral Interventions." These simulations primarily examine the behavioral dynamics of smoking cessation.

4. This model uses deterministic thresholds for all simulations. See details in appendix C. Thresholds of 40% and 60% are reported here; however, a complete description of results for all threshold values can be found in Soojong Kim and Damon Centola, "Seeding Strategies for Social Network Interventions in Public Health" (working paper, Annenberg School for Communication, University of Pennsylvania, Philadelphia, 2016, Adobe PDF file).

5. The results here do not depend on the number of initial rounds of diffusion that are used before seeds become susceptible. Fewer initial rounds of diffusion reduce spreading in the random seeding experiments but do not noticeably affect diffusion in the clustered seeding experiments; a greater number of maintenance rounds can increase the effectiveness of random seeding, however does not qualitatively change the results, see details in appendix C.

6. Successful examples of this strategy are found in Centola, Willer, and Macy, "Emperor's Dilemma," and discussed in D. J. Watts and P. S. Dodds, "Threshold Models of Social Influence," in *The Oxford Handbook of Analytical*

Sociology, ed. Peter Hedström and Peter Bearman (Oxford: Oxford University Press, 2009), 475–497.

7. An important extension of these results is to consider the effects of neighborhood boundaries relating to group identity and status; see Max Weber, *Economy and Society: An Outline of Interpretive Sociology,* ed. Guenther Roth and Claus Wittich (Berkeley: University of California Press, 1978); and DiMaggio and Garip, "Network Effects and Social Inequality." Related topics will be addressed using empirical methods in part 3 of this book.

8. These computational results on seeding strategies for behavioral interventions apply to situations where the treatment behavior is relatively costly or difficult to administer (such that only a modest fraction of a population can be treated) and the members of the population have a high level of resistance to the intervention (such that thresholds for adoption are high). Across several hundred trials of these computational experiments, stochastic variation can occasionally enable random seeding to diffuse the intervention with moderate success, when, for instance, seeds are co-located in the same neighborhood, or a seed neighborhood is small enough that a single seed has sufficient influence to trigger a chain reaction of adoption. However, on average, clustered seeding is a significantly more effective strategy for increasing diffusion and maintenance of the intervention behavior. Considering the boundary conditions of these results, there are two important factors that affect the success of an intervention strategy: (i) the size of the seed group and (ii) the level of resistance to the intervention. (I) First, the experimental trials presented here were designed to test the effects of seeding interventions in populations with high thresholds for adoption (40% in the first two experiments, and 60% in the final experiment). If thresholds are lowered, then random seeding approaches can be more effective than clustered seeding. This is because interventions that do not encounter resistance will be simple contagions, which can benefit more from exposure than from reinforcement. (II) Second, the results also depend upon the size of the treated group. The assumption in the computational trials presented here is that intervention treatments are expensive and therefore treating a large fraction of the population is impossible. These experiments show how clustered seeding strategies can enable a relatively small fraction of the population to trigger a sustained change in behavior in a sizable fraction of the community. The results will be different, however, if an intervention treatment is relatively inexpensive and easy to administer. For a seed group that comprises a larger fraction of the population, a random seeding strategy may be more effective at generating widespread change than a clustered one. This is because a relatively large fraction of randomly distributed seeds can saturate neighborhoods throughout the population with reinforcing adopters, generating widespread behavior change. A detailed analysis of these boundary conditions can be found in Kim and Centola, "Seeding Strategies."

9. These implications for seeding contested public-health interventions resonate with earlier research on how "islands" of altruists might be used to seed cooperation into populations of defectors. Granovetter has also noted that similar kinds of approaches might be useful for thinking about how to seed integration norms into segregated schools; Boorman and Levitt, *Genetics of Altruism*; Mark Granovetter, "The Micro-Structure of School Desegregation," in *School Desegregation Research: New Directions in Situational Analysis,* ed. Jeffrey Prager, Douglas Longshore, and Melvin Seeman, 81–110 (New York: Plenum, 1986).

10. Glenn Ellison, "Learning, Local Interaction, and Coordination," *Econometrica* 61, no. 5 (1993): 1047–1071; Andrea Montanari and Amin Saberi, "The Spread of Innovations in Social Networks," *Proceedings of the National Academy of Sciences* 107, no. 47 (2010): 20196–20201; H. Peyton Young—in "Innovation Diffusion in Heterogeneous Populations: Contagion, Social Influence and Social Learning," *American Economic Review* 99 (2009): 1899–1924 and *Individual Strategy and Social Structure: An Evolutionary Theory of Institutions* (Princeton, NJ: Princeton University Press, 1998), 98–102—gives one of the earliest models of stochastic diffusion on networks and explains why clustering accelerates this process. While random networks will ultimately converge on the challenger alternative, expected convergence times are significantly improved by network clustering.

11. Simmel, *Sociology of Georg Simmel*, 123.

12. Cf. Montanari and Saberi, "Spread of Innovations"; Ellison, "Learning"; Young, "Evolution of Conventions"; Centola, Willer, and Macy, "Emperor's Dilemma."

13. Axelrod, *Evolution of Cooperation*; Boorman and Levitt, 1983; Michael D. Cohen, Rick L. Riolo, and Robert Axelrod, "The Role of Social Structure in the Maintenance of Cooperative Regimes," *Rationality and Society* 13, no. 1 (2001): 5–32; Jason Alexander and Brian Skyrms, "Bargaining with Neighbors: Is Justice Contagious?," *Journal of Philosophy* 96, no. 11 (1999): 588–598; Montanari and Saberi, "Spread of Innovations"; Young, *Individual Strategy*.

14. Axelrod, *Evolution of Cooperation*; Alexander and Skyrms, "Bargaining with Neighbors"; cf. Gladwell, *Tipping Point* and Gladwell, "Small Change."

CHAPTER 7. DIFFUSING CHANGE IN ORGANIZATIONS

1. Ronald S. Burt, "Structural Holes and Good Ideas," *American Journal of Sociology* 110, no. 2 (2004): 349–399; Ronald S. Burt, "The Network Structure of Social Capital," *Research in Organizational Behavior* 22 (2000): 345–423; Ronald S. Burt, *Structural Holes: The Social Structure of Competition* (Cambridge, MA: Harvard University Press, 1992).

2. Burt, *Structural Holes*; Burt, "Structural Holes and Good Ideas"; Collins, *Sociology of Philosophies*.

3. Ronald S. Burt, "The Social Capital of Structural Holes," in *The New Economic Sociology*, ed. Mauro F. Guillen et al. (New York: Russell Sage Foundation, 2002), 156–157.

4. Scott E. Page, *The Difference: How the Power of Diversity Creates Better Groups, Firms, Schools, and Societies* (Princeton, NJ: Princeton University Press, 2007); Burt, "Network Structure"; Burt, "Social Capital"; Morten T. Hansen, "The Search-Transfer Problem: The Role of Weak Ties in Sharing Knowledge across Organization Subunits," *Administrative Science Quarterly* 44, no. 1 (1999): 82–111.

5. Syed M. Ahmed and Salman Azhar, "Adoption and Implementation of Total Quality Management (TQM) in the Florida Construction Industry" (paper, Associated Schools of Construction, 42nd Annual Conference, Colorado State University, Ft. Collins, April 20–22, 2006); Mohammed Al-Omiri, "The Factors Influencing the Adoption of Total Quality Management with Emphasis on Innovative/Strategic Management Accounting Techniques: Evidence from Saudi Arabia," *International Journal of Customer Relationship Marketing and Management (IJCRMM)* 3, no. 3 (2012): 33–54; John M. Barron and Kathy Paulson Gjerde, "Who Adopts Total Quality Management (TQM): Theory and An

Empirical Test," *Journal of Economics & Management Strategy* 5, no. 1 (1996): 69–106; Nelson P. Repenning, "A Simulation-Based Approach to Understanding the Dynamics of Innovation Implementation," *Organization Science* 13, no. 2 (2002): 109–127; Hansen, "Search-Transfer Problem," 82; Deborah G. Ancona and David Caldwell, "Beyond Boundary Spanning: Managing External Dependence in Product Development Teams," *Journal of High Technology Management Research* 1, no. 2 (1990): 119–135; Deborah G. Ancona and David F. Caldwell, "Bridging the Boundary: External Activity and Performance in Organizational Teams," *Administrative Science Quarterly* 37 (1992): 651.

6. Centola, "Social Origins of Networks"; Hansen, "Search-Transfer Problem."

7. Cf. Jay R. Galbraith, "Matrix Organization Designs: How to Combine Functional and Project Forms," *Business Horizons* 14, no. 1 (February 1971): 29–40.

8. Centola and Macy, "Complex Contagions."

9. Burt, "Network Structure"; Hansen, "Search-Transfer Problem"; John F. Padgett and Christopher K. Ansell, "Robust Action and the Rise of the Medici, 1400–1434," *American Journal of Sociology* 98, no. 6 (1993): 1259–1319; Burt, "Social Capital," 157.

10. Simmel, *Sociology of Georg Simmel*; David Krackhardt, "The Ties That Torture: Simmelian Tie Analysis in Organizations," *Research in the Sociology of Organizations* 16, no. 1 (1999): 183–210; Repenning, "Simulation-Based Approach"; David Krackhardt, "The Strength of Strong Ties: The Importance of Philos in Organizations," in *Networks in the Knowledge Economy*, ed. Rob Cross, Andrew Parker, and Lisa Sasson (New York: Oxford University Press, 2003), 82–108; Coleman, "Social Capital."

11. Hansen, "Search-Transfer Problem"; Ancona and Caldwell, "Bridging the Boundary."

12. These points connect to a very large literature on the structural antecedents of innovation and team success. Most work on this topic emphasizes the importance of structure because of its implications for diversity. However, related to the discussion here, there are a few studies that concern the structure of overlapping groups and the growth of innovations, e.g., Mathijs de Vaan, Balazs Vedres, and David Stark, "Game Changer: The Topology of Creativity," *American Journal of Sociology* 120, no. 4 (2015): 1144–1194, and their idea of *structural folding*. As they say, "Teams are most likely to be creatively successful when their cognitively heterogeneous groups have points of intersection" (1147). The emphasis in the discussion here is that the key to the successful growth of innovations is not just having points of intersection between heterogeneous groups, but also having *multiple, overlapping points of intersection*, which create wide bridges between cohesive groups. Other related work includes Ray Reagans and Bill McEvily. "Network Structure and Knowledge Transfer: The Effects of Cohesion and Range," *Administrative Science Quarterly* 48, no. 2 (2003): 240–267; Brian Uzzi and Jarrett Spiro, "Collaboration and Creativity: The Small World Problem," *American Journal of Sociology* 111, no. 2 (2005): 447–504; and David Obstfeld, "Social Networks, the Tertius Iungens Orientation, and Involvement in Innovation," *Administrative Science Quarterly* 50, no. 1 (2005): 100–130.

13. Gerald Davis and Henrich Greve, "Corporate Elite Networks and Governance Changes in the 1980s," *American Journal of Sociology* 103, no. 1 (1997): 1–37; Krackhardt, "Strength of Strong Ties"; Coleman, "Social Capital."

14. Walter W. Powell and Paul J. DiMaggio, *The New Institutionalism in Organizational Analysis* (Chicago: University of Chicago Press, 1991).

15. Burt, "Social Capital"; Burt, *Structural Holes*.

16. Peter M. Blau and Joseph E. Schwartz, *Crosscutting Social Circles* (Orlando, FL: Academic Press, 1984); Paul F. Lazarsfeld and Robert K. Merton, "Friendship as a Social Process: A Substantive and Methodological Analysis," *Freedom and Control in Modern Society* 18, no. 1 (1954): 18–66; Feld, "Focused Organization"; Mario Small, *Unanticipated Gains: Origins of Network Inequality in Everyday Life* (Oxford: Oxford University Press, 2009).

17. The application I discuss here concerns organizational networks; however, these same ideas apply more broadly to institutional design in any setting. Moreover, related implications from Thomas Piketty (*Capital in the Twenty-First Century*, trans. Arthur Goldhammer [Cambridge, MA: Belknap Press of Harvard University Press, 2014]) suggest that overlapping networks of wide bridges throughout a society may be necessary for diffusing innovations and complex information essential for reducing wealth inequality. See also Centola, "Social Origins of Networks," for applications to intermarriage, collective action, etc.

18. Centola, "Social Origins of Networks"; Small, *Unanticipated Gains*.

19. Thomas J. Allen, *Managing the Flow of Technology: Technology Transfer and the Dissemination of Technological Information within the R&D Organization* (Cambridge, MA: MIT Press, 1984).

20. Blau and Schwartz, *Crosscutting Social Circles*; Centola, "Social Origins of Networks." Assuming normal levels of homophily, see Jon M. Kleinberg, "Navigation in a Small World," Nature 406, no. 6798 (2000): 845; Duncan J. Watts, Peter S. Dodds, and Mark E. J. Newman, "Identity and Search in Social Networks," *Science* 296 (2002): 1302–1305.

21. As Blau and Schwartz (*Crosscutting Social Circles*, 12) put it, "The degree to which social differences intersect [i.e., the degree to which identities are "expansive" or "focused"] is of prime significance for intergroup relations, and a community's integration. . . . [This] is the central concept of the theory under consideration." The theory of organizational identities presented here is a direct application of Blau and Schwartz, *Crosscutting Social Circles*, and Centola, "Social Origins of Networks."

22. This is tantamount to Blau and Schwartz's concept of "consolidation." See Centola, "Social Origins of Networks."

23. Distinct from homophily, Blau and Schwartz (*Crosscutting Social Circles*) refer to correlated positions across multiple social contexts as "consolidation." This is the central idea developed here.

24. This is sometimes referred to as a "tight" organizational culture; see Michelle J. Gelfand, Lisa Nishii, and Jana Raver, "On the Nature and Importance of Cultural Tightness-Looseness," *Journal of Applied Psychology* 91 (2006):1225–1244.

25. Centola, "Social Origins of Networks"; technical details are provided in appendix C.

26. Ellison, "Learning"; Centola and Baronchelli, "Spontaneous Emergence"; David Lazer and Allan Friedman, "The Network Structure of Exploration and Exploitation," *Administrative Science Quarterly* 52, no. 4 (2007): 667–694; Carroll and Hannan, *Demography of Corporations*. Outside of an organizational context, these structural insights might also be applied to facilitating conflict resolution through the construction of so-called "gateway communities"—that is, network clusters composed of overlapping ties between multiple, conflicting

communities. Research on the Israeli/Palestinian conflict has suggested that networks in which individuals have cross-cutting memberships, thus establishing wide bridges across conflicting groups, may be used to diffuse reconciliation attitudes; see Levy et al., "Ingroups, Outgroups."

27. Cf. H. Russell Bernard, P. Killworth, and L. Sailer, "Informant Accuracy in Social Network Data IV," *Social Networks* 2 (1980): 191–218.

28. This discussion is focused on organizational networks; however, these methodological ideas generalize to sociological research on institutions more broadly; see Centola, "Social Origins of Networks."

29. Cf. Harrison White, *Identity and Control* (Princeton, NJ: Princeton University Press: 2008).

30. Mechanical solidarity; Emile Durkheim, *The Division of Labor in Society*, trans. W. D. Halls (New York: Free Press, 1997).

31. Cf. de Vaan, Vedres, and Stark, "Game Changer," on structural folding; Centola, "Social Origins of Networks."

INTRODUCTION TO PART III

1. A similar sociological lament dates back to Alexis de Tocqueville's (*Democracy in America*, trans. Harvey C. Mansfield and Delba Winthrop [Chicago: University of Chicago Press, 2000]) worries about the integrity of civic life during his increasingly disconnected age, as well as Durkheim's (*Suicide*) well-known fears about increasing anomie in cosmopolitan Europe and Weber's (*Economy and Society*) concerns about the thinning of social relations and its impact on social discourse. Perhaps the main difference here is that this discussion brings attention to the unexpected dangers of an increasingly *connected* age, drawing out the implications of the changing structure of social networks, and what the surfeit of social interactions online may mean for the civic expectations that citizens may come to have of one another, and the resulting implications for the empirical landscape of data-driven social science that studies these interactions (cf. Putnam, *Bowling Alone*).

2. John Seely Brown and Paul Duguid, "Knowledge and Organization: A Social-Practice Perspective," *Organization Science* 12, no. 2 (2001): 198–213; John Seely Brown and Paul Duguid, *The Social Life of Information* (Brighton, MA: Harvard Business Press Publishing, 2000).

3. Emile Durkheim, *Suicide: A Study in Sociology*, trans. J.A. Spaulding and G. Simpson (Glencoe, Illinois: Free Press, 1951); Putnam, *Bowling Alone*; Ferdinand Tonnies, *Community and Society* (New Brunswick, NJ: Transaction Publishers, 1988). As John Seely Brown and Paul Duguid (*Social Life of Information*) put it, "The tight focus on information, with the implicit assumption that if we look after information everything else will fall into place, is ultimately a sort of social and moral blindness" (30).

4. As Robert Putnam wrote, "Social movements and social capital are so closely connected that it is sometimes hard to see which is chicken and which egg. . . . Precisely because social capital is essential for social movements, its erosion could shroud their prospects for the future" (*Bowling Alone*, 152–153).

5. Ralph Waldo Emerson, *Journals of Ralph Waldo Emerson: With Annotations*, ed. Edward Waldo Emerson and Waldo Emerson Forbes, vol. 8, *1849–1855* (Boston: Houghton Mifflin, 1912), 528.

6. W. Brian Arthur, "Competing Technologies, Increasing Returns, and Lock-in by Historical Events," *Economic Journal* 99, no. 394 (1989): 116–131; Paul

A. David, "Clio and the Economics of QWERTY," *American Economic Review* 75, no. 2 (1985): 332–337; I. C. Bupp and J. C. Derian, *Light Water: How the Nuclear Dream Dissolved* (New York: Basic Books, 1978); Robin Cowan, "Backing the Wrong Horse: Sequential Choice among Technologies of Unknown Merit" (PhD diss., Stanford University, 1987); W. Brian Arthur, "Positive Feedbacks in the Economy," *Scientific American* 262, no. 2 (1990): 92–99; Eberhard Bruckner et al., "Hyperselection and Innovation Described by a Stochastic Model of Technological Evolution," in *Evolutionary Economics and Chaos Theory: New Directions in Technology Studies*, ed. Loet Leydesdorff and Peter Van den Besselaar (London: Palgrave Macmillan, 1994), 79–90; W. Brian Arthur, "Competing Technologies: An Overview," in *Technical Change and Economic Theory*, ed. G. Dosi et al. (London: Pinter, 1988), 590–607; W. Brian Arthur, "Self-Reinforcing Mechanisms in Economics," in *The Economy as an Evolving Complex System*, ed. P. W. Anderson, K. Arrow, and D. Pines (Redwood City, CA: Addison-Wesley, 1988), 9–32.

7. Daniel C. Dennett, *Darwin's Dangerous Idea: Evolution and the Meanings of Life* (New York: Simon and Schuster, 1995); Berger, *Contagious*; Carroll and Hannan, *Demography of Corporations*; Glenn R. Carroll and Michael T. Hannan, "Organizational Ecology," in *International Encyclopedia of Social and Behavioral Sciences*, ed. J. Wright, 2nd ed., vol. 17 (Amsterdam: Elsevier, 2015), 358–363; Charles Darwin, *On the Origin of Species by Means of Natural Selection, or the Preservation of Favoured Races in the Struggle for Life.* (London: John Murray, 1859).

8. Leigh Van Valen, "A New Evolutionary Law," *Evolutionary Theory* 1 (1973): 1–30; Lewis Carroll, *Through the Looking Glass: And What Alice Found There* (Chicago: Rand McNally, 1917).

9. Carroll, *Through the Looking Glass*, 34.

10. Berger, *Contagious*; Sinan Aral and Dylan Walker, "Creating Social Contagion through Viral Product Design: A Randomized Trial of Peer Influence in Networks," *Management Science* 57, no. 9 (2011): 1623–1639; Sinan Aral, Lev Muchnik, and Arun Sundararajan, "Engineering Social Contagions: Optimal Network Seeding in the Presence of Homophily," *Network Science* 1, no. 2 (2013): 125–153; Brown and Duguid, *Social Life of Information*.

11. Lee Rainie, Kristen Purcell, and Aaron Smith, "The Social Side of the Internet," Pew Research Center: Internet, Science & Tech, January 18, 2011.

12. Ibid.; Anderson and Rainie, "Millennials"; Aaron Smith, "Why Americans Use Social Media," Pew Research Center: Internet, Science & Tech, November 15, 2011; Susannah Fox and Maeve Duggan, "Health Online 2013," Pew Research Center: Internet, Science & Tech, January 15, 2013; Wen-Ying Sylvia Chou et al., "Social Media Use in the United States: Implications for Health Communication," *Journal of Medical Internet Research* 11, no. 4 (2009): e48.

13. Centola et al., "Homophily, Cultural Drift"; Damon Centola and Arnout van de Rijt, "Choosing Your Network: Social Preferences in an Online Health Community," *Social Science & Medicine* 125 (January 2015): 19–31.

CHAPTER 8. DESIGNING SOCIAL NETWORKS FOR DIFFUSION

1. Putnam, *Bowling Alone*.

2. Rainie, Purcell, and Smith, "Social Side"; Smith, "Why Americans Use Social Media"; Fox and Duggan, "Health Online 2013"; Centola, "Social Media"; Chou et al., "Social Media Use"; Grace C. Huang et al., "Peer Influences: The

Impact of Online and Offline Friendship Networks on Adolescent Smoking and Alcohol Use," *Journal of Adolescent Health* 54, no. 5 (May 2014): 508–514.

3. Avi Asher-Schapiro, "The Virtual Surgeons of Syria," *Atlantic*, August 24, 2016; Jeana Frost and Michael Massagli, "Social Uses of Personal Health Information Within PatientsLikeMe, an Online Patient Community: What Can Happen When Patients Have Access to One Another's Data," *Journal of Medical Internet Research* 10, no. 3 (2008): e15; Chou et al., "Social Media Use"; Centola, "Social Media"; C. Lee Ventola, "Social Media and Health Care Professionals: Benefits, Risks, and Best Practices," *Pharmacy and Therapeutics* 39, no. 7 (2014): 491; Sara LaJeunesse, "Mobile Health Apps Lack Behavior-Change Techniques," Penn State News, May 6, 2014.

4. Recent work on social influence suggests that there are influential and susceptible "types" of people; see Sinan Aral and Dylan Walker, "Identifying Influential and Susceptible Members of Social Networks," *Science* 337 (2012): 337–341. By contrast, the approach developed here suggests that influence and susceptibility typically vary with social context.

5. http://PatientsLikeMe.com.

6. Ibid.; Chou et al., "Social Media Use"; Frost and Massagli, "Social Uses."

7. All quotations from Frost and Massagli, "Social Uses," 5.

8. Lazarsfeld and Merton, "Friendship as a Social Process"; Robert Axelrod, "The Dissemination of Culture: A Model with Local Convergence and Global Polarization," *Journal of Conflict Resolution* 41, no. 2 (1997): 203–226; Miller McPherson, Lynn Smith-Lovin, and James M. Cook, "Birds of a Feather: Homophily in Social Networks," *Annual Review of Sociology* 27 (2001): 415–444; J. Miller McPherson and Lynn Smith-Lovin, "Homophily in Voluntary Organizations: Status Distance and the Composition of Face-to-Face Groups," *American Sociological Review* 52, no. 3 (1987): 370–379.

9. As Lazarsfeld and Merton ("Friendship as a Social Process") put it, "The problem of selection [is] not adequately formulated by the familiar and egregiously misleading question: When it comes to close friendships, do birds of a feather actually flock together? Rather it is a more complex problem of determining the degree to which such selectivity varies for different kinds of social attributes, how it varies within different kinds of social structure, and how such selective patterns come about." In other words, selection preferences, like social relevance, vary by context, which makes them hard to identify.

10. This solution is also the suggestion that emerges from Lazarsfeld and Merton ("Friendship as a Social Process"), but without any direct means of implementation.

11. I am indebted to Maryanne Kirkbride and Kim Schive of MIT's medical office for their assistance implementing these studies into the GetFit program.

12. My colleague Arnout van de Rijt collaborated on this project; see Centola and van de Rijt, "Choosing Your Network."

13. 710 program members signed up to participate in this study. Each of the 710 participants was randomly assigned to one of the ten communities until 71 people were assigned to each network. Because each network had 72 nodes, this left one "unoccupied" node in each network. This spot was reserved for a special seed node, which was used to initiate the diffusion process. The seed node was the same individual in all ten networks. Thus, the fitness profile (age, gender, BMI, and so on) of the first adopter was the same in all ten communities. In every community, the seed node who initiated the diffusion process had a health profile typical of early adopters of health innovations—that is,

healthy (BMI = 23), young (28 years old), and female. By using the same seed profile in every network, it was possible to identify how the homophilous arrangement of social ties affected the reach of the diffusion process, traveling from a healthy seed individual to influence the least healthy members of each population. Additional robustness tests also examined the effects of using alternative seeding strategies. See Centola, "Experimental Study."

14. In this study, participants could not add or remove their ties. Further, none of the subjects in this study had participated in the study where ties could be changed, so there were no confounding effects of having made past social selections in the program.

15. Centola, "Experimental Study."

16. Erving Goffman, *The Presentation of Self in Everyday Life* (New York: Anchor Books, 1959); Amartya Sen, *Identity and Violence: The Illusion of Destiny* (New York: W. W. Norton, 2006); George Akerlof and Rachel Kranton, *Identity Economics* (Princeton, NJ: Princeton University Press, 2010).

17. Berger, *Contagious*; Aral and Walker, "Creating Social Contagion."

18. In some settings, "relational context" can refer to the way that the affective strength of social ties can influence network interactions, as in situations where two close friends may interact differently with a mutual acquaintance than with each other. It can also refer to the temporal arrangement of social interactions, such as situations where there is an important difference between people interacting with all of their network contacts simultaneously, in a group, versus interacting with their contacts one at a time. Each of these features of the relational context may shape how network ties transmit behavioral contagions.

CHAPTER 9. CREATING SOCIAL CONTEXTS FOR BEHAVIOR CHANGE

1. Mary C. Brinton and Victor Nee, *The New Institutionalism in Sociology* (New York: Russell Sage Foundation, 1988); Powell and DiMaggio, *New Institutionalism*; Paul DiMaggio and Walter W. Powell, "The Iron Cage Revisited: Collective Rationality and Institutional Isomorphism in Organizational Fields," *American Sociological Review* 48, no. 2 (1983): 147–160; James G. March, *Primer on Decision Making: How Decisions Happen* (New York: Simon and Schuster, 1994); Mario Small, *Someone to Talk To* (Oxford: Oxford University Press, 2017).

2. Georg Simmel, "How Is Society Possible?," in *Georg Simmel, 1858–1918: A Collection of Essays, with Translations and a Bibliography*, ed. Kurt H. Wolff (Columbus: Ohio State University Press, 1959).

3. Daniel C. Dennett, *Consciousness Explained* (Boston: Back Bay Books, 1991); Edmund Husserl, *Cartesian Meditations: An Introduction to Phenomenology*, trans. Dorion Cairns (The Hague: Martinus Nijhoff, 1950).

4. For a similar reason, anonymity can also be an effective way to improve behavioral influence among strangers. There are many social contexts in which people actively seek out contacts who are not embedded in their friendship networks—for instance, to avoid possible reputation effects that might arise from discussing a potential diagnosis with HIV/AIDS or admitting the challenges of financial hardship. In these cases, casual acquaintances are safer, and in some ways more trusted, than one's close friends or family, who might use this information in future interactions. In most offline settings, these weak ties are random contacts who do not provide any social reinforcement for behavior change. Online, however, social settings may be designed to combine the relational advantages of weak ties—that is, freedom from undesirable reputation

effects—with the structural advantages of clustered ties—namely, reinforcing signals from relevant peers who can encourage desirable behavior change. Online social worlds present a timely opportunity for designing social relationships that are both anonymous and influential. See Small, *Someone To Talk*.

5. Zhang et al., "Efficacy and Causal Mechanism"; Zhang et al., "Support or Competition?"

6. Kenneth J. Arrow, "Gifts and Exchanges," *Philosophy & Public Affairs* 1, no. 4 (1972): 343–362; Robert M. Solow, "The Economist's Approach to Pollution and Its Control," *Science* 173, no. 3996 (1971): 498–503; Samuel Bowles and Sandra Polanía-Reyes, "Economic Incentives and Social Preferences: Substitutes or Complements?," *Journal of Economic Literature* 50, no. 2 (June 1, 2012): 368–425.

7. Centola, "Experimental Study"; Centola and van de Rijt, "Choosing Your Network"; Jason D. Flatt, Yll Agimi, and Steve M. Albert, "Homophily and Health Behavior in Social Networks of Older Adults," *Family & Community Health* 35, no. 4 (2012): 312–321; Thomas W. Valente et al., "Adolescent Affiliations and Adiposity: A Social Network Analysis of Friendships and Obesity," *Journal of Adolescent Health* 45, no. 2 (2009): 202–204.

8. Noah J. Goldstein, Robert B. Cialdini, and Vladas Griskevicius, "A Room with a Viewpoint: Using Social Norms to Motivate Environmental Conservation in Hotels," *Journal of Consumer Research* 35, no. 3 (2008): 472–482; Gregory M. Walton, "The New Science of Wise Psychological Interventions," *Current Directions in Psychological Science* 23, no. 1 (2014): 73–82.

9. Clarissa David, Joseph N. Cappella, and Martin Fishbein, "The Social Diffusion of Influence among Adolescents: Group Interaction in a Chat Room Environment about Antidrug Advertisements," *Communication Theory* 16, no. 1 (2006): 118–140; Robert Hornik et al., "Effects of the National Youth Anti-Drug Media Campaign on Youths," *American Journal of Public Health* 98, no. 12 (2008): 2229–2236.

10. Willemieke Kroeze, Andrea Werkman, and Johannes Brug, "A Systematic Review of Randomized Trials on the Effectiveness of Computer-Tailored Education on Physical Activity and Dietary Behaviors," *Annals of Behavioral Medicine* 31, no. 3 (2006): 205–223; Dariush Mozaffarian et al., "Population Approaches to Improve Diet, Physical Activity, and Smoking Habits A Scientific Statement from the American Heart Association," *Circulation* 126, no. 12 (2012): 1514–1563; Pechmann et al., "Randomised Controlled Trial Evaluation"; S. L. Williams and D. P. French, "What Are the Most Effective Intervention Techniques for Changing Physical Activity Self-Efficacy and Physical Activity Behaviour—And Are They the Same?," *Health Education Research* 26, no. 2 (2011): 308–322; Liliana Laranjo et al., "The Influence of Social Networking Sites on Health Behavior Change: A Systematic Review and Meta-analysis," *Journal of the American Medical Informatics Association*, 22, no. 1 (2014): 243–256; Carol A. Maher et al., "Are Health Behavior Change Interventions That Use Online Social Networks Effective? A Systematic Review," *Journal of Medical Internet Research* 16, no. 2 (2014): e40; Nathan K. Cobb et al., "Initial Evaluation of a Real-World Internet Smoking Cessation System," *Nicotine & Tobacco Research* 7, no. 2 (2005): 207–216; Anna Khaylis et al., "A Review of Efficacious Technology-Based Weight-Loss Interventions: Five Key Components," *Telemedicine and E-Health* 16, no. 9 (2010): 931–938; Kroeze, Werkman, and Brug, "Systematic Review"; Nathan K. Cobb and Amanda L. Graham, "Health Behavior Interventions in the Age of Facebook," *American Journal of Preventive Medicine* 43, no. 5 (2012): 571–572.

11. Jingwen Zhang and I have reviewed a wide range of situations where social comparison can have both positive and negative effects on collective

behavior, and discussed how social design may be used to control these influences; see Jingwen Zhang and Damon Centola, "How Social Networks Shape Social Comparison," in *Social Comparison, Judgment & Behavior*, edited by Jerry Suls (New York: Oxford University Press, forthcoming).

EPILOGUE: EXPERIMENTAL SOCIOLOGY

1. Iain D. Couzin et al., "Uninformed Individuals Promote Democratic Consensus in Animal Groups," *Science* 334, no. 6062 (2011): 1578–1580.

2. Mitchel Resnick, *Turtles, Termites, and Traffic Jams: Explorations in Massively Parallel Microworlds* (Cambridge, MA: MIT Press, 1997); Dirk Helbing, "Traffic and Related Self-Driven Many-Particle Systems," *Reviews of Modern Physics* 73, no. 4 (2001): 1067–1141.

3. Michael Li and Raymond Perkins, "The Perils of Polling in a Brexit and Donald Trump World," *TechCrunch*.

4. Important new work in this area has come from the experimental approach described in this epilogue; see Colin F. Camerer, George Loewenstein, and Matthew Rabin, *Advances in Behavioral Economics* (Princeton, NJ: Princeton University Press, 2003).

5. Gustave Le Bon, *The Crowd: A Study of the Popular Mind* (Fischer, 1897); Charles Mackay, *Memoirs of Extraordinary Popular Delusions and the Madness of Crowds* (London: Office of National Illustrated Library, 1852).

6. Robert K. Merton, *The Sociology of Science: Theoretical and Empirical Investigations* (Chicago: University of Chicago Press, 1973).

7. Edward Dolnick, *The Clockwork Universe: Isaac Newton, the Royal Society, and the Birth of the Modern World* (New York: Harper Collins, 2011); Philip Ball, *Critical Mass: How One Thing Leads to Another* (New York: Farrar, Straus and Giroux, 2006); Alex Pentland, *Social Physics: How Social Networks Can Make Us Smarter* (New York: Penguin Books, 2014).

8. Thomas Ernst Uebel, *Overcoming Logical Positivism from Within: The Emergence of Neurath's Naturalism in the Vienna Circle's Protocol Sentence Debate* (Amsterdam: Editions Rodopi, 1992), 205. In practice, no scientist actually holds this view; however, popular espousals of data science have come close to embracing it.

9. Ann Blair, "Tycho Brahe's Critique of Copernicus and the Copernican System," *Journal of the History of Ideas* 51, no. 3 (1990): 355–377; R. Taton and C. Wilson, eds., *Planetary Astronomy from the Renaissance to the Rise of Astrophysics, Part A, Tycho Brahe to Newton* (Cambridge: Cambridge University Press, 1989).

10. Paul B. Scheurer and Guy Debrock, *Newton's Scientific and Philosophical Legacy*, vol. 123 of the International Archives of the History of Ideas (Dordrecht: Kluwer Academic, 1988); These tests were famously done by Huygens and Hooke, whose work informed Newton's theory of gravitation. Cf. Arthur Ernest Bell and A. E. Bell, *Christian Huygens and the Development of Science in the Seventeenth Century* (London: Edward Arnold, 1947); G. E. Smith, "The Methodology of the Principia," in *The Cambridge Companion to Newton*, ed. I. B. Cohen and G. E. Smith (Cambridge: Cambridge University Press, 2002); mostly Huygens and Hooke conducted these tests, not Newton; Dolnick, *Clockwork Universe*; also, see Hooke's intuition on this prior to Newton, Scheurer and Debrock, *Newton's Scientific and Philosophical Legacy*.

11. Durkheim, *Suicide*; Karl Marx, *Capital: Critique of Political Economy*, trans. Samuel Moore and Edward Aveling (Moscow: Progress Publishers, 1867); Max

Weber, *The Protestant Ethic and the Spirit of Capitalism: And Other Writings* (New York: Penguin, 2002).

12. I do not think that Popperian falsification is itself a basis for evaluating scientific theories. There are stronger and weaker kinds of tests, and there are situations in which keeping a theory means abandoning so many commitments (e.g., to physics or to bimodal logic), that the theory is, in practice if not in principle, falsified. I refer here to these strong tests, which have not been available for evaluating classical theories of causation in research on the dynamics of collective behavior; see Willard Van Orman Quine, "Two Dogmas of Empiricism," *Philosophical Review* 60 (1951): 20–43.

13. Robert K. Merton, *Social Theory and Social Structure* (New York: Free Press, 1968); Robert K. Merton, "The Unanticipated Consequences of Purposive Social Action," *American Sociological Review* 1, no. 6 (1936): 894–904; Peter Hedström and Richard Swedberg, eds., *Social Mechanisms: An Analytical Approach to Social Theory* (Cambridge: Cambridge University Press, 1998); Jon Elster, *Nuts and Bolts for the Social Sciences* (Cambridge: Cambridge University Press, 1989); Granovetter, "Threshold Models"; Schelling, *Micromotives*; Ellison, "Learning"; Lars-Erik Cederman, *Emergent Actors in World Politics: How States and Nations Develop and Dissolve* (Princeton, NJ: Princeton University Press, 1997); Andrew V. Papachristos, Tracey L. Meares, and Jeffrey Fagan, "Attention Felons: Evaluating Project Safe Neighborhoods in Chicago," *Journal of Empirical Legal Studies* 4, no. 2 (2007): 223–272; Andrew V. Papachristos, Tracey L. Meares, and Jeffrey Fagan, "Why Do Criminals Obey the Law? The Influence of Legitimacy and Social Networks on Active Gun Offenders," *Journal of Criminal Law and Criminology* 102, no. 2 (2012): 397–440; Robert J. Sampson, Stephen W. Raudenbush, and Felton Earls, "Neighborhoods and Violent Crime: A Multilevel Study of Collective Efficacy," *Science* 277, no. 5328 (1997): 918–924; Marwell and Oliver, *Critical Mass*; Gould, "Collective Action"; Damon Centola, "Homophily, Networks, and Critical Mass: Solving the Start-up Problem in Large Group Collective Action," *Rationality and Society* 25, no. 1 (2013): 3–40; Michael Suk-Young Chwe, "Structure and Strategy in Collective Action," *American Journal of Sociology* 105, no. 1 (1999): 128–156; March, "Exploration and Exploitation"; David Lazer and Allan Friedman, "The Network Structure of Exploration and Exploitation," *Administrative Science Quarterly* 52, no. 4 (2007): 667–694; Rosabeth Moss Kanter, *Men and Women of the Corporation* (New York: Basic Books, 1977); Berkman and Kawachi, eds., *Social Epidemiology*.

14. Rosabeth Moss Kanter, "Some Effects of Proportions on Group Life: Skewed Sex Ratios and Responses to Token Women," *American Journal of Sociology* 82, no. 5 (1977): 965–990; Kanter, *Men and Women*; Vicki W. Kramer et al., *Critical Mass on Corporate Boards: Why Three or More Women Enhance Governance* (Boston: Wellesley Centers for Women, 2006).

15. Centola and Baronchelli, "Spontaneous Emergence."

16. Matthew J. Salganik, Peter Sheridan Dodds, and Duncan J. Watts, "Experimental Study of Inequality and Unpredictability in an Artificial Cultural Market," *Science* 311, no. 5762 (2006): 854–856; Arnout van de Rijt et al., "Field Experiments of Success-Breeds-Success Dynamics," *Proceedings of the National Academy of Sciences* 111, no. 19 (2014): 6934–6939; Akihiro Nishi et al., "Inequality and Visibility of Wealth in Experimental Social Networks," *Nature* 526, no. 7573 (2015): 426–429.

17. For an excellent overview of the practical advantages of web-based approaches, my colleague, Matthew Salganik, has recently published a very

useful handbook showing the variety of strategies for conducting social research online at http://www.bitbybitbook.com/.

18. Cecilia L. Ridgeway et al., "How Do Status Beliefs Develop? The Role of Resources and Interactional Experience," *American Sociological Review* 63, no. 3 (1998): 331–350; Quincy Thomas Stewart, "Big Bad Racists, Subtle Prejudice and Minority Victims: An Agent-Based Analysis of the Dynamics of Racial Inequality" (paper, Annual Meeting of the Population Association of America, Dallas, TX, April 2010); Centola, "Experimental Study"; Centola, "Spread of Behavior"; Winter Mason and Duncan J. Watts, "Collaborative Learning in Networks," *Proceedings of the National Academy of Sciences* 109, no. 3 (2012): 764–769; Winter Mason, Andy Jones, and Robert L. Goldstone, "Propagation of Innovations in Networked Groups," *Journal of Experimental Psychology: General* 137, no. 3 (2008): 422–433; Joshua A. Becker, Devon Brackbill, and Damon Centola, "The Network Dynamics of Social Influence in the Wisdom of Crowds," *Proceedings of the National Academy of Science* 114, no. 26 (2017): 5070–5076; Devon Brackbill and Damon Centola, "The Network Structure of Solution Discovery" (working paper, Annenberg School for Communication, University of Pennsylvania, PA, 2016, Adobe PDF file).

19. Peter M. Blau, *Inequality and Heterogeneity: A Primitive Theory of Social Structure* (New York: Free Press, 1977).

20. Cecilia L. Ridgeway, "Status Construction Theory," in *The Wiley Blackwell Encyclopedia of Race, Ethnicity, and Nationalism* (Wiley Online Library, 2015), 1–3; Shelley J. Correll and Cecilia L. Ridgeway, "Expectation States Theory," in *Handbook of Social Psychology*, ed. John Delameter (New York: Springer, 2006), 29–51; Cecilia L. Ridgeway and Shelley J. Correll, "Consensus and the Creation of Status Beliefs," *Social Forces* 85, no. 1 (2006): 431–453; William Peters, *A Class Divided: Then and Now* (New Haven, CT: Yale University Press, 1987); William Peters, dir., "A Class Divided," *Frontline*, aired March 26, 1985, on PBS.

21. Ridgeway, "Status Construction Theory"; Ridgeway et al., "How Do Status Beliefs Develop?"; Cecilia L. Ridgeway and Joseph Berger, "Expectations, Legitimation, and Dominance Behavior in Task Groups," *American Sociological Review* 51, no. 5 (1986): 603–617; Ridgeway and Correll, "Consensus"; Correll and Ridgeway, "Expectation States Theory."

22. Shelley J. Correll et al., "It's the Conventional Thought That Counts: How Third-Order Inference Produces Status Advantage," *American Sociological Review* 82 (2017): 297–327.

23. Burt, *Structural Holes*.

24. Vincent Buskens and Arnout van de Rijt, "Dynamics of Networks if Everyone Strives for Structural Holes," *American Journal of Sociology* 114, no. 2 (2008): 371–407.

25. Asch, "Effects of Group Pressure"; Peter M. Krafft, Michael Macy, and Alex Pentland, "Bots as Virtual Confederates: Design and Ethics," *Proceedings of the 2017 ACM Conference on Computer-Supported Cooperative Work and Social Computing* (New York: ACM, 2017).

26. Douglas Guilbeault and Samuel Woolley, "How Twitter Bots Are Shaping the Election," *Atlantic*, November 1, 2016; Amanda Hess, "On Twitter, a Battle among Political Bots," *New York Times*, December 14, 2016. I am indebted to Douglas Guilbeault for this discussion.

27. Amy Gutmann and Dennis F. Thompson, *Democracy and Disagreement* (Cambridge, MA: Harvard University Press, 1996); James S. Fishkin, *When the*

People Speak: Deliberative Democracy and Public Consultation (Oxford: Oxford University Press, 2009); Vincent Price, Joseph N. Cappella, and Lilach Nir, "Does Disagreement Contribute to More Deliberative Opinion?," *Political Communication* 19, no. 1 (2002): 95–112; Joseph N. Cappella, Vincent Price, and Lilach Nir, "Argument Repertoire as a Reliable and Valid Measure of Opinion Quality: Electronic Dialogue during Campaign 2000," *Political Communication* 19, no. 1 (2002): 73–93; Richard E. Petty, John T. Cacioppo, and Rachel Goldman, "Personal Involvement as a Determinant of Argument-Based Persuasion," *Journal of Personality and Social Psychology* 41, no. 5 (1981): 847–855; Diana C. Mutz, "The Consequences of Cross-Cutting Networks for Political Participation," *American Journal of Political Science* 46, no. 4 (2002): 838–855; Andrew F. Hayes, Dietram A. Scheufele, and Michael E. Huge, "Nonparticipation as Self-Censorship: Publicly Observable Political Activity in a Polarized Opinion Climate," *Political Behavior* 28, no. 3 (2006): 259–283; Elisabeth Noelle-Neumann, "The Spiral of Silence: A Theory of Public Opinion," *Journal of Communication* 24, no. 2 (1974): 43–51; Kurt Neuwirth, Edward Frederick, and Charles Mayo, "The Spiral of Silence and Fear of Isolation," *Journal of Communication* 57, no. 3 (2007): 450–468.

28. David G. Myers and George D. Bishop, "Discussion Effects on Racial Attitudes," *Science* 169, no. 3947 (19970): 778–779; Daniel J. Isenberg, "Group Polarization: A Critical Review and Meta-analysis," *Journal of Personality and Social Psychology* 50, no. 6 (1986): 1141–51; Cass R. Sunstein, *Going to Extremes: How Like Minds Unite and Divide* (Oxford: Oxford University Press, 2009); Boaz Hameiri et al., "Moderating Attitudes in Times of Violence Through Paradoxical Thinking Intervention," *Proceedings of the National Academy of Sciences* 113, no. 43 (2016): 12105–12110.

APPENDIX A: THE ETHICS OF SOCIAL DESIGN

1. National Commission for the Protection of Human Subjects of Biomedical and Behavioral Research, *The Belmont Report: Ethical Principles and Guidelines for the Protection of Human Subjects of Research* (Washington, DC: US Department of Health, Education, and Welfare, 1978).

2. To date, the best treatment of this topic is found in Cass R. Sunstein, *The Ethics of Influence: Government in the Age of Behavioral Science* (New York: Cambridge University Press, 2016). My discussion here extends beyond behavioral economics and concerns the uses of computational social science and network science research to influence behavior change.

3. Mancur Olson, *The Logic of Collective Action: Public Goods and the Theory of Groups* (Cambridge, MA: Harvard University Press, 1965).

4. Axelrod, *Evolution of Cooperation*.

5. Goldstein, Cialdini, and Griskevicius, "Room with a Viewpoint"; John C. Hershey et al., "The Roles of Altruism, Free Riding, and Bandwagoning in Vaccination Decisions," *Organizational Behavior and Human Decision Processes* 59, no. 2 (1994): 177–187; Rogers, *Diffusion of Innovations*; Gary King, Jennifer Pan, and Margaret E. Roberts, "How the Chinese Government Fabricates Social Media Posts for Strategic Distraction, Not Engaged Argument," *American Political Science Review* 111, no. 3 (August 2017): 484--501; Gary King, Jennifer Pan, and Margaret E. Roberts, "Reverse-Engineering Censorship in China: Randomized Experimentation and Participant Observation," *Science* 345, no. 6199 (2014): 1–10; Gary King, Jennifer Pan, and Margaret Roberts, "How Censorship in China Allows Government Criticism but Silences Collective Expression," *American Political Science Review* 107, no. 2 (May 2013): 1–18; Chen-fong

Wu, "The Relationship between Business Ethics Diffusion, Knowledge Sharing and Service Innovation," *Management Decision* 54, no. 6 (2016): 1343–1358; Filiz Garip, *On the Move: The Changing Mechanisms of Mexico-U.S. Migration* (Princeton, NJ: Princeton University Press, 2016); Filiz Garip, "Social Capital and Migration: How Do Similar Resources Lead to Divergent Outcomes?" *Demography* 45, no. 3 (2008): 591–617; Laurence R. Iannaccone, "Why Strict Churches Are Strong," *American Journal of Sociology* 99, no. 5 (1994): 1180–1211; Elizabeth Levy Paluck and Hana Shepherd, "The Salience of Social Referents: A Field Experiment on Collective Norms and Harassment Behavior in a School Social Network," *Journal of Personality and Social Psychology* 103, no. 6 (2012): 899; Elizabeth Levy Paluck, Hana Shepherd, and Peter M. Aronow, "Changing Climates of Conflict: A Social Network Experiment in 56 Schools," *Proceedings of the National Academy of Sciences* 113, no. 3 (2016): 566–571; Durkheim, *Suicide*; Bond et al., "61-Million-Person Experiment."

6. Sunstein, *Ethics of Influence*; Thaler and Sunstein, *Nudge*.

7. Kirk H. Smith and Martha Rogers, "Effectiveness of Subliminal Messages in Television Commercials: Two Experiments," *Journal of Applied Psychology* 79, no. 6 (1994): 866–874; S. J. Brooks et al., "Exposure to Subliminal Arousing Stimuli Induces Robust Activation in the Amygdala, Hippocampus, Anterior Cingulate, Insular Cortex and Primary Visual Cortex: A Systematic Meta-Analysis of fMRI Studies," *NeuroImage* 59, no. 3 (2012): 2962–2973; Friederike Schlaghecken and Martin Eimer, "Subliminal Stimuli Can Bias 'Free' Choices between Response Alternatives," *Psychonomic Bulletin & Review* 11 (2004): 463–468; Ap Dijksterhuis et al., "The Unconscious Consumer: Effects of Environment on Consumer Behavior," *Journal of Consumer Psychology* 15, no. 3 (2005): 193–202; Norman F. Dixon, *Subliminal Perception: The Nature of a Controversy* (New York: McGraw-Hill, 1971).

8. Simon Ruch, Marc Alain Züst, and Katharina Henke, "Subliminal Messages Exert Long-Term Effects on Decision-Making," *Neuroscience of Consciousness* 2016, no. 1 (2016): niw013. doi: 10.1093/nc/niw013.

9. Kramer, Guillory, and Hancock, "Experimental Evidence."

10. Lucien A. Bebchuk and Jesse M. Fried, "Executive Compensation at Fannie Mae: A Case Study of Perverse Incentives, Nonperformance Pay, and Camouflage," *Journal of Corporation Law* 30, no. 4 (2005): 807–822; James Surowiecki, "Open Season," *New Yorker*, October 13, 2013.

11. Uri Gneezy and Aldo Rustichini. "A Fine Is a Price," *Journal of Legal Studies* 29 (2000): 1–17.

APPENDIX B. METHODS OF COMPUTATIONAL SOCIAL SCIENCE

1. Were it not for my ignorance, I would include ethnography (and other qualitative approaches) in this list of methods. Qualitative methods are omitted here only because I do not know enough about them to know how they would be incorporated into the approach I have described. But I have no doubt that they have a meaningful role to play.

APPENDIX C. TECHNICAL APPENDIX FOR MODELS

1. Watts and Strogatz, "Collective Dynamics."
2. Newman and Watts, "Scaling and Percolation."
3. Maslov and Sneppen, "Specificity and Stability."

4. Centola and Macy, "Complex Contagions."

5. Grannovetter, "Threshold Models."

6. Duncan J. Watts, "A Simple Model of Global Cascades on Random Networks," *Proceedings of the National Academy of Sciences* 99, no. 9 (2002): 5766–5771.

7. Ties are nonredundant so long as there are no more than a bridge ties to a single member of D. Suppose $a = 2$. If there were three bridge ties to any node in D, then one of these ties would be redundant, leaving only two nonredundant ties in the bridge.

8. This probability can be calculated on a ring lattice of known size and degree. For any large network, the probability approaches zero.

9. Note that it is also the case that $R = 0$ if $a = 1$ and $z = 2$, giving $W_c = W_{max} = 1$. The rewired tie now creates a break along the ring but also creates a bridge across the ring, allowing the contagion to fan out from three locations instead of just two (prior to rewiring). However, if $a > 1$ and $R = 0$, the first tie that is randomly rewired will break the ring but cannot create a shortcut.

10. Ellison, "Learning"; Young, "Evolution of Conventions."

11. Watts, Dodds, and Newman, "Identity and Search," 1303.

References

ACOR.org—Association of Cancer Online Resources. Accessed February 5, 2017. http://www.acor.org/.

Ahmed, Syed M., and Salman Azhar. "Adoption and Implementation of Total Quality Management (TQM) in the Florida Construction Industry." Paper presented at Associated Schools of Construction: 42nd Annual Conference, Colorado State University, Ft. Collins, April 20–22, 2006. http://ascpro0.asc web.org/archives/cd/2006/2006pro/2006/CPRT27_Ahmed06_7500.htm.

Ajzen, Icek. "The Theory of Planned Behavior." *Organizational Behavior and Human Decision Processes* 50, no. 2 (1991): 179–211.

Ajzen, Icek, and Martin Fishbein. *Understanding Attitudes and Predicting Social Behaviour.* Englewood Cliffs, NJ: Prentice-Hall, 1980.

Akerlof, George, and Rachel Kranton. *Identity Economics.* Princeton, NJ: Princeton University Press, 2010.

Albert, Réka, Hawoong Jeong, and Albert-László Barabási. "Error and Attack Tolerance of Complex Networks." *Nature* 406, no. 6794 (2000): 378–382.

Alexander, Jason, and Brian Skyrms, "Bargaining with Neighbors: Is Justice Contagious?" *Journal of Philosophy* 96, no. 11 (1999): 588–598.

Allen, Thomas J. *Managing the Flow of Technology: Technology Transfer and the Dissemination of Technological Information within the R&D Organization.* Cambridge, MA: MIT Press, 1984.

Al-Omiri, Mohammed. "The Factors Influencing the Adoption of Total Quality Management with Emphasis on Innovative/Strategic Management Accounting Techniques: Evidence from Saudi Arabia." *International Journal of Customer Relationship Marketing and Management (IJCRMM)* 3, no. 3 (2012): 33–54.

Ancona, Deborah G., and David Caldwell. "Beyond Boundary Spanning: Managing External Dependence in Product Development Teams." *Journal of High Technology Management Research* 1, no. 2 (1990): 119–135.

———. "Bridging the Boundary: External Activity and Performance in Organizational Teams." *Administrative Science Quarterly* 37 (1992): 634–665.

Anderson, Janna, and Lee Rainie. "Millennials Will Make Online Sharing in Networks a Lifelong Habit." Pew Research Center: Internet & Technology, July 9, 2010. http://www.pewinternet.org/2010/07/09/millennials-will-make -online-sharing-in-networks-a-lifelong-habit/.

Anderson, Philip W. "More Is Different." *Science* 177, no. 4047 (1972): 393–396.

Aral, Sinan, Lev Muchnik, and Arun Sundararajan. "Engineering Social Contagions: Optimal Network Seeding in the Presence of Homophily." *Network Science* 1, no. 2 (2013): 125–153.

Aral, Sinan, and Christos Nicolaides. "Exercise Contagion in a Global Social Network." *Nature Communications* 8: 14753 (2017). doi:10.1038/ncomms14753.

Aral, Sinan, and Dylan Walker. "Creating Social Contagion through Viral Product Design: A Randomized Trial of Peer Influence in Networks." *Management Science* 57, no. 9 (2011): 1623–1639.

———. "Identifying Influential and Susceptible Members of Social Networks." *Science* 337 (2012): 337–341.

Arendt, Hannah. *The Origins of Totalitarianism.* London: Schocken Books, 1951.

Arrow, Kenneth J. "Gifts and Exchanges." *Philosophy & Public Affairs* 1, no. 4 (1972): 343–362.

Arthur, W. Brian. "Competing Technologies: An Overview." In *Technical Change and Economic Theory*, edited by G. Dosi, C. Freeman, R. Nelson, G. Silverberg, and L. Soete, 590–607. London: Pinter, 1988.

———. "Competing Technologies, Increasing Returns, and Lock-In by Historical Events." *Economic Journal* 99, no. 394 (1989): 116–131.

———. "Positive Feedbacks in the Economy." *Scientific American* 262, no. 2 (1990): 92–99.

———. "Self-Reinforcing Mechanisms in Economics." In *The Economy as an Evolving Complex System*, edited by P. W. Anderson, K. Arrow, and D. Pines, 9–32. Redwood City, CA: Addison-Wesley, 1988.

Asch, Solomon E. "Effects of Group Pressure upon the Modification and Distortion of Judgments." *Groups, Leadership, and Men: Research in Human Relations*, edited by Harold S. Guetzkow, 222–236. Pittsburgh: Carnegie Press, 1951.

Asher-Schapiro, Avi. "The Virtual Surgeons of Syria." *Atlantic*, August 24, 2016. http://www.theatlantic.com/international/archive/2016/08/syria-madaya-doctors-whatsapp-facebook-surgery-assad/496958/.

Auvert, Bertran, Dirk Taljaard, Emmanuel Lagarde, Joelle Sobngwi-Tambekou, Rémi Sitta, and Adrian Puren. "Randomized, Controlled Intervention Trial of Male Circumcision for Reduction of HIV Infection Risk: The ANRS 1265 Trial." *PLOS Medicine* 2, no. 11 (2005): e298.

Axelrod, Robert. "The Dissemination of Culture: A Model with Local Convergence and Global Polarization." *Journal of Conflict Resolution* 41, no. 2 (1997): 203–226.

———. *The Evolution of Cooperation.* Rev. ed. New York: Basic Books, 1984.

Backstrom, Lars, Dan Huttenlocher, Jon Kleinberg, and Xiangyang Lan. "Group Formation in Large Social Networks: Membership, Growth, and Evolution." In *Proceedings of the 12th ACM SIGKDD International Conference on Knowledge Discovery and Data Mining*, 44–54. New York: Association of Computing Machinery, 2006.

Baer, John S. "Effects of College Residence on Perceived Norms for Alcohol Consumption: An Examination of the First Year in College." *Psychology of Addictive Behaviors* 8, no. 1 (1994): 43–50.

Bailey, Norman T. J., *The Mathematical Theory of Infectious Diseases and Its Application.* London: Griffin, 1975.

Bailey, Robert C., Stephen Moses, Corette B. Parker, Kawango Agot, Ian Maclean, John N. Krieger, Carolyn F. M. Williams, Richard T. Campbell, and

Jeckoniah O. Ndinya-Achola. "Male Circumcision for HIV Prevention in Young Men in Kisumu, Kenya: A Randomised Controlled Trial." *Lancet* 369, no. 9562 (2007): 643–656.

Bakshy, Etan, B. Karrer, and L. Adamic, "Social Influence and the Diffusion of User-Created Content." In *Proceedings of the 10th ACM Conference on Electronic Commerce*, 325–334. New York: Association of Computing Machinery, 2009.

Balkundi, Prasad, and David A. Harrison. "Ties, Leaders, and Time in Teams: Strong Inference about Network Structure's Effects on Team Viability and Performance." *Academy of Management Journal* 49, no. 1 (2006): 49–68.

Ball, Philip. *Critical Mass: How One Thing Leads to Another*. New York: Farrar, Straus and Giroux, 2006.

Bankole, A., G. Rodríguez, and C. F. Westoff. "Mass Media Messages and Reproductive Behaviour in Nigeria." *Journal of Biosocial Science* 28, no. 2 (1996): 227–239.

Barabási, Albert-László. *Linked: How Everything Is Connected to Everything Else and What It Means for Business, Science, and Everyday Life*. New York: Perseus Books, 2002.

Barabási, Albert-László, and Réka Albert. "Emergence of Scaling in Random Networks." *Science* 286, no. 5439 (1999): 509–512.

Barabási, Albert-László, Réka Albert, and Hawoong Jeong. "Scale-Free Characteristics of Random Networks: The Topology of the World-Wide Web." *Physica A: Statistical Mechanics and Its Applications* 281, no. 1 (2000): 69–77.

Barash, Vladimir, Christopher Cameron, and Michael Macy. "Critical Phenomena in Complex Contagions." *Social Networks* 34 (2012): 451–461.

Barclay, Michael J., William Christie, Jeffrey Harris, Eugene Kandel, and Paul H. Schultz. "Effects of Market Reform on the Trading Costs and Depths of Nasdaq Stocks." *Journal of Finance* 54, no. 1 (1999): 1–34.

Barron, John M., and Kathy Paulson Gjerde. "Who Adopts Total Quality Management (TQM): Theory and an Empirical Test." *Journal of Economics & Management Strategy* 5, no. 1 (1996): 69–106.

Bass, Frank M. "A New Product Growth for Model Consumer Durables." *Management Science* 15, no. 5 (1969): 215–227.

BBC News. "Ebola Outbreak: Guinea Health Team Killed." September 19, 2014, sec. Africa. http://www.bbc.com/news/world-africa-29256443.

Beaman, Lori, Ariel B. Yishay, Jeremy Magruder, and Ahmed M. Mobarak. "Can Network Theory-Based Targeting Increase Technology Adoption?" Working paper, Northwestern University, Evanston, IL, June 2015. http://faculty.wcas.northwestern.edu/~lab823/MNW_june15.pdf.

Bebchuk, Lucien A., and Jesse M. Fried. "Executive Compensation at Fannie Mae: A Case Study of Perverse Incentives, Nonperformance Pay, and Camouflage." *Journal of Corporation Law* 30, no. 4 (2005): 807–822.

Becker, Joshua A., Devon Brackbill, and Damon Centola. "The Network Dynamics of Social Influence in the Wisdom of Crowds." *Proceedings of the National Academy of Science* 114, no. 26 (2017): 5070–5076.

Begum, Hamida A., and Eliza Ahmed. "Individual Risk Taking and Risky Shift as a Function of Cooperation-Competition Proneness of Subjects." *Psychological Studies* 31, no. 1 (1986): 21–25.

Bell, Arthur E., and A. E. Bell. *Christian Huygens and the Development of Science in the Seventeenth Century.* London: Edward Arnold, 1947.

Berezow, Alex, and Hank Campbell. *Science Left Behind: Feel-Good Fallacies and the Rise of the Anti-scientific Left.* New York: PublicAffairs, 2012.

Berg, Howard C. *Random Walks in Biology.* Princeton, NJ: Princeton University Press, 1993.

Berg, Ivar. *Education and Jobs: The Great Training Robbery.* New York: Praeger Publishers, 1970.

Berger, Jonah. *Contagious: Why Things Catch On.* New York: Simon and Schuster, 2013.

Berkman, Lisa F., and Ichiro Kawachi. *Social Epidemiology.* Oxford: Oxford University Press, 2000.

Berkman, Lisa F., Ichiro Kawachi, and M. Maria Glymour. *Social Epidemiology.* 2nd. ed. Oxford: Oxford University Press, 2014.

Bernard, H. Russell, P. Killworth, and L. Sailer. "Informant Accuracy in Social Network Data IV." *Social Networks* 2 (1980): 191–218.

Bicchieri, Cristina. *The Grammar of Society: The Nature and Dynamics of Social Norms.* Cambridge: Cambridge University Press, 2006.

———. *Norms in the Wild: How to Diagnose, Measure and Change Social Norms.* Oxford: Oxford University Press, 2016.

Biggs, Michael. "Positive Feedback in Collective Mobilization: The American Strike Wave of 1886." *Theory and Society* 32, no. 2 (2003): 217–254.

———. "Strikes as Forest Fires: Chicago and Paris in the Late Nineteenth Century." *American Journal of Sociology* 110, no. 6 (2005): 1684–1714.

Blair, Ann. "Tycho Brahe's Critique of Copernicus and the Copernican System." *Journal of the History of Ideas* 51, no. 3 (1990): 355–377.

Blau, Peter M. *Inequality and Heterogeneity: A Primitive Theory of Social Structure.* New York: Free Press, 1977.

Blau, Peter M., Terry C. Blum, and Joseph E. Schwartz. "Heterogeneity and Intermarriage." *American Sociological Review* 47, no. 1 (1982): 45–62.

Blau, Peter M., and Joseph E. Schwartz. *Crosscutting Social Circles.* Orlando, FL: Academic Press, 1984.

Boguñá, Marián, Dmitri Krioukov, and K. C. Claffy. "Navigability of Complex Networks." *Nature Physics* 5, no. 1 (2009): 74–80.

Bond, Robert M., Christopher J. Fariss, Jason J. Jones, Adam D. I. Kramer, Cameron Marlow, Jaime E. Settle, and James H. Fowler. "A 61-Million-Person Experiment in Social Influence and Political Mobilization." *Nature* 489, no. 7415 (2012): 295–298.

Boorman, Scott A., and Paul R. Levitt. *The Genetics of Altruism.* New York: Academic Press, 1983.

Borsari, Brian, and Kate B. Carey. "Peer Influences on College Drinking: A Review of the Research." *Journal of Substance Abuse* 13, no. 4 (2001): 391–424.

Bowles, Samuel, and Sandra Polanía-Reyes. "Economic Incentives and Social Preferences: Substitutes or Complements?" *Journal of Economic Literature* 50, no. 2 (June 1, 2012): 368–425.

Brackbill, Devon, and Damon Centola. "The Network Structure of Scientific Discovery." Working Paper, Annenberg School for Communication, University of Pennsylvania, Philadelphia, 2016. Adobe PDF file.

Breiger, Ronald L. "The Duality of Persons and Groups." *Social Forces* 53, no. 2 (1974): 181–190.

Brinton, Mary C., and Victor Nee. *The New Institutionalism in Sociology*. New York: Russell Sage Foundation, 1988.

Brooks, S. J., V. Savov, E. Allzén, C. Benedict, R. Fredriksson, and H. B. Schiöth. "Exposure to Subliminal Arousing Stimuli Induces Robust Activation in the Amygdala, Hippocampus, Anterior Cingulate, Insular Cortex and Primary Visual Cortex: A Systematic Meta-analysis of fMRI Studies." *NeuroImage* 59, no. 3 (2012): 2962–2973.

Brown, John S., and Paul Duguid. "Knowledge and Organization: A Social-Practice Perspective." *Organization Science* 12, no. 2 (2001): 198–213.

———. *The Social Life of Information*. Brighton, MA: Harvard Business Review Press, 2000.

Bruckner, Eberhard, Werner Ebeling, M. A. Jiménez Montaño, and Andrea Scharnhorst. "Hyperselection and Innovation Described by a Stochastic Model of Technological Evolution." In *Evolutionary Economics and Chaos Theory: New Directions in Technology Studies*, edited by Loet Leydesdorff and Peter Van den Besselaar, 79–90. London: Palgrave Macmillan, 1994.

Bupp, Irvin C., and Jean-Claude Derian. *Light Water: How the Nuclear Dream Dissolved*. New York: Basic Books, 1978.

Burgess, Matthew, Eytan Adar, and Michael Cafarella. "Link-Prediction Enhanced Consensus Clustering for Complex Networks." *PLOS ONE* 11, no. 5 (2016): e0153384.

Burt, Ronald S. "The Network Structure of Social Capital." *Research in Organizational Behavior* 22 (2000): 345–423.

———. "The Social Capital of Structural Holes." In The *New Economic Sociology: Developments in an Emerging Field*, edited by Mauro F. Guillén, Randall Collins, Paula England, and Marshall Meyer, 148–191. New York: Russell Sage Foundation, 2002.

———. "Structural Holes and Good Ideas." *American Journal of Sociology* 110, no. 2 (2004): 349–399.

———. *Structural Holes: The Social Structure of Competition*. Cambridge, MA: Harvard University Press, 1992.

Buskens, Vincent, and Arnout van de Rijt. "Dynamics of Networks if Everyone Strives for Structural Holes." *American Journal of Sociology* 114, no. 2 (2008): 371–407.

Cacioppo, John T., Richard E. Petty, Chuan Feng Kao, and Regina Rodriguez. "Central and Peripheral Routes to Persuasion: An Individual Difference Perspective." *Journal of Personality and Social Psychology* 51, no. 5 (1986): 1032–1043.

Camerer, Colin F., George Loewenstein, and Matthew Rabin. *Advances in Behavioral Economics*. Princeton, NJ: Princeton University Press, 2003.

Campbell, Ellsworth, and Marcel Salathé. "Complex Social Contagion Makes Networks More Vulnerable to Disease Outbreaks." *Scientific Reports* 3 (2013): 1–6.

Cappella, Joseph N., Vincent Price, and Lilach Nir. "Argument Repertoire as a Reliable and Valid Measure of Opinion Quality: Electronic Dialogue during Campaign 2000." *Political Communication* 19, no. 1 (2002): 73–93.

Carrington, Peter J., John Scott, and Stanley Wasserman, eds. *Models and Methods in Social Network Analysis*. New York: Cambridge University Press, 2005.

Carroll, Glenn R., and Michael T. Hannan. *The Demography of Corporations and Industries*. Princeton, NJ: Princeton University Press, 2000.

———. "Organizational Ecology." In *International Encyclopedia of Social and Behavioral Sciences*, 2nd ed., edited by J. Wright, 17:358–363. Amsterdam: Elsevier, 2015.

Carroll, Lewis. *Through the Looking Glass: And What Alice Found There*. Chicago: Rand, McNally, 1917.

Cederman, Lars-Erik. *Emergent Actors in World Politics: How States and Nations Develop and Dissolve*. Princeton, NJ: Princeton University Press, 1997.

Centola, Damon. "An Experimental Study of Homophily in the Adoption of Health Behavior." *Science* 334, no. 6060 (2011): 1269–1272.

———. "Failure in Complex Social Networks." *Journal of Mathematical Sociology* 33, no. 1 (2008): 64–68.

———. "Homophily, Networks, and Critical Mass: Solving the Start-up Problem in Large Group Collective Action." *Rationality and Society* 25, no. 1 (2013): 3–40.

———. "Social Media and the Science of Health Behavior." *Circulation* 127, no. 21 (2013): 2135–2144.

———. "The Social Origins of Networks and Diffusion." *American Journal of Sociology* 120, no. 5 (2015): 1295–1338.

———. "The Spread of Behavior in an Online Social Network Experiment." *Science* 329, no. 5996 (2010): 1194–1197.

Centola, Damon, and Andrea Baronchelli. "The Spontaneous Emergence of Conventions: An Experimental Study of Cultural Evolution." *Proceedings of the National Academy of Sciences* 112, no. 7 (2015): 1989–1994.

Centola, Damon, Juan Carlos Gonzalez-Avella, Victor M. Eguiluz, and Maxi San Miguel. "Homophily, Cultural Drift, and the Co-evolution of Cultural Groups." *Journal of Conflict Resolution* 51, no. 6 (2007): 905–929.

Centola, Damon, and Michael Macy. "Complex Contagions and the Weakness of Long Ties." *American Journal of Sociology* 113, no. 3 (2007): 702–734.

———. "Social Life in Silico." In *The Handbook of Group Research and Practice*, edited by Susan A. Wheelan, 273–281. Thousand Oaks, CA: SAGE Publications, 2005.

Centola, Damon, and Arnout van de Rijt. "Choosing Your Network: Social Preferences in an Online Health Community." *Social Science & Medicine* 125 (January 2015): 19–31.

Centola, Damon, Robb Willer, and Michael Macy. "The Emperor's Dilemma: A Computational Model of Self-Enforcing Norms." *American Journal of Sociology* 110, no. 4 (2005): 1009–1040.

Chan, Jason, and Anindya Ghose, "Internet's Dirty Secret: Assessing the Impact of Online Intermediaries on HIV Transmission." *MIS Quarterly* 38, no. 4 (2013): 955–976.

Chetty, Raj, Nathaniel Hendren, and Lawrence F. Katz. "The Effects of Exposure to Better Neighborhoods on Children: New Evidence from the Moving to Opportunity Experiment." NBER Working Paper No. 21156, National

Bureau of Economic Research, Cambridge, MA, May 2015. http://www.nber.org/papers/w21156.

Chong, Dennis. *Collective Action and the Civil Rights Movement*. Chicago: University of Chicago Press, 2014.

Chou, Wen-Ying Sylvia, Yvonne M. Hunt, Ellen B. Beckjord, Richard P. Moser, and Bradford W. Hesse. "Social Media Use in the United States: Implications for Health Communication." *Journal of Medical Internet Research* 11, no. 4 (2009): e48.

Christakis, Nicholas A., and James H. Fowler. "The Collective Dynamics of Smoking in a Large Social Network." *New England Journal of Medicine* 358, no. 21 (2008): 2249–2258.

Christakis, Nicholas A., and James H. Fowler. "Social Contagion Theory: Examining Dynamic Social Networks and Human Behavior." *Statistics in Medicine* 61, no.4 (2013): 556-577.

———. *Connected: The Surprising Power of Our Social Networks and How They Shape Our Lives*. New York: Little, Brown, 2009.

———. "The Spread of Obesity in a Large Social Network over 32 Years." *New England Journal of Medicine* 357, no. 4 (2007): 370–379.

Chwe, Michael Suk-Young. "Structure and Strategy in Collective Action." *American Journal of Sociology* 105, no. 1 (1999): 128–156.

Cialdini, Robert B. *Influence: The Psychology of Persuasion*. New York: Collins Business, 2007.

Clampet-Lundquist, Susan, and Douglas S. Massey. "Neighborhood Effects on Economic Self-Sufficiency: A Reconsideration of the Moving to Opportunity Experiment." *American Journal of Sociology* 114, no. 1 (2008): 107–143.

Coates, Thomas J., Linda Richter, and Carlos Caceres. "Behavioural Strategies to Reduce HIV Transmission: How to Make Them Work Better." *Lancet* 372, no. 9639 (2008): 669–684.

Cobb, Nathan K., and Amanda L. Graham. "Health Behavior Interventions in the Age of Facebook." *American Journal of Preventive Medicine* 43, no. 5 (2012): 571–572.

Cobb, Nathan K., Amanda L. Graham, Beth C. Bock, George Papandonatos, and David B. Abrams. "Initial Evaluation of a Real-World Internet Smoking Cessation System." *Nicotine & Tobacco Research* 7, no. 2 (2005): 207–216.

Cohen, Michael D., Rick L. Riolo, and Robert Axelrod. "The Role of Social Structure in the Maintenance of Cooperative Regimes." *Rationality and Society* 13, no. 1 (2001): 5–32.

Cohen-Cole, Ethan, and Jason M. Fletcher. "Is Obesity Contagious? Social Networks vs. Environmental Factors in the Obesity Epidemic." *Journal of Health Economics* 27, no. 5 (2008): 1382–1387.

Coleman, James S. "Social Capital in the Creation of Human Capital." *American Journal of Sociology* 94 (1988): S95–S120.

Coleman, James S., Elihu Katz, and Herbert Menzel. *Medical Innovation: A Diffusion Study*. New York: Bobbs-Merrill, 1966.

Collins, Randall. "Emotional Energy as the Common Denominator of Rational Action." *Rationality and Society* 5, no. 2 (1993): 203–230.

———. *The Sociology of Philosophies: A Global Theory of Intellectual Change.* Cambridge, MA: Belknap Press of Harvard University Press, 1998.

———. "Three Faces of Cruelty: Towards a Comparative Sociology of Violence." *Theory and Society* 1, no. 4 (1974): 415–440.

"Collusion in the Stockmarket." *Economist,* January 15, 1998. http://www.econ omist.com/node/111273.

Compagnone, Claude, and Peter Hamilton. "Burgundy Winemakers and Respect of the Environment." *Revue Française de Sociologie* 55, no. 2 (2014): 319–358.

Correll, Shelley J., and Cecilia L. Ridgeway. "Expectation States Theory." In *Handbook of Social Psychology,* edited by John Delameter, 29–51. New York: Springer, 2006.

Correll, Shelley J., Cecilia L. Ridgeway, Ezra W. Zuckerman, Sharon Jank, Sara Jordan-Bloch, and Sandra Nakagawa. "It's the Conventional Thought That Counts: How Third-Order Inference Produces Status Advantage." *American Sociological Review* 82 (2017): 297–327.

Couzin, Iain D., Christos C. Ioannou, Güven Demirel, Thilo Gross, Colin J. Torney, Andrew Hartnett, Larissa Conradt, Simon A. Levin, and Naomi E. Leonard. "Uninformed Individuals Promote Democratic Consensus in Animal Groups." *Science* 334, no. 6062 (2011): 1578–1580.

Cowan, Robin. "Backing the Wrong Horse: Sequential Choice among Technologies of Unknown Merit." PhD diss., Stanford University, 1987.

Crane, Diana. "Diffusion Models and Fashion: A Reassessment." *Annals of the American Academy of Political and Social Science* 566, no. 1 (1999): 13–24.

Crosnoe, Robert, Anna Strassmann Mueller, and Kenneth Frank. "Gender, Body Size and Social Relations in American High Schools." *Social Forces* 86, no. 3 (2008): 1189–1216.

Damani, R., M. W. Ross, S. O. Aral, S. Berman, J. St. Lawrence, and M. L. Williams. "Emotional Intimacy Predicts Condom Use: Findings in a Group at High Sexually Transmitted Disease Risk." *International Journal of STD & AIDS* 20, no. 11 (2009): 761–764.

Darwin, Charles. *On the Origin of Species by Means of Natural Selection, or the Preservation of Favoured Races in the Struggle for Life.* London: John Murray, 1859.

David, Clarissa, Joseph N. Cappella, and Martin Fishbein. "The Social Diffusion of Influence among Adolescents: Group Interaction in a Chat Room Environment about Antidrug Advertisements." *Communication Theory* 16, no. 1 (2006): 118–140.

David, Paul A. "Clio and the Economics of QWERTY." *American Economic Review* 75, no. 2 (1985): 332–337.

Davis, Gerald, and Henrich Greve. "Corporate Elite Networks and Governance Changes in the 1980s." *American Journal of Sociology* 103 no. 1 (1997): 1–37.

Davis, Gerald F., and Mayer Zald. "Social Change, Social Theory, and the Convergence of Movements and Organizations. In *Social Movements and Organization Theory,* edited by Gerald F. Davis, Doug McAdam, W. Richard Scott, and Mayer N. Zald, 335–350. New York: Cambridge University Press, 2005.

Dawkins, Richard. *The Blind Watchmaker: Why the Evidence of Evolution Reveals a Universe without Design*. New York: W. W. Norton, 1986.

Dean, Tim. *Unlimited Intimacy: Reflections on the Subculture of Barebacking*. Chicago: University of Chicago Press, 2009.

DellaPosta, Daniel, Victor Nee, and Sonja Opper. "Endogenous Dynamics of Institutional Change." *Rationality and Society* (2016): 1–44.

Dennett, Daniel C. *Consciousness Explained*. Boston: Back Bay Books, 1991.

———. *Darwin's Dangerous Idea: Evolution and the Meanings of Life*. New York: Simon and Schuster, 1995.

De Sola Pool, Ithiel, and Manfred Kochen. "Contacts and Influence." *Social Networks* 1, no. 1 (1978–79): 5–51.

Dietler, Michael, and Ingrid Herbich. "Habitus, Techniques, Style: An Integrated Approach to the Social Understanding of Material Culture and Boundaries." In *The Archaeology of Social Boundaries*, edited by Miriam T. Stark, 232–263. Washington, DC: Smithsonian Institution Press, 1998.

Dijksterhuis, Jan., Pamela K. Smith, Rick B. van Baaren, and Daniël H. J. Wigboldus. "The Unconscious Consumer: Effects of Environment on Consumer Behavior." *Journal of Consumer Psychology* 15, no. 3 (2005): 193–202.

DiMaggio, Paul, and Filiz Garip, "Network Effects and Social Inequality." *Annual Review of Sociology* 38 (2012): 93–118.

DiMaggio, Paul, E. Hargittai, C. Celeste, and S. Shafer. "Digital Inequality: From Unequal Access to Differentiated Use." In *Social Inequality*, edited by K. Neckerman, 355–400. New York: Russell Sage Foundation, 2004.

DiMaggio, Paul, and Walter W. Powell. "The Iron Cage Revisited: Collective Rationality and Institutional Isomorphism in Organizational Fields." *American Sociological Review* 48, no. 2 (1983): 147–160.

Dixon, Norman F. *Subliminal Perception: The Nature of a Controversy*. New York: McGraw-Hill, 1971.

Dodds, Peter S., Roby Muhamad, and Duncan J. Watts. "An Experimental Study of Search in Global Social Networks." *Science* 301, no. 5634 (2003): 827–829.

Dolnick, Edward. *The Clockwork Universe: Isaac Newton, the Royal Society, and the Birth of the Modern World*. New York: Harper Collins, 2011.

Douglas, Mary. *How Institutions Think*. Syracuse, NY: Syracuse University Press, 1986.

Dunbar, R.I.M. "Neocortex Size as a Constraint on Group Size in Primates." *Journal of Human Evolution* 22, no. 6 (1992): 469–493.

Durkheim, Emile. *The Division of Labor in Society*. Translated by W. D. Halls. New York: Free Press, 1997. Originally published as *De la division du travail social* (Paris: F. Alcan, 1893).

———. *Suicide: A Study in Sociology*. Translated by J. A. Spaulding and G. Simpson. New York: Free Press, 1951. Originally published as *Le suicide* (Paris: F. Alcan, 1897).

Eagle, Nathan, Michael Macy, and Rob Claxton. "Network Diversity and Economic Development." *Science* 328, no. 5981 (2010): 1029–1031.

Easley, David, and Jon Kleinberg. *Networks, Crowds, and Markets: Reasoning about a Highly Connected World*. New York: Cambridge University Press, 2010.

Ellison, Glenn. "Learning, Local Interaction, and Coordination." *Econometrica* 61, no. 5 (1993): 1047–1071.

Elster, Jon. *Nuts and Bolts for the Social Sciences*. Cambridge: Cambridge University Press, 1989.

Eltantawy, Nahed, and Julie B. Wiest. "Social Media in the Egyptian Revolution: Reconsidering Resource Mobilization Theory." *International Journal of Communication* 5 (2011): Feature 1207–1224.

Emerson, Ralph Waldo. *Journals of Ralph Waldo Emerson: With Annotations*. Edited by Edward Waldo Emerson and Waldo Emerson Forbes. Vol. 8, *1849–1855*. Boston: Houghton Mifflin, 1912.

Entwisle, Barbara, John B. Casterline, and Hussein A. A. Sayed. "Villages as Contexts for Contraceptive Behavior in Rural Egypt." *American Sociological Review* 54, no. 6 (1989): 1019–1034.

Entwisle, Barbara, Ronald R. Rindfuss, David K. Guilkey, Aphichat Chamratrithirong, Sara R. Curran, and Yothin Sawangdee. "Community and Contraceptive Choice in Rural Thailand: A Case Study of Nang Rong." *Demography* 33, no. 1 (1996): 1–11.

Erikson, Kai T. *Wayward Puritans: A Study in the Sociology of Deviance*. New York: Wiley and Sons, 1966.

Evans-Pritchard, E. E. *The Nuer: A Description of the Modes of Livelihood and Political Institutions of a Nilotic People*. Oxford: Clarendon Press, 1940.

Feld, Scott L. "The Focused Organization of Social Ties." *American Journal of Sociology* 86, no. 5 (1981): 1015–1035.

Feld, Scott L., and William C. Carter. "When Desegregation Reduces Interracial Contact: A Class Size Paradox for Weak Ties." *American Journal of Sociology* 103, no. 5 (1998): 1165–1186.

Festinger, Leon. *A Theory of Cognitive Dissonance*. Stanford, CA: Stanford University Press, 1957.

Fick, Adolph. "On Liquid Diffusion." *Poggendorffs Annalen* 94, no. 59 (1855). Reprinted in *Journal of Membrane Science* 100 (1995): 33–38.

Finkel, Steven E., Edward N. Muller, and Karl-Dieter Opp. "Personal Influence, Collective Rationality, and Mass Political Action." *American Political Science Review* 83, no. 3 (1989): 885–903.

Fisher, Jeffrey D., Stephen J. Misovich, William A. Fisher, and Ralph J. DiClemente. "Impact of Perceived Social Norms on Adolescents' AIDS-Risk Behavior and Prevention." In *Adolescents and AIDS: A Generation in Jeopardy*, edited by Ralph Diclemente, 117–136. Newberry Park, CA: SAGE Publications, 1992.

Fishkin, James S. *When the People Speak: Deliberative Democracy and Public Consultation*. Oxford: Oxford University Press, 2009.

Flatt, Jason D., Yll Agimi, and Steve M. Albert. "Homophily and Health Behavior in Social Networks of Older Adults." *Family & Community Health* 35, no. 4 (2012): 312–321.

Fleming, D. T., and J. N. Wasserheit. "From Epidemiological Synergy to Public Health Policy and Practice: The Contribution of Other Sexually Transmitted Diseases to Sexual Transmission of HIV Infection." *Sexually Transmitted Infections* 75, no. 1 (1999): 3–17.

Forsyth, Donelson R. *Group Dynamics*. Pacific Grove, CA: Brooks/Cole, 1990.

Fox, Susannah, and Maeve Duggan. "Health Online 2013." Pew Research Center: Internet, Science & Technology, January 15, 2013. http://www.pewinternet .org/2013/01/15/health-online-2013/.

Framingham Heart Study. Framingham Heart Study: A Project of the National Heart, Lung, and Blood Institute and Boston University. Accessed January 18, 2017. https://www.framinghamheartstudy.org/.

Frank, Robert H. *Luxury Fever: Money and Happiness in an Era of Excess*. Princeton, NJ: Princeton University Press, 2000.

Freud, Sigmund. *Beyond the Pleasure Principle: Group Psychology and Other Works*. Translated by C.J.M. Hubback. London: International Psycho-Analytical, 1922.

Frost, Jeana, and Michael Massagli. "Social Uses of Personal Health Information within PatientsLikeMe, an Online Patient Community: What Can Happen When Patients Have Access to One Another's Data." *Journal of Medical Internet Research* 10, no. 3 (2008): e15.

Gabbriellini, Simone, Gianluca Manzo, Valentine Roux, and Freda Nkirote M'Mbogori. "Complex Contagions in Ethnically Diverse Non-Western Societies: Explaining Diffusion Dynamics among Indian and Kenyan Potters." Paper presented at the DIFFCERAM Workshop, Paris, France, June 16, 2016.

Galbraith, Jay R. "Matrix Organization Designs: How to Combine Functional and Project Forms." *Business Horizons* 14, no. 1 (February 1971): 29–40.

Gandomi, A., and M. Haider, "Beyond the Hype: Big Data Concepts, Methods, and Analytics." *International Journal of Information Management* 35, no. 2, (2015): 137–144.

Garip, Filiz. *On the Move: The Changing Mechanisms of Mexico-U.S. Migration*. Princeton, NJ: Princeton University Press, 2016.

———. "Social Capital and Migration: How Do Similar Resources Lead to Divergent Outcomes?" *Demography* 45, no. 3 (2008): 591–617.

Gelfand, Michele J., Lisa H. Nishii, and Jana L. Raver. "On the Nature and Importance of Cultural Tightness-Looseness." *Journal of Applied Psychology* 91 (2006):1225–1244.

Gennetian, Lisa A., Lisa Sanbonmatsu, and Jens Ludwig. "An Overview of Moving to Opportunity: A Random Assignment Housing Mobility Study in Five U.S. Cities." In *Neighborhood and Life Chances: How Place Matters in Modern America*, edited by Harriet B. Newburger, Eugenie L. Birch, and Susan M. Wachter, 163–178. Philadelphia: University of Pennsylvania Press, 2011.

Gladwell, Malcolm. "Q and A with Malcolm." Gladwell.com. Accessed January 5, 2017. http://gladwell.com/the-tipping-point/the-tipping-point-q-and-a/.

———. "Small Change: Why the Revolution Will Not Be Tweeted." *New Yorker*, October 4, 2010. http://www.newyorker.com/magazine/2010/10/04/small -change-malcolm-gladwell.

———. *The Tipping Point: How Little Things Can Make a Big Difference*. Boston: Little, Brown, 2000.

Gneezy, Uri, and Aldo Rustichini. "A Fine Is a Price." *Journal of Legal Studies* 29 (2000): 1–17.

Goffman, Erving. *The Presentation of Self in Everyday Life*. New York: Anchor Books, 1959.

Goldstein, Noah J., Robert B. Cialdini, and Vladas Griskevicius. "A Room with a Viewpoint: Using Social Norms to Motivate Environmental Conservation in Hotels." *Journal of Consumer Research* 35, no. 3 (2008): 472–482.

González, Marta C., César A. Hidalgo, and Albert-László Barabási. "Understanding Individual Human Mobility Patterns." *Nature* 453, no. 7196 (2008): 779–782.

Gould, Roger V. "Collective Action and Network Structure." *American Sociological Review* 58, no. 2 (1993): 182–196.

———. "Multiple Networks and Mobilization in the Paris Commune, 1871." *American Sociological Review* 56, no. 6 (1991): 716–729.

———. "The Origins of Status Hierarchies: A Formal Theory and Empirical Test." *American Journal of Sociology* 107, no. 5 (2002): 1143–1178.

Granovetter, Mark. *Getting a Job: A Study of Contacts and Careers*. Chicago: University Of Chicago Press, 1974.

———. "The Micro-Structure of School Desegregation." In J. Prager et al, *School Desegregation Research: New Directions in Situational Analysis*, edited by Jeffrey Prager, Douglas Longshore, and Melvin Seeman, 81–110. New York: Plenum, 1986.

———. "The Strength of Weak Ties." *American Journal of Sociology* 78, no. 6 (1973): 1360–1380.

———. "The Strength of Weak Ties: A Network Theory Revisited." *Sociological Theory* 1, no. 1 (1983): 201–233.

———. "Threshold Models of Collective Behavior." *American Journal of Sociology* 83, no. 6 (1978): 1420–1443.

Gray, Ronald H., Godfrey Kigozi, David Serwadda, Frederick Makumbi, Stephen Watya, Fred Nalugoda, Noah Kiwanuka, et al. "Male Circumcision for HIV Prevention in Men in Rakai, Uganda: A Randomised Trial." *Lancet* 369, no. 9562 (2007): 657–666.

Grindereng, Margaret P. "Fashion Diffusion." *Journal of Home Economics* 59, no. 3 (1967): 171–174.

Guare, John. *Six Degrees of Separation: A Play*. New York: Random House, 1990.

Guilbeault, Douglas, Joshua Becker, and Damon Centola. "Complex Contagions: A Decade in Review." In *Spreading Dynamics in Social Systems*, edited by Yong Yeol Ahn and Sune Lehmann. New York: Springer Nature, forthcoming.

Guilbeault, Douglas, and Samuel Woolley. "How Twitter Bots Are Shaping the Election." *Atlantic*, November 1, 2016. https://www.theatlantic.com/technology/archive/2016/11/election-bots/506072/.

Gupta, Sunetra, Roy M. Anderson, and Robert M. May. "Networks of Sexual Contacts: Implications for the Pattern of Spread of HIV." *AIDS* 3, no. 12 (1989): 807–818.

Gurevich, Michael. *The Social Structure of Acquaintanceship Networks*. Cambridge, MA: MIT Press, 1961.

Gutmann, Amy, and Dennis F. Thompson. *Democracy and Disagreement*. Cambridge, MA: Harvard University Press, 1996.

Hagerstrand, Torsten. *Innovation Diffusion as a Spatial Process.* Chicago: University of Chicago Press, 1968.

Hameiri, Boaz, Roni Porat, Daniel Bar-Tal, and Eran Halperin. "Moderating Attitudes in Times of Violence through Paradoxical Thinking Intervention." *Proceedings of the National Academy of Sciences* 113, no. 43 (2016): 12105–12110.

Hansen, Morten T. "The Search-Transfer Problem: The Role of Weak Ties in Sharing Knowledge across Organization Subunits." *Administrative Science Quarterly* 44, no. 1 (1999): 82–111.

Harlow, Summer. "Social Media and Social Movements: Facebook and an Online Guatemalan Justice Movement That Moved Offline." *New Media & Society* 14, no. 2 (2012): 225–243.

Harrigan, Nicholas, Palakorn Achananuparp, and Ee-Peng Lim. "Influentials, Novelty, and Social Contagion: The Viral Power of Average Friends, Close Communities, and Old News." *Social Networks* 34, no. 4 (2012): 470–480.

Haub, Carl. "Did South Korea's Population Policy Work Too Well?" Population Reference Bureau, March 2010. http://www.prb.org/Publications/Articles/2010/koreafertility.aspx.

Hayes, Andrew F., Dietram A. Scheufele, and Michael E. Huge. "Nonparticipation as Self-Censorship: Publicly Observable Political Activity in a Polarized Opinion Climate." *Political Behavior* 28, no. 3 (2006): 259–283.

Heath, Chip, Chris Bell, and Emily Sternberg. "Emotional Selection in Memes: The Case of Urban Legends." *Journal of Personality and Social Psychology* 81, no. 6 (2001): 1028–1041.

Hébert-Dufresne, Laurent, and Benjamin M. Althouse. "Complex Dynamics of Synergistic Coinfections on Realistically Clustered Networks." *Proceedings of the National Academy of Sciences* 112, no. 33 (2015): 10551–10556.

Hedström, Peter. "Contagious Collectivities: On the Spatial Diffusion of Swedish Trade Unions, 1890–1940." *American Journal of Sociology* 99, no. 5 (1994): 1157–1179.

Hedström, Peter, and Richard Swedberg, eds. *Social Mechanisms: An Analytical Approach to Social Theory.* Cambridge: Cambridge University Press, 1998.

Helbing, Dirk. "Traffic and Related Self-Driven Many-Particle Systems." *Reviews of Modern Physics* 73, no. 4 (2001): 1067–1141.

Hense, Burkhard A., Christina Kuttler, Johannes Müller, Michael Rothballer, Anton Hartmann, and Jan-Ulrich Kreft. "Does Efficiency Sensing Unify Diffusion and Quorum Sensing?" *Nature Reviews Microbiology* 5, no. 3 (2007): 230–239.

Hershey, John C., David A. Asch, Thi Thumasathit, Jacqueline Meszaros, and Victor V. Waters. "The Roles of Altruism, Free Riding, and Bandwagoning in Vaccination Decisions." *Organizational Behavior and Human Decision Processes* 59, no. 2 (1994): 177–187.

Hess, Amanda. "On Twitter, a Battle among Political Bots." *New York Times,* December 14, 2016. https://www.nytimes.com/2016/12/14/arts/on-twitter-a-battle-among-political-bots.html.

Hess, George. "Disease in Metapopulation Models: Implications for Conservation." *Ecology* 77, no. 5 (1996): 1617–1632.

Hodas, Nathan O., and Kristina Lerman, "How Visibility and Divided Attention Constrain Social Contagion." In *Proceedings, 2012 ASE/IEEE International Conference on Privacy, Security, Risk and Trust and 2012 ASE/IEEE International Conference on Social Computing*, 249–257. Piscataway, NJ: Institute of Electrical and Electronic Engineers, 2012.

Holt, John G. *Bergey's Manual of Determinative Bacteriology*. 9th ed. Philadelphia: Lippincott Williams & Wilkins, 1994.

Hornik, Robert. "Channeling Effectiveness in Development Communication Programs." In *Public Communication Campaigns*, edited by R. Rice and C. Atkins, 309–330. Newbury Park, CA: SAGE Publications, 1989.

Hornik, Robert, Lela Jacobsohn, Robert Orwin, Andrea Piesse, and Graham Kalton. "Effects of the National Youth Anti-Drug Media Campaign on Youths." *American Journal of Public Health* 98, no. 12 (2008): 2229–2236.

Howard, Philip N., and Muzammil M. Hussain. "The Role of Digital Media." *Journal of Democracy* 22, no. 3 (2011): 35–48.

Huang, Grace C., Jennifer B. Unger, Daniel Soto, Kayo Fujimoto, Mary Ann Pentz, Maryalice Jordan-Marsh, and Thomas W. Valente. "Peer Influences: The Impact of Online and Offline Friendship Networks on Adolescent Smoking and Alcohol Use." *Journal of Adolescent Health* 54, no. 5 (May 2014): 508–514.

Huisman, Mark. "Imputation of Missing Network Data: Some Simple Procedures." *Journal of Social Structure* 10, no. 1 (2009): 1–29.

Husserl, Edmund. *Cartesian Meditations: An Introduction to Phenomenology*. Translated by Dorion Cairns. The Hague: Martinus Nijhoff, 1950.

Iannaccone, Laurence R. "Why Strict Churches Are Strong." *American Journal of Sociology* 99, no. 5 (1994): 1180–1211.

Isenberg, Daniel J. "Group Polarization: A Critical Review and Meta-analysis." *Journal of Personality and Social Psychology* 50, no. 6 (1986): 1141–1151.

Jackson, Matthew O. *Social and Economic Networks*. Princeton, NJ: Princeton University Press, 2008.

Jamieson, Kathleen Hall, and Bruce W. Hardy. "Leveraging Scientific Credibility about Arctic Sea Ice Trends in a Polarized Political Environment." *Proceedings of the National Academy of Sciences* 111, no. S4 (2014): 13598–13605.

Kanter, Rosabeth Moss. *Men and Women of the Corporation*. New York: Basic Books, 1977.

———. "Some Effects of Proportions on Group Life: Skewed Sex Ratios and Responses to Token Women." *American Journal of Sociology* 82, no. 5 (1977): 965–990.

Karsai, Márton, Gerardo Iñiguez, Riivo Kikas, Kimmo Kaski, and János Kertész. "Local Cascades Induced Global Contagion: How Heterogeneous Thresholds, Exogenous Effects, and Unconcerned Behaviour Govern Online Adoption Spreading." *Scientific Reports* (2016): 27178. doi.org/10.1038/srep27178.

Katz, Elihu, and Paul Lazarsfeld. *Personal Influence*. New York: Free Press, 1955.

Kawachi, Ichiro, and Lisa Berkman. "Social Cohesion, Social Capital, and Health." In *Social Epidemiology*, edited by Lisa Berkman and Ichiro Kawachi, 174–190. New York: Oxford University Press, 2000.

Keller, Sarah N., and Jane D. Brown. "Media Interventions to Promote Responsible Sexual Behavior." *Journal of Sex Research* 39, no. 1 (2002): 67–72.

Kelley, Eric K., and Paul C. Tetlock. "How Wise Are Crowds? Insights from Retail Orders and Stock Returns." *Journal of Finance* 68, no. 3 (2013): 1229–1265.

Khaylis, Anna, Themis Yiaslas, Jessica Bergstrom, and Cheryl Gore-Felton. "A Review of Efficacious Technology-Based Weight-Loss Interventions: Five Key Components." *Telemedicine and E-Health* 16, no. 9 (2010): 931–938.

Kim, Hyojoung, and Peter S. Bearman. "The Structure and Dynamics of Movement Participation." *American Sociological Review* 62, no. 1 (1997): 70–93.

Kim, Soojong, and Damon Centola, "Seeding Strategies for Social Network Interventions in Public Health." Working Paper, Annenberg School for Communication, University of Pennsylvania, Philadelphia, 2016. Adobe PDF file.

King, Gary, Jennifer Pan, and Margaret Roberts. "How Censorship in China Allows Government Criticism but Silences Collective Expression." *American Political Science Review* 107, no. 2 (May 2013): 1–18.

———. "How the Chinese Government Fabricates Social Media Posts for Strategic Distraction, Not Engaged Argument." *American Political Science Review* 111, no. 3 (August 2017): 484–501.

———. "Reverse-Engineering Censorship in China: Randomized Experimentation and Participant Observation." *Science* 345, no. 6199 (2014): 1–10.

Kitts, James A. "Egocentric Bias or Information Management? Selective Disclosure and the Social Roots of Norm Misperception." *Social Psychology Quarterly* 66, no. 3 (2003): 222–237.

Klandermans, Bert. "The Formation and Mobilization of Consensus." *International Social Movement Research* 1 (1988): 173–196.

Kleinberg, Jon M. "Navigation in a Small World." *Nature* 406, no. 6798 (2000): 845.

Klemm, Konstantin, and Víctor M. Eguíluz. "Highly Clustered Scale-Free Networks." *Physical Review E* 65, no. 3 (2002): 36123.

Knappett, Carl, and Sander Van Der Leeuw. "A Developmental Approach to Ancient Innovation: The Potter's Wheel in the Bronze Age East Mediterranean." *Pragmatics & Cognition* 22, no. 1 (2014): 64–92.

Kohler, Hans-Peter. "Learning in Social Networks and Contraceptive Choice." *Demography* 34, no. 3 (1997): 369–383.

Kooti, Farshad, Winter A. Mason, Krishna P. Gummadi, and Meeyoung Cha. "Predicting Emerging Social Conventions in Online Social Networks." In *CIKM '12, Proceedings of the 21st ACM International Conference on Information and Knowledge Management*, 445–454 (New York: Association of Computing Machinery, 2012).

Kossinets, Gueorgi, and Duncan J. Watts. "Empirical Analysis of an Evolving Social Network." *Science* 311, no. 5757 (2006): 88–90.

———. "Origins of Homophily in an Evolving Social Network." *American Journal of Sociology* 115, no. 2 (2009): 405–450.

Kow, Yong Ming, Yubo Kou, Bryan Semaan, and Waikuen Cheng, "Mediating the Undercurrents: Using Social Media to Sustain a Social Movement." In *Proceedings of the 2016 CHI Conference on Human Factors in Computing Systems*, 3883–3894. New York: Association of Computing Machinery, 2016.

Krackhardt, David. "The Strength of Strong Ties: The Importance of Philos in Organizations." In *Networks in the Knowledge Economy*, edited by Rob Cross, Andrew Parker, and Lisa Sasson, 82–108. New York: Oxford University Press, 2003.

———. "The Ties That Torture: Simmelian Tie Analysis in Organizations." *Research in the Sociology of Organizations* 16, no. 1 (1999): 183–210.

Krafft, Peter M., Michael Macy, and Alex Pentland. "Bots as Virtual Confederates: Design and Ethics." In *CSCW '17, Proceedings of the 2017 ACM Conference on Computer-Supported Cooperative Work and Social Computing*, 183–190. New York: Association of Computing Machinery, 2017. https://doi.org/10.1145 /2998181.2998354.

Krafft, Peter M., Julia Zheng, Wei Pan, Nicolás Della Penna, Yaniv Altshuler, Erez Shmueli, Joshua B. Tenenbaum, and Alex Pentland. "Human Collective Intelligence as Distributed Bayesian Inference." Unpublished manuscript, August 5, 2016. http://arxiv.org/abs/1608.01987.

Kramer, Adam D. I., Jamie E. Guillory, and Jeffrey T. Hancock. "Experimental Evidence of Massive-Scale Emotional Contagion through Social Networks." *Proceedings of the National Academy of Sciences* 111, no. 24 (2014): 8788–8790.

Kramer, Vicki W., Alison M. Konrad, Sumru Erkut, and Michele J. Hooper. *Critical Mass on Corporate Boards: Why Three or More Women Enhance Governance*. Boston: Wellesley Centers for Women, 2006.

Kroeze, Willemieke, Andrea Werkman, and Johannes Brug. "A Systematic Review of Randomized Trials on the Effectiveness of Computer-Tailored Education on Physical Activity and Dietary Behaviors." *Annals of Behavioral Medicine* 31, no. 3 (2006): 205–223.

Kuhlman, Chris, V. S. Anil Kumar, Madhav V. Marathe, S. S. Ravi, and Daniel J. Rosenkrantz. "Effects of Opposition on the Diffusion of Complex Contagions in Social Networks: An Empirical Study." In *Social Computing, Behavioral-Cultural Modeling and Prediction, SBP 2011*, edited by J. Salerno, S. J. Yang, D. Nau, and S. K. Chai, 188–196. Vol. 6589 of Lecture Notes in Computer Science (Heidelberg: Springer, 2011).

Kuhlman, Chris, V. S. Anil Kumar, Madhav Marathe, Samarth Swarup, Gaurav Tuli, S. S. Ravi, Daniel J. Rosenkrantz. "A Bi-Threshold Model of Complex Contagion and its Application to the Spread of Smoking Behavior." Paper presented at the Fifth SIGKDD Workshop on Social Network Mining and Analysis (SNA-KDD), San Diego, CA, 2011.

Kuran, Timur. *Private Truths, Public Lies: The Social Consequences of Preference Falsification*. Cambridge, MA: Harvard University Press, 1995.

LaJeunesse, Sara. "Mobile Health Apps Lack Behavior-Change Techniques." *Penn State News*, May 6, 2014. http://news.psu.edu/story/314757/2014/05/06 /research/mobile-health-apps-lack-behavior-change-techniques.

Lakon, Cynthia M., Cornelia Pechmann, Cheng Wang, Li Pan, Kevin Delucchi, and Judith J. Prochaska. "Mapping Engagement in Twitter-Based Support Networks for Adult Smoking Cessation." *American Journal of Public Health* 106, no. 8 (2016): 1374–1380.

Laranjo, Liliana, Amaël Arguel, Ana L. Neves, Aideen M. Gallagher, Ruth Kaplan, Nathan Mortimer, Guilherme A. Mendes, and Annie Y. S. Lau. "The

Influence of Social Networking Sites on Health Behavior Change: A Systematic Review and Meta-analysis." *Journal of the American Medical Informatics Association* 22, no. 1 (2014): 243–256.

Lazarsfeld, Paul F., and Robert K. Merton. "Friendship as a Social Process: A Substantive and Methodological Analysis." *Freedom and Control in Modern Society* 18, no. 1 (1954): 18–66.

Lazer, David, and Allan Friedman. "The Network Structure of Exploration and Exploitation." *Administrative Science Quarterly* 52, no. 4 (2007): 667–694.

Lazer, David, Alex Sandy Pentland, Lada Adamic, Sinan Aral, Albert Laszlo Barabasi, Devon Brewer, Nicholas Christakis, et al. "Life in the Network: The Coming Age of Computational Social Science." *Science* 323, no. 5915 (2009): 721–723.

Le Bon, Gustave. *The Crowd: A Study of the Popular Mind*. Fischer, 1897.

Levin, Carl, and Tom Coburn. *Wall Street and the Financial Crisis: Anatomy of a Financial Collapse*. Majority and Minority Staff Report, Permanent Subcommittee on Investigations, Committee on Homeland Security and Governmental Affairs, United States Senate, April 13, 2011, Washington, DC.

Levy, Aharon, Tamar Saguy, Martijn van Zomeren, and Eran Halperin. "Ingroups, Outgroups, and the Gateway Groups Between: The Potential of Dual Identities to Improve Intergroup Relations." *Journal of Experimental Social Psychology* 70 (2016): 260–271.

Lewis, Kevin, Jason Kaufman, and Nicholas Christakis. "The Taste for Privacy: An Analysis of College Student Privacy Settings in an Online Social Network." *Journal of Computer-Mediated Communication* 14, no. 1 (2008): 79–100.

Li, Michael, and Raymond Perkins. "The Perils of Polling in a Brexit and Donald Trump World." TechCrunch, October 19, 2016. http://social.tech crunch.com/2016/10/19/the-perils-of-polling-in-a-brexit-and-donald -trump-world/.

Liljeros, Fredrik, Christofer R. Edling, Luís A. Nunes Amaral, H. Eugene Stanley, and Yvonne Åberg. "The Web of Human Sexual Contacts." *Nature* 411, no. 6840 (2001): 907–908.

Liljeros, Fredrik, Christofer R. Edling, H. Eugene Stanley, Y. Åberg, and Luis A. N. Amaral. "Social Networks (Communication Arising): Sexual Contacts and Epidemic Thresholds." *Nature* 423, no. 6940 (2003): 606–606.

Liu, Ka-Yuet, Marissa King, and Peter S. Bearman. "Social Influence and the Autism Epidemic." *American Journal of Sociology* 115, no. 5 (2010): 1387–1434.

Longini, Ira M., Jr. "A Mathematical Model for Predicting the Geographic Spread of New Infectious Agents." *Mathematical Biosciences* 90, no. 1–2 (1988): 367–383.

Lotan, Gilad, Erhardt Graeff, Mike Ananny, Devin Gaffney, Ian Pearce, and Danah Boyd. "The Revolutions Were Tweeted: Information Flows during the 2011 Tunisian and Egyptian Revolutions." *International Journal of Communication* 5 (2011): 1375–1405.

Luke, Douglas A., and Jenine K. Harris. "Network Analysis in Public Health: History, Methods, and Applications." *Annual Review of Public Health* 28, no. 1 (2007): 69–93.

MacDonald, John, and Leatrice MacDonald. "Chain Migration, Ethnic Neighborhood Formation, and Social Networks." In *An Urban World*, edited by Charles Tilly, 226–236. Boston: Little, Brown, 1974.

Mackay, Charles. *Memoirs of Extraordinary Popular Delusions and the Madness of Crowds.* London: Office of National Illustrated Library, 1852.

Mackie, Diane, Eliot R. Smith, and Devin G. Ray, "Intergroup Emotions and Intergroup Relations." *Social and Personality Psychology Compass* 2, no. 5 (2008): 1866–1880.

MacPhail, Catherine, and Catherine Campbell. " 'I Think Condoms Are Good But, Aai, I Hate Those Things': Condom Use among Adolescents and Young People in a Southern African Township." *Social Science and Medicine* 52, no. 11 (2001): 1613–1627.

Madigan, Michael T., John M. Martinko, Kelly S. Bender, Daniel H. Buckley, David A. Stahl, and Thomas Brock. *Brock Biology of Microorganisms.* 14th ed. Boston: Pearson, 2014.

Maher, Carol A., Lucy K. Lewis, Katia Ferrar, Simon Marshall, Ilse De Bourdeaudhuij, and Corneel Vandelanotte. "Are Health Behavior Change Interventions That Use Online Social Networks Effective? A Systematic Review." *Journal of Medical Internet Research* 16, no. 2 (2014): e40.

Majumdar, Sarangam, and Subhoshmita Mondal. "Conversation Game: Talking Bacteria." *Journal of Cell Communication and Signaling* 10, no. 4 (2016): 331–335.

Manning, Rachel, Mark Levine, and Alan Collins. "The Kitty Genovese Murder and the Social Psychology of Helping: The Parable of the 38 Witnesses." *American Psychologist* 62, no. 6 (2007): 555–562.

March, James G. "Exploration and Exploitation in Organizational Learning." *Organization Science* 2, no. 1 (1991): 71–87.

———. *Primer on Decision Making: How Decisions Happen.* New York: Simon and Schuster, 1994.

Marcus, Bess H., LeighAnn H. Forsyth, Elaine J. Stone, Patricia M. Dubbert, Thomas L. McKenzie, Andrea L. Dunn, and Steven N. Blair. "Physical Activity Behavior Change: Issues in Adoption and Maintenance." *Health Psychology* 19, no. 1, suppl. (2000): 32–41.

Markus, M. Lynne. "Toward a 'Critical Mass' Theory of Interactive Media Universal Access, Interdependence and Diffusion." *Communication Research* 14, no. 5 (1987): 491–511.

Marrazzo, Jeanne M., Gita Ramjee, Barbra A. Richardson, Kailazarid Gomez, Nyaradzo Mgodi, Gonasagrie Nair, Thesla Palanee, et al. "Tenofovir-Based Preexposure Prophylaxis for HIV Infection among African Women." *New England Journal of Medicine* 372, no. 6 (2015): 509–518.

Marsden, Peter V. "Homogeneity in Confiding Relations." *Social Networks* 10, no. 1 (1988): 57–76.

———. "Network Data and Measurement." *Annual Review of Sociology* 16 (1990): 435–463.

———. *Social Trends in American Life: Findings from the General Social Survey since 1972.* Princeton, NJ: Princeton University Press, 2012.

Marwell, Gerald, and Pamela Oliver. *The Critical Mass in Collective Action: A Micro-Social Theory.* Cambridge: Cambridge University Press, 1993.

Marx, Karl. *Capital: Critique of Political Economy.* Translated by Samuel Moore and Edward Aveling. Moscow: Progress Publishers, 1867.

Maslov, Sergei, and Kim Sneppen. "Specificity and Stability in Topology of Protein Networks." *Science* 296, no. 5569 (2002): 910–913.

Mason, Winter, Andy Jones, and Robert L. Goldstone. "Propagation of Innovations in Networked Groups." *Journal of Experimental Psychology: General* 137, no. 3 (2008): 422–433.

Mason, Winter, and Duncan J. Watts. "Collaborative Learning in Networks." *Proceedings of the National Academy of Sciences* 109, no. 3 (2012): 764–69.

McAdam, Doug. *Freedom Summer.* Oxford: Oxford University Press, 1988.

———. "Recruitment to High-Risk Activism: The Case of Freedom Summer." *American Journal of Sociology* 92, no. 1 (1986): 64–90.

McAdam, Doug, and Ronnelle Paulsen. "Specifying the Relationship between Social Ties and Activism." *American Journal of Sociology* 99, no. 3 (1993): 640–667.

McCarthy, John D., and Mayer N. Zald. "Resource Mobilization and Social Movements: A Partial Theory." *American Journal of Sociology* 82, no. 6 (1977): 1212–1241.

McFarland Daniel, and Heili Pals. "Motives and Contexts of Identity Change: A Case for Network Effects." *Social Psychology Quarterly* 68 no. 4 (2005): 289–315.

McLean, Bethany, and Joe Nocera. *All the Devils Are Here: The Hidden History of the Financial Crisis.* New York: Portfolio/Penguin, 2011.

McPhail, Clark. *The Myth of the Madding Crowd.* Piscataway, NJ: Transaction Publishers, 1991.

McPherson, J. Miller, and Lynn Smith-Lovin. "Homophily in Voluntary Organizations: Status Distance and the Composition of Face-to-Face Groups." *American Sociological Review* 52, no. 3 (1987): 370–379.

McPherson, Miller, Lynn Smith-Lovin, and James M. Cook. "Birds of a Feather: Homophily in Social Networks." *Annual Review of Sociology* 27 (2001): 415–444.

Merton, Robert K. *Social Theory and Social Structure.* New York: Free Press, 1968.

———. *The Sociology of Science: Theoretical and Empirical Investigations.* Chicago: University of Chicago Press, 1973.

———. "The Unanticipated Consequences of Purposive Social Action." *American Sociological Review* 1, no. 6 (1936): 894–904.

Milgram, Stanley. "The Small World Problem." *Psychology Today* 2 (1967): 60–67.

Miller, Melissa B., and Bonnie L. Bassler. "Quorum Sensing in Bacteria." *Annual Review of Microbiology* 55 (2001): 165–199.

Montanari, Andrea, and Amin Saberi. "The Spread of Innovations in Social Networks." *Proceedings of the National Academy of Sciences* 107, no. 47 (2010): 20196–20201.

Montgomery, Elizabeth T., B. Mensch, P. Musara, M Hartmann, K. Woeber, J. Etima, and A. van der Straten. "Misreporting of Product Adherence in the MTN-003/VOICE Trial for HIV Prevention in Africa: Participants' Explanations for Dishonesty." *AIDS and Behavior* 21, no. 2 (2017): 481–491.

Montgomery, Mark R., and John B. Casterline. "The Diffusion of Fertility Control in Taiwan: Evidence from Pooled Cross-Section Time-Series Models." *Population Studies* 47, no. 3 (1993): 457–479.

Moreno, Jacob Levy. *Sociometry, Experimental Method and the Science of Society.* New York: Beacon House, 1951.

Morenoff, Jeffrey D., and Robert J. Sampson. "Violent Crime and the Spatial Dynamics of Neighborhood Transition: Chicago, 1970–1990." *Social Forces* 76, no. 1 (1997): 31–64.

Morgenson, Gretchen, and Louise Story. "Senate Report Names Culprits of the Financial Crisis." *New York Times*, April 13, 2011. http://www.nytimes .com/2011/04/14/business/14crisis.html.

Morris, Stephen. "Contagion." *Review of Economic Studies* 67, no. 1 (2000): 57–78.

Mozaffarian, Dariush, Ashkan Afshin, Neal L. Benowitz, Vera Bittner, Stephen R. Daniels, Harold A. Franch, David R. Jacobs, et al. "Population Approaches to Improve Diet, Physical Activity, and Smoking Habits: A Scientific Statement from the American Heart Association." *Circulation* 126, no. 12 (2012): 1514–1563.

Mutz, Diana C. "The Consequences of Cross-Cutting Networks for Political Participation." *American Journal of Political Science* 46, no. 4 (2002): 838–855.

Myneni, Sahiti, Kayo Fujimoto, Nathan Cobb, and Trevor Cohen. "Content-Driven Analysis of an Online Community for Smoking Cessation: Integration of Qualitative Techniques, Automated Text Analysis, and Affiliation Networks." *American Journal of Public Health* 105, no. 6 (2015): 1206–1212. doi: 0.2105/AJPH.2014.302464.

Myers, David G., and George D. Bishop. "Discussion Effects on Racial Attitudes." *Science* 169, no. 3947 (19970): 778–779.

Nagoshi, Craig T., Mark D. Wood, Christopher C. Cote, and Steven M. Abbit. "College Drinking Game Participation within the Context of Other Predictors of Alcohol Use and Problems." *Psychology of Addictive Behaviors* 8, no. 4 (1994): 203–213.

National AIDS Control Council. *Kenya Aids Strategic Framework 2014/2015–2018 /2019.* Nairobi: Kenya Ministry of Health, 2015. http://nacc.or.ke/wp-con tent/uploads/2015/09/KASF_Final.pdf.

National Commission for the Protection of Human Subjects of Biomedical and Behavioral Research. *The Belmont Report: Ethical Principles and Guidelines for the Protection of Human Subjects of Research.* Washington, DC: US Department of Health, Education, and Welfare, 1978.

Neuwirth, Kurt, Edward Frederick, and Charles Mayo. "The Spiral of Silence and Fear of Isolation." *Journal of Communication* 57, no. 3 (2007): 450–468.

Newman, Mark E. J. "Models of the Small World." *Journal of Statistical Physics* 101, no. 3–4 (2000): 819–841.

Newman, Mark E. J., Albert-László Barabási, and Duncan J. Watts. *The Structure and Dynamics of Networks.* Princeton, NJ: Princeton University Press, 2006.

Newman, Mark E. J., and Duncan J. Watts. "Scaling and Percolation in the Small-World Network Model." *Physical Review E* 60, no. 6 (1999): 7332.

Nishi, Akihiro, Hirokazu Shirado, David G. Rand, and Nicholas A. Christakis. "Inequality and Visibility of Wealth in Experimental Social Networks." *Nature* 526, no. 7573 (2015): 426–29.

Noar, Seth M., and Patricia J. Morokoff, "The Relationship between Masculinity Ideology, Condom Attitudes, and Condom Use: Stage of Change; A

Structural Equation Modeling Approach." *International Journal of Men's Health* 1, no. 1 (2002): 43–58.

Noelle-Neumann, Elisabeth. "The Spiral of Silence: A Theory of Public Opinion." *Journal of Communication* 24, no. 2 (1974): 43–51.

Obstfeld, David. "Social Networks, the Tertius Iungens Orientation, and Involvement in Innovation." *Administrative Science Quarterly* 50, no. 1 (2005): 100–130.

Okeyo, Verah. "Lessons from Voluntary Medical Male Circumcision." *Daily Nation*, June 14, 2016. http://www.nation.co.ke/lifestyle/DN2/Lessons-from-voluntary-medical-male-circumcision/957860–3249398–7r161t/index.html.

Oliver, Pamela, Gerald Marwell, and Ruy Teixeira. "A Theory of the Critical Mass. I. Interdependence, Group Heterogeneity, and the Production of Collective Action." *American Journal of Sociology* 91, no. 3 (1985): 522–556.

Olson, Mancur. *The Logic of Collective Action: Public Goods and the Theory of Groups*. Cambridge, MA: Harvard University Press, 1965.

Opp, Karl-Dieter, and Christiane Gern. "Dissident Groups, Personal Networks, and Spontaneous Cooperation: The East German Revolution of 1989." *American Sociological Review* 58, no. 5 (1993): 659–680.

Orr, Larry, Judith Feins, Robin Jacob, Eric Beecroft, Lisa Sanbonmatsu, Lawrence Katz, Jeffrey Liebman, and Jeffrey Kling. *Moving to Opportunity: Interim Impacts Evaluation*. Washington, DC: US Department of Housing and Urban Development, Office of Policy and Development Research, 2003.

O'Shea-Wheller, Thomas A., Ana B. Sendova-Franks, and Nigel R. Franks. "Migration Control: A Distance Compensation Strategy in Ants." *Science of Nature* 103, no. 7–8 (2016): art. 60. doi: 10.1007/s00114-016-1386-8.

Padgett, John F., and Christopher K. Ansell. "Robust Action and the Rise of the Medici, 1400–1434." *American Journal of Sociology* 98, no. 6 (1993): 1259–1319.

Page, Scott E. *The Difference: How the Power of Diversity Creates Better Groups, Firms, Schools, and Societies*. Princeton, NJ: Princeton University Press, 2007.

Paluck, Elizabeth Levy, and Hana Shepherd. "The Salience of Social Referents: A Field Experiment on Collective Norms and Harassment Behavior in a School Social Network." *Journal of Personality and Social Psychology* 103, no. 6 (2012): 899–915.

Paluck, Elizabeth Levy, Hana Shepherd, and Peter M. Aronow. "Changing Climates of Conflict: A Social Network Experiment in 56 Schools." *Proceedings of the National Academy of Sciences* 113, no. 3 (2016): 566–571.

Pampel, Fred C., Patrick M. Krueger, and Justin T. Denney. "Socioeconomic Disparities in Health Behaviors." *Annual Review of Sociology* 36, no. 1 (2010): 349–370.

Papachristos, Andrew V., Tracey L. Meares, and Jeffrey Fagan. "Attention Felons: Evaluating Project Safe Neighborhoods in Chicago." *Journal of Empirical Legal Studies* 4, no. 2 (2007): 223–72.

———. "Why Do Criminals Obey the Law? The Influence of Legitimacy and Social Networks on Active Gun Offenders." *Journal of Criminal Law and Criminology* 102, no. 2 (2012): 397–440.

Parkhurst, Justin O., David Chilongozi, and Eleanor Hutchinson. "Doubt, Defiance, and Identity: Understanding Resistance to Male Circumcision for HIV Prevention in Malawi." *Social Science & Medicine* 135 (2015): 15–22.

PatientsLikeMe. Accessed January 19, 2017. https://www.patientslikeme.com/.

Pechmann, Cornelia, Kevin Delucchi, Cynthia M. Lakon, and Judith J. Prochaska. "Randomised Controlled Trial Evaluation of Tweet2Quit: A Social Network Quit-Smoking Intervention." *Tobacco Control* 26, no. 2 (2017): 188–194.

Peleg, David, and Eli Upfal. "A Trade-Off between Space and Efficiency for Routing Tables." *Journal of the Association for Computing Machinery* 36, no. 3 (1989): 510–530.

Pentland, Alex. *Social Physics: How Social Networks Can Make Us Smarter*. New York: Penguin Books, 2014.

Perkins, H. Wesley, and Henry Wechsler. "Variation in Perceived College Drinking Norms and Its Impact on Alcohol Abuse: A Nationwide Study." *Journal of Drug Issues* 26, no. 4 (1996): 961–974.

Peters, William, dir. "A Class Divided." *Frontline*. Aired March 26, 1985, on PBS. http://www.pbs.org/wgbh/frontline/film/class-divided/.

———. *A Class Divided: Then and Now*. New Haven, CT: Yale University Press, 1987.

Petty, Richard E., John T. Cacioppo, and Rachel Goldman. "Personal Involvement as a Determinant of Argument-Based Persuasion." *Journal of Personality and Social Psychology* 41, no. 5 (1981): 847–855.

Phelan, Jo C., Bruce G. Link, and Parisa Tehranifar. "Social Conditions as Fundamental Causes of Health Inequalities: Theory, Evidence, and Policy Implications." *Journal of Health and Social Behavior* 51, no. 1, suppl. (2010): S28–S40.

Phillips, Damon J., and Ezra W. Zuckerman. "Middle-Status Conformity: Theoretical Restatement and Empirical Demonstration in Two Markets." *American Journal of Sociology* 107, no. 2 (2001): 379–429.

Piketty, Thomas. *Capital in the Twenty-First Century*. Translated by Arthur Goldhammer. Cambridge, MA: Belknap Press of Harvard University Press, 2014.

Podolny, Joel M. "Networks as the Pipes and Prisms of the Market." *American Journal of Sociology* 107, no. 1 (2001): 33–60.

Polletta, Francesca. "'It Was Like A Fever . . .': Narrative and Identity in Social Protest." *Social Problems* 45, no. 2 (1998): 137–159.

Powell, Walter W., and Paul J. DiMaggio. *The New Institutionalism in Organizational Analysis*. Chicago: University of Chicago Press, 1991.

Prentice, Deborah A., and Dale T. Miller. "Pluralistic Ignorance and Alcohol Use on Campus: Some Consequences of Misperceiving the Social Norm." *Journal of Personality and Social Psychology* 64, no. 2 (1993): 243–256.

Price, Vincent, Joseph N. Cappella, and Lilach Nir. "Does Disagreement Contribute to More Deliberative Opinion?" *Political Communication* 19, no. 1 (2002): 95–112.

Putnam, Robert D. *Bowling Alone: The Collapse and Revival of American Community*. New York: Simon and Schuster, 2001.

Quine, Willard Van Orman. "Two Dogmas of Empiricism." *Philosophical Review* 60 (1951): 20–43.

Rainie, Lee, Kristen Purcell, and Aaron Smith. "The Social Side of the Internet." Pew Research Center: Internet, Science & Tech, January 18, 2011. http://www.pewinternet.org/2011/01/18/the-social-side-of-the-internet/.

Reagans, Ray, and Bill McEvily. "Network Structure and Knowledge Transfer: The Effects of Cohesion and Range." *Administrative Science Quarterly* 48, no. 2 (2003): 240–267.

Reagans, Ray, and Ezra W. Zuckerman. "Networks, Diversity, and Productivity: The Social Capital of Corporate R&D Teams." *Organization Science* 12, no. 4 (2001): 502–517.

Repenning, Nelson P. "A Simulation-Based Approach to Understanding the Dynamics of Innovation Implementation." *Organization Science* 13, no. 2 (2002): 109–127.

Resnick, Mitchel. *Turtles, Termites, and Traffic Jams: Explorations in Massively Parallel Microworlds*. Cambridge, MA: MIT Press, 1997.

Ridgeway, Cecilia L. "Status Construction Theory." In *The Wiley Blackwell Encyclopedia of Race, Ethnicity, and Nationalism*. Wiley Online Library, 2015. doi: 10.1002/9781118663202.wberen200.

Ridgeway, Cecilia L., and Joseph Berger. "Expectations, Legitimation, and Dominance Behavior in Task Groups." *American Sociological Review* 51, no. 5 (1986): 603–617.

Ridgeway, Cecilia L., Elizabeth Heger Boyle, Kathy J. Kuipers, and Dawn T. Robinson. "How Do Status Beliefs Develop? The Role of Resources and Interactional Experience." *American Sociological Review* 63, no. 3 (1998): 331–350.

Ridgeway, Cecilia L., and Shelley J. Correll. "Consensus and the Creation of Status Beliefs." *Social Forces* 85, no. 1 (2006): 431–453.

Rijt, Arnout van de, Soong Moon Kang, Michael Restivo, and Akshay Patil. "Field Experiments of Success-Breeds-Success Dynamics." *Proceedings of the National Academy of Sciences* 111, no. 19 (2014): 6934–6939.

Rogers, Everett M. *Diffusion of Innovations*. 5th ed. New York: Free Press, 2003.

Rogers, Everett M., and D. Lawrence Kincaid. *Communication Networks: Toward a New Paradigm for Research*. New York: Free Press, 1981.

Romero, Daniel M., Brendan Meeder, and Jon Kleinberg. "Differences in the Mechanics of Information Diffusion across Topics: Idioms, Political Hashtags, and Complex Contagion on Twitter." In *Proceedings of the 20th International Conference on World Wide Web*, 695–704. New York: Association of Computing Machinery, 2011.

Ross, Philip. "Marin County and California's Measles Outbreak: A Look into the Epicenter of the Anti-vaccination Trend." *International Business Times*, February 6, 2015. http://www.ibtimes.com/marin-county-californias-measles-outbreak-look-epicenter-anti-vaccination-trend-1808182.

Ruch, Simon, Marc Alain Züst, and Katharina Henke. "Subliminal Messages Exert Long-Term Effects on Decision-Making." *Neuroscience of Consciousness* 2016, no. 1 (2016): niw013. doi: 10.1093/nc/niw013.

Ryan, Bryce, and Neil C. Gross. "The Diffusion of Hybrid Seed Corn in Two Iowa Communities." *Rural Sociology* 8, no. 1 (1943): 15–24.

Saavedra, Serguei, Kathleen Hagerty, and Brian Uzzi. "Synchronicity, Instant Messaging, and Performance among Financial Traders." *Proceedings of the National Academy of Sciences* 108, no. 13 (2011): 5296–5301.

Sahin, Erol, and Nigel R. Franks. "Measurement of Space: From Ants to Robots." Paper presented at WGW 2002: EPSRC/BBSRC International Workshop Biologically-Inspired Robotics: The Legacy of W. Grey Walter, HP Bristol Labs, UK, August 2002.

Salathé, Marcel, and Sebastian Bonhoeffer. "The Effect of Opinion Clustering on Disease Outbreaks." *Journal of the Royal Society: Interface* 5, no. 29 (2008): 1505–1508.

Salganik, Matthew J., Peter Sheridan Dodds, and Duncan J. Watts. "Experimental Study of Inequality and Unpredictability in an Artificial Cultural Market." *Science* 311, no. 5762 (2006): 854–856.

Sampson, Robert J., Stephen W. Raudenbush, and Felton Earls. "Neighborhoods and Violent Crime: A Multilevel Study of Collective Efficacy." *Science* 277, no. 5328 (1997): 918–924.

Sanbonmatsu, Lisa, Jens Ludwig, Lawrence F. Katz, Lisa A. Gennetian, Greg J. Duncan, Ronald C. Kessler, Emma Adam, Thomas W. McDade, and Stacy Tessler Lindau. *Moving to Opportunity for Fair Housing Demonstration Program: Final Impacts Evaluation.* Washington, DC: U.S. Department of Housing and Urban Development, 2011.

Sattenspiel, Lisa, and Carl P. Simon. "The Spread and Persistence of Infectious Diseases in Structured Populations." *Mathematical Biosciences* 90, no. 1–2 (1988): 341–366.

Schachter, Stanley. "Leon Festinger." *Biographical Memoirs of the National Academy of Sciences* 64 (1994): 99–110.

Schelling, Thomas C. *Micromotives and Macrobehavior.* New York: Norton, 1978.

Scheurer, Paul B., and Guy Debrock, eds. *Newton's Scientific and Philosophical Legacy.* Vol. 123 of the International Archives of the History of Ideas. Dordrecht: Kluwer Academic, 1988.

Schlaghecken, Friederike, and Martin Eimer. "Subliminal Stimuli Can Bias 'Free' Choices between Response Alternatives." *Psychonomic Bulletin & Review* 11 (2004): 463–468.

Schneider, John A., Benjamin Cornwell, David Ostrow, Stuart Michaels, Phil Schumm, Edward O. Laumann, and Samuel Friedman. "Network Mixing and Network Influences Most Linked to HIV Infection and Risk Behavior in the HIV Epidemic among Black Men Who Have Sex with Men." *American Journal of Public Health* 103, no. 1 (2012): e28–e36.

Seeley, Thomas, and P. Kirk Visscher. "Group Decision Making in Nest-Site Selection by Honey Bees." *Apidologie* 35, no. 2 (2004): 101–116.

Seeley, Thomas D., P. Kirk Visscher, and Kevin M. Passino. "Group Decision Making in Honey Bee Swarms." *American Scientist* 94, no. 3 (2006): 220–229.

Sen, Amartya, *Identity and Violence: The Illusion of Destiny.* New York: W. W. Norton, 2006.

Shalizi, Cosma Rohilla, and Andrew C. Thomas. "Homophily and Contagion Are Generically Confounded in Observational Social Network Studies." *Sociological Methods & Research* 40, no. 2 (2011): 211–239.

Sharma, Sanjay. "Black Twitter?: Racial Hashtags, Networks and Contagion." *New Formations* 78, no. 1 (2013): 46–64.

Shaw, M. E. *Group Dynamics: The Psychology of Small Group Behavior.* 2nd ed. New York: McGraw-Hill, 1976.

Sherif, Muzafer. *Experimental Study of Positive and Negative Intergroup Attitudes between Experimentally Produced Groups: Robbers Cave Study.* Norman: Institute of Group Relations, University of Oklahoma, 1954.

Simmel, Georg. *Conflict and the Web of Group Affiliations.* New York: Free Press, 1955.

———. "How Is Society Possible?" In *Georg Simmel, 1858–1918: A Collection of Essays, with Translations and a Bibliography,* edited by Kurt H. Wolff. Columbus: Ohio State University Press, 1959.

———. *The Sociology of Georg Simmel.* Translated by Kurt H. Wolff. New York: Free Press, 1950.

Small, Mario. *Someone to Talk To.* Oxford: Oxford University Press, 2017.

———. *Unanticipated Gains: Origins of Network Inequality in Everyday Life.* Oxford: Oxford University Press, 2009.

Smelser, Neil J. *The Sociology of Economic Life.* Englewood Cliffs, NJ: Prentice-Hall, 1976.

Smith, Aaron. "Why Americans Use Social Media." Pew Research Center: Internet, Science & Tech, November 15, 2011. http://www.pewinternet .org/2011/11/15/why-americans-use-social-media/.

Smith, Dawn K., Jeffrey H. Herbst, Xinjiang Zhang, and Charles E. Rose. "Condom Effectiveness for HIV Prevention by Consistency of Use among Men Who Have Sex with Men in the United States." *JAIDS: Journal of Acquired Immune Deficiency Syndromes* 68, no. 3 (2015): 337–344.

Smith, Eliot R., and Diane Mackie, "Dynamics of Group-Based Emotions: Insights from Intergroup Emotions Theory," *Emotion Review* 7, no. 4 (October 2015): 349–354.

Smith, G. E. "The Methodology of the Principia." In *The Cambridge Companion to Newton,* edited by I. B. Cohen and G. E. Smith, 138–173. Cambridge: Cambridge University Press, 2002.

Smith, Kirk H., and Martha Rogers. "Effectiveness of Subliminal Messages in Television Commercials: Two Experiments." *Journal of Applied Psychology* 79, no. 6 (1994): 866–874.

Snijders, Tom A. B. "The Statistical Evaluation of Social Network Dynamics." *Sociological Methodology* 31, no. 1 (2001): 361–395.

———. "Stochastic Actor-Oriented Models for Network Change." *Journal of Mathematical Sociology* 21, no. 1–2 (1996): 149–172.

Snijders, Tom A. B., Gerhard G. Van de Bunt, and Christian E. G. Steglich. "Introduction to Stochastic Actor-Based Models for Network Dynamics." *Social Networks* 32, no. 1 (2010): 44–60.

Solow, Robert M. "The Economist's Approach to Pollution and Its Control." *Science* 173, no. 3996 (1971): 498–503.

Soule, Sarah A. "The Student Divestment Movement in the United States and Tactical Diffusion: The Shantytown Protest." *Social Forces* 75, no. 3 (1997): 855–882.

State, Bogdan, and Lada Adamic. "The Diffusion of Support in an Online Social Movement: Evidence from the Adoption of Equal-Sign Profile Pictures." In *Proceedings of the 18th ACM Conference on Computer Supported Cooperative Work & Social Computing*, 1741–1750. New York: Association of Computing Machinery, 2015.

Steinert-Threlkeld, Zachary C. "Spontaneous Collective Action: Peripheral Mobilization during the Arab Spring." *American Political Science Review* 111, no. 2 (2017): 379–403.

Stewart, Quincy Thomas. "Big Bad Racists, Subtle Prejudice and Minority Victims: An Agent-Based Analysis of the Dynamics of Racial Inequality." Paper presented at the Annual Meeting of the Population Association of America, Dallas, TX, April 2010.

Strang, David, and John W. Meyer. "Institutional Conditions for Diffusion." *Theory and Society* 22, no. 4 (1993): 487–511.

Strang, David, and Sarah A. Soule. "Diffusion in Organizations and Social Movements: From Hybrid Corn to Poison Pills." *Annual Review of Sociology* 24 (January 1, 1998): 265–290.

Sunstein, Cass R. *The Ethics of Influence: Government in the Age of Behavioral Science*. Cambridge: Cambridge University Press, 2016.

———. *Going to Extremes: How Like Minds Unite and Divide*. Oxford: Oxford University Press, 2009.

Surowiecki, James. "Open Season." *New Yorker*, October 13, 2013.

Tarde, Gabriel. *The Laws of Imitation*. Translated by E. C. Parsons. New York: Henry Holt, 1903.

Taton, R., and C. Wilson. *Planetary Astronomy from the Renaissance to the Rise of Astrophysics, Part A, Tycho Brahe to Newton*. Cambridge: Cambridge University Press, 1989.

Thaler, Richard H., and Cass R. Sunstein. *Nudge: Improving Decisions About Health, Wealth, and Happiness*. New Haven, CT: Yale University Press, 2008.

Timm, Jonathan. "When the Boss Says, 'Don't Tell Your Coworkers How Much You Get Paid.'" *Atlantic*, July 15, 2014. http://www.theatlantic.com/business/archive/2014/07/when-the-boss-says-dont-tell-your-coworkers-how-much-you-get-paid/374467/.

Tobian, Aaron A. R., Seema Kacker, and Thomas C. Quinn. "Male Circumcision: A Globally Relevant but Under-Utilized Method for the Prevention of HIV and Other Sexually Transmitted Infections." *Annual Review of Medicine* 65 (2014): 293–306.

Tocqueville, Alexis de. *Democracy in America*. Translated by Harvey C. Mansfield and Delba Winthrop. Chicago: University of Chicago Press, 2000. Originally published as *De la démocratie en Amérique* (London: Saunders and Otley, 1835–40).

Tonnies, Ferdinand. *Community and Society*. New Brunswick, NJ: Transaction, 1988.

Toole, Jameson L., Meeyoung Cha, and Marta C. González. "Modeling the Adoption of Innovations in the Presence of Geographic and Media Influences." *PLOS ONE* 7, no. 1 (2012): e29528. https://doi.org/10.1371/journal.pone.0029528.

Totterdell, Peter. "Catching Moods and Hitting Runs: Mood Linkage and Subjective Performance in Professional Sport Teams." *Journal of Applied Psychology* 85, no. 6 (2000): 848–859.

Traag, Vincent. "Complex Contagion of Campaign Donations." *PLOS One* 11 no. 4 (2016): e0153539.

Travers, Jeffrey, and Stanley Milgram. "An Experimental Study of the Small World Problem." *Sociometry* 32, no. 4 (1969): 425–443.

Tucker, Boima. "Beats, Rhymes and Ebola." *Cultural Anthropology*, October 7, 2014. https://culanth.org/fieldsights/592-beats-rhymes-and-ebola.

Uebel, Thomas Ernst. *Overcoming Logical Positivism from Within: The Emergence of Neurath's Naturalism in the Vienna Circle's Protocol Sentence Debate.* Amsterdam: Editions Rodopi, 1992.

Ugander, Johan, Lars Backstrom, Cameron Marlow, and Jon Kleinberg. "Structural Diversity in Social Contagion." *Proceedings of the National Academy of Sciences* 109, no. 16 (2012): 5962–5966.

Umberson, Debra, Robert Crosnoe, and Corinne Reczek. "Social Relationships and Health Behavior across the Life Course." *Annual Review of Sociology* 36, no. 1 (2010): 139–157.

University of North Carolina at Chapel Hill. Add Health: The National Longitudinal Study of Adolescent to Adult Health. Carolina Population Center. Accessed January 18, 2017. http://www.cpc.unc.edu/projects/addhealth.

Uzzi, Brian, and Jarrett Spiro. "Collaboration and Creativity: The Small World Problem." *American Journal of Sociology* 111, no. 2 (2005): 447–504.

Vaan, Mathijs de, Balazs Vedres, and David Stark. "Game Changer: The Topology of Creativity." *American Journal of Sociology* 120, no. 4 (2015): 1144–1194.

Valente, Thomas W. "Mass-Media-Generated Interpersonal Communication as Sources of Information about Family Planning." *Journal of Health Communication* 1, no. 3 (1996): 247–266.

———. *Network Models of the Diffusion of Innovations.* Cresskill, NJ: Hampton Press, 1995.

———. *Social Networks and Health: Models, Methods, and Applications.* Oxford: Oxford University Press, 2010.

Valente, Thomas W., Kayo Fujimoto, Chih-Ping Chou, and Donna Spruijt-Metz. "Adolescent Affiliations and Adiposity: A Social Network Analysis of Friendships and Obesity." *Journal of Adolescent Health* 45, no. 2 (2009): 202–204.

Valente, Thomas W., Susan C. Watkins, Miriam N. Jato, Ariane Van Der Straten, and Louis-Philippe M. Tsitsol. "Social Network Associations with Contraceptive Use among Cameroonian Women in Voluntary Associations." *Social Science & Medicine* 45, no. 5 (1997): 677–687.

Van der Straten, Andrea, J. Stadler, E. Leucke, N. Laborde, M Hartmann, E. T. Montgomery, and the VOICE-C Study Team. "Perspectives on Use of Oral and Vaginal Antiretrovirals for HIV Prevention: The VOICE-C Qualitative Study in Johannesburg, South Africa." *Journal of the International AIDS Society* 17, no. 3 (2014): 19146. doi: 10.7448/IAS.17.3.19146.

Van Valen, Leigh. "A New Evolutionary Law." *Evolutionary Theory* 1 (1973): 1–30.

Venkatesh, Viswanath. "Where to Go from Here? Thoughts on Future Directions for Research on Individual-Level Technology Adoption with a Focus on Decision Making." *Decision Sciences* 37, no. 4 (2006): 497–518.

Ventola, C. Lee. "Social Media and Health Care Professionals: Benefits, Risks, and Best Practices." *Pharmacy and Therapeutics* 39, no. 7 (2014): 491–499.

Verster, Francois, dir. *Protection: Masculinity & Condom Use in Sub-Saharan Africa*. DVD. 114 min. Johannesburg: Fireworx Media Production, 2009.

Walton, Gregory M. "The New Science of Wise Psychological Interventions." *Current Directions in Psychological Science* 23, no. 1 (2014): 73–82.

Watkins, Susan, and I. Warriner. "How Do We Know We Need to Control for Selectivity?" *Demographic Research*, Special Collection 1 (2003):109–142.

Watts, Duncan J. "Networks, Dynamics, and the Small-World Phenomenon." *American Journal of Sociology* 105, no. 2 (1999): 493–527.

———. "A Simple Model of Global Cascades on Random Networks." *Proceedings of the National Academy of Sciences* 99, no. 9 (2002): 5766–5771.

———. *Small Worlds: The Dynamics of Networks between Order and Randomness*. Princeton, NJ: Princeton University Press, 1999.

Watts, Duncan J., and Peter S. Dodds, "Threshold Models of Social Influence." In *The Oxford Handbook of Analytical Sociology*, edited by Peter Hedström and Peter Bearman, 475–497. Oxford: Oxford University Press, 2009.

Watts, Duncan J., Peter S. Dodds, and Mark E. J. Newman. "Identity and Search in Social Networks." *Science* 296 (2002): 1302–1305.

Watts, Duncan J., and Steven H. Strogatz. "Collective Dynamics of 'Small-World' Networks." *Nature* 393, no. 6684 (1998): 440–442.

Weber, Max. *Economy and Society: An Outline of Interpretive Sociology*. Edited by Guenther Roth, and Claus Wittich. Berkeley: University of California Press, 1978. Originally published as *Wirtschaft und Gesellschaft: Grundriß der verstehenden Soziologie* (Tübingen: J.C.B. Mohr, 1922).

———. *The Protestant Ethic and the Spirit of Capitalism: And Other Writings*. Edited and translated by Peter Baehr and Gordon C. Wells. New York: Penguin, 2002.

Weiss, Helen A., Maria A. Quigley, and Richard J. Hayes. "Male Circumcision and Risk of HIV Infection in Sub-Saharan Africa: A Systematic Review and Meta-analysis." *AIDS* 14, no. 15 (2000): 2361–2370.

Werfel, Justin, Kirstin Petersen, and Radhika Nagpal. "Designing Collective Behavior in a Termite-Inspired Robot Construction Team." *Science* 343, no. 6172 (2014): 754–758.

Wellman, Barry, and Scot Wortley. "Different Strokes from Different Folks: Community Ties and Social Support." *American Journal of Sociology* 96, no. 3 (1990): 558–588.

White, Harrison. *Identity and Control*. Princeton, NJ: Princeton University Press: 2008.

———. "Search Parameters for the Small World Problem." *Social Forces* 49, no. 2 (1970): 259–264.

Whyte, William H., Jr. "The Web of Word of Mouth." *Fortune* 50, no. 5 (1954): 140–143.

Williams, S. L., and D. P. French. "What Are the Most Effective Intervention Techniques for Changing Physical Activity Self-Efficacy and Physical

Activity Behaviour—And Are They the Same?" *Health Education Research* 26, no. 2 (2011): 308–322.

Wolfers, Justin, and Eric Zitzewitz. "Prediction Markets." *Journal of Economic Perspectives* 18, no. 2 (2004): 107–126.

World Health Organization (WHO). "Ebola Outbreak 2014–2015." December 23, 2016. http://www.who.int/csr/disease/ebola/en/.

World Health Organization (WHO). "HIV/AIDS." Global Health Observatory Data. Accessed January 5, 2017. http://www.who.int/gho/hiv/en/.

World Health Organization (WHO) and Joint United Nations Programme on HIV/AIDS (UNAIDS). *Joint Strategic Action Framework to Accelerate the Scale-Up of Voluntary Medical Male Circumcision for HIV Prevention in Eastern and Southern Africa (2012–2016).* Geneva: UNAIDS, 2011. http://files.unaids.org /en/media/unaids/contentassets/documents/unaidspublication/2011/JC 2251_Action_Framework_circumcision_en.pdf.

Wu, Chen-fong. "The Relationship between Business Ethics Diffusion, Knowledge Sharing and Service Innovation." *Management Decision* 54, no. 6 (2016): 1343–1358.

Xie, Jierui, Sameet Sreenivasan, Gyorgy Korniss, Weituo Zhang, Chjan Lim, and Boleslaw K. Szymanski. "Social Consensus through the Influence of Committed Minorities." *Physical Review E* 84, no. 1 (2011): 011130.

Yaqub, Ohid, Sophie Castle-Clarke, Nick Sevdalis, and Joanna Chataway. "Attitudes to Vaccination: A Critical Review." *Social Science & Medicine* 112 (2014): 1–11.

Young, H. Peyton. "The Dynamics of Social Innovation." *Proceedings of the National Academy of Sciences* 108, no. 4 (2011): 21285–21291.

———. "The Evolution of Conventions." *Econometrica* 61, no. 1 (1993): 57–84.

———. *Individual Strategy and Social Structure: An Evolutionary Theory of Institutions.* Princeton, NJ: Princeton University Press, 1998.

———. "Innovation Diffusion in Heterogeneous Populations: Contagion, Social Influence and Social Learning." *American Economic Review* 99 (2009): 1899–1924.

Young, H. Peyton, and Gabriel E. Kreindler. "Rapid Innovation Diffusion in Social Networks." *Proceedings of the National Academy of Sciences* 111, suppl. 3 (2014): 10881–10888.

Zhang, Jingwen and Damon Centola, "How Social Networks Shape Social Comparison," in *Social Comparison, Judgment & Behavior,* edited by Jerry Suls. New York: Oxford University Press, forthcoming.

Zhang, Jingwen, Devon Brackbill, Sijia Yang, Joshua Becker, Natalie Herbert, and Damon Centola. "Support or Competition? How Online Social Networks Increase Physical Activity: A Randomized Controlled Trial." *Preventive Medicine Reports* 4 (2016): 453–458.

Zhang, Jingwen, Devon Brackbill, Sijia Yang, and Damon Centola. "Efficacy and Causal Mechanism of an Online Social Media Intervention to Increase Physical Activity: Results of a Randomized Controlled Trial." *Preventive Medicine Reports* 2 (2015): 651–657.

Zhao, Dingxin. "Ecologies of Social Movements: Student Mobilization during the 1989 Prodemocracy Movement in Beijing." *American Journal of Sociology* 103, no. 6 (1998): 1493–1529.

Index

Page references in italics refer to illustrations and their captions.